Kitchen and Bathroom
Cabinets

Percy W. Blandford

TAB BOOKS Inc.
Blue Ridge Summit, PA

FIRST EDITION
FIRST PRINTING

Copyright © 1989 by **TAB BOOKS Inc.**
Printed in the United States of America

Library of Congress Cataloging-in-Publication Data

Blandford, Percy W.
   Kitchen and bathroom cabinets / by Percy W. Blandford.
     p. cm.
   ISBN 0-8306-9244-4   ISBN 0-8306-3244-1 (pbk.)
   1. Kitchen cabinets. 2. Bathroom cabinets. I. Title.
TT197.5.K57B59 1989
684.1'6—dc 20
                        89-36597
                        CIP

TAB BOOKS Inc. offers software for sale. For information and a catalog, please contact
TAB Software Department, Blue Ridge Summit, PA 17294-0850.

Questions regarding the content of this book
should be addressed to:

   Reader Inquiry Branch
   TAB BOOKS Inc.
   Blue Ridge Summit, PA 17294-0214

Acquisitions Editor: Kimberly Tabor
Book Editor: Mark Kmetzko
Production: Katherine Brown

Cover photograph courtesy of Kohler Company Inc.

Contents

Introduction   vii

1 Preparations   **1**
Measurements 2
Access 5
Design 7

2 Materials   **11**
Wood 11
Plywood 13
Other Materials 15

3 Construction   **17**
Screws 18
Dowels 19
Edges 21
Drawers 22
Hinges 28
Handles and Catches 32

4 Doors and Drawer Fronts   **36**
Plain Doors 37
Framed Doors 40
Molded Doors 43
Raised Panels 43
Shaped Frames 45
Sliding Doors 48

5 Basic Cabinets   **52**
Fitted Two-part Cabinet 54
Enclosed Two-drawer Cabinet 58

6 Unit Construction   64

Unit Choice 65
Unit Sizes 67
Shell Construction 67
Cabinet with Shelves 70
Sliding Trays 71
Cabinet with Drawers 71
Vertical Storage 75
Cloth-hanging Compartment 78
Breadboard Slide 79
Tilt Bin 80
Bottle Rack 82
Wide Unit 84
End Shelves 86
Unit Assembly 88

7 Dealing with Corners   89

Overlapped Corner 92
Top-access Corner 94
Corner Unit 96
Folding Doors 96
Diagonal Corner Unit 99
External Corners 101
Square Corner 101
Large Shelf Corner 102
Small Shelf Corner 105

8 Cabinet Ends   108

Ledged Shelves 108
Railed Shelves 110
Angled End Cabinet 112
Raised End Cabinet 117
Tall End Cabinet 121
Tall Cabinet with Oven 125

9 Countertops   130

Planning 131
Wood Worktops 131
Laminated Plastic Counters 133
Stone Countertops 139
Tiled Countertops 140
Insetting a Sink 142
Accommodating Other Appliances 143

10 Island Units   144

Kitchen Table 145
Square Island Cabinets 149
Multiple Island Units 153
Island Bench 155

Side Shelf Unit   158
Island Unit with Trays   164

11   Built-in Tables   172

Sliding Shelf   172
Folding Table   174
End Table   177
Counter-height Table   181
Breakfast Bar   184
Cabinet Extension   188

12   Shelves   194

Simple Shelf   195
Block of Shelves   196
Basic Shelf Unit   198
Corner Shelves   201
Display Shelves   203
Countertop Shelves   206
Tall Shelves   212
Wide Shelves   217
Spindle-supported Shelves   222
Plate Rack   225

13   Basic Hanging Wall Cabinets   229

Single Cupboard   230
Small Mirror Cabinet   233
Matching Cabinet   236
Cook's Tool Cabinet   240
Corner Cupboard   245
Writing-flap Cabinet   249
Cabinet with Lifting Door   253

14   Multiple Hanging Wall Cabinets   256

Planning   257
Carcass Construction   262
Long Cabinet   265
Corner Unit   270

15   Special Bathroom Cabinets   274

Vanity Unit   275
Modular Units   280
Storage Cabinet   283

Glossary   287

Index   290

Introduction

Not so many years ago a kitchen was just a workplace with a miscellaneous collection of equipment, tables, and other cooking and washing paraphernalia, with no particular order and no consideration given to appearance. Cooks were able to do their work but probably did not get much enjoyment from it.

Things have changed dramatically. Cooking and food preparation have become more mechanized, and there are far more aids. Clothes washing has been moved elsewhere. With all this has come an appreciation of the need to get things organized and to make the kitchen more efficient and better looking. The result: It is a joy to work in a modern kitchen.

Much of the ease and efficiency of working in a modern kitchen are due to the use of countertops with storage below and above, arranged to tie in with the stove and the other appliances needed by the modern cook. Careful planning can lead to a far better use of space, resulting in a kitchen more pleasing to use *and* to view. Ideally, as the cook enjoys the surroundings more, the results of his efforts should be better.

Bathrooms have not advanced as quickly or as much as kitchens. Many bathrooms are simply functional, yet their basic problem is the same as that of kitchens: space and organization. Most bathrooms benefit from the addition of cabinets, even if the cabinets are compact. In addition to being useful, they bring order into the room and improve its appearance. Although there might not be as much room for the development of cabinets in a bathroom as in a kitchen, the two rooms can make use of the same basic cabinet designs.

This book is devoted to the making of all kinds of wooden cabinets for kitchens and bathrooms. It is hoped that you will find plenty of designs to follow or adapt—to make your kitchen or bathroom a much better place and at much less expense than buying kits or employing a professional to do the work. Cabinets must be arranged to suit particular situations, but by following instructions in this book and using unit construction where appropriate, you can make cabinets and worktops to suit your needs. Moreover, you will have the satisfaction of knowing you did the work yourself.

All sizes in this book are in inches. In materials lists, widths and thicknesses are mostly finished sizes, but lengths are full to allow for cutting and fitting.

1

Preparations

In your enthusiasm to refurbish a kitchen or bathroom, you may be tempted to begin by making cabinets and adding other furniture, either built-in or freestanding. However, you should first spend some time planning the work. Treat the project as a whole, even if all you intend to do is make one small cabinet now and add to it later. Wouldn't it be frustrating to find when you move on to later work that the first item has to be altered or even discarded as you arrange other developments?

It is unlikely that you will be able to alter the size of the room. There must be space for the cook and others to move about and do their work. Be careful, therefore, to avoid overcrowding with cabinets, worktops, storage items, and bulky things that might have uses in a bigger room. What you make might be competing for space and has to justify itself, particularly if it is competing with human beings.

In a kitchen there are appliances and equipment that must be there: a range, a sink, and other things. And you cannot have a bathroom without a bath, hand basin, and toilet. Anything you make must complement these essential items. Your additions should make use of the room more comfortable and efficient, and should certainly not impede the use of the room's functional items.

The main layout consideration is floor space, particularly in relation to the occupants of the room. After allowing for space to move around, you want to make the most use of what is left. As you consider this challenge, remember that you must be able to open doors and drawers without having to close or move something else first and that such things as range and refrigerator must be able to be moved for maintenance.

Floor layout is usually about the same as worktop layout. Farther up the walls there is quite a lot of space that can be used. Shelves and cabinets can go to the ceiling, if necessary. Use of this space needs to be related to movements of the cook and others over the worktop. There has to be working clearance, and anything mounted on the wall should not project enough to be hit by a bending head. Also, consider the opening of room doors and interference with natural light when planning wall attachments.

In general, plan equipment and additions around the walls. It would have to be a very big bathroom to do otherwise, but if a kitchen is big enough a cook will find a central work area attractive. This could be just a table to use with chairs for meals, or perhaps a workbench with storage underneath. It need not be fixed and could be on casters.

If there is sufficient height, there could be some sort of hanging arrangement from the ceiling. A frame, for example, could support pots and pans or some of the cook's tools, but do not arrange anything to hang too low. It must all be above head level; a tightly packed, low-slung mass in the center of the room will have a depressing effect on a kitchen. Likewise, trying to put too much in a kitchen or bathroom will have a claustrophobic effect. Keeping to light colors will help counteract this problem, as will breaking up closed masses with open storage, latticework, or glass panels.

Good natural or artificial lighting also will produce a roomier effect. Consider the placement of electric lights as you plan the new layout. In some rooms in a house, lighting might be primarily decorative, but in a kitchen or bathroom it is functional. Strip lights of various forms spread light well. You can conceal some, but check that they put light where you want it. The placement of lighting should not be an afterthought.

MEASUREMENTS

In the early stages, measurements are crucial. At first you need to know overall sizes, which can then be broken down into individual units. Most important are the horizontal measurements, which show you the layout and thus should be dealt with first. From them you have to project upward and decide on heights and vertical positions. Make every attempt to measure accurately, so you do not make something that will not fit or does not have the proper relationship to other things.

You can do a certain amount of layout work on the actual floor, either by chalking outlines or laying out strips of wood (FIG. 1-1A). You can use any scrap wood or wood that will be used later in cabinet construction. For an idea of heights and projections, you can use one or more pieces of plywood or hardboard (FIG. 1-1B). If such things as range and refrigerator are not already there, ascertain their sizes and mark them out or even make a mock-up, so what you will be making can be related to them. Obviously it would be wrong to first make your cabinets and then try to find a range or other appliance to fit them.

If you have to convince the cook that what you plan is the right way, you might need to rig temporary pieces of plywood of the right size at countertop level and put strips underneath to show divisions. Templates would show wall fittings. These preliminaries might show you some snags that you had not anticipated, before you make expensive mistakes in construction.

You also will have to make a scale drawing, which can be simple but should be accurate. You do not have to be a draftsman and you do not need much drafting equipment.

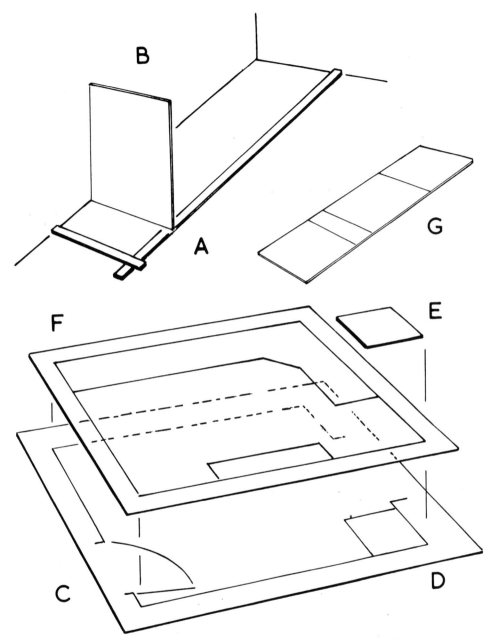

Fig. 1-1. The first step in planning a kitchen is to check layout and sizes.

You can manage without scale rules if you choose the right scale. If you settle on ¾ inch equals 1 foot, each ¹⁄₁₆ inch on your shop rule will represent 1 inch. It might be better to double that so that 1½ inch represents 1 foot and ⅛ inch on the rule is 1 inch on the scale drawing. At ¾ inch equals 1 foot, your drawing will be ¹⁄₁₆ full size. At

1½ inch equals 1 foot, it will be ⅛ full size. Converting this to a sheet of typing paper, you can put a room about 5 feet × 7 feet on it at 1½ inch equals 1 foot. At ¾ inch equals 1 foot, however, you can fit a room about 10 feet by 14 feet on a sheet of typing paper. For more scope, use larger paper or join pieces together. You can also deal with some rooms in two parts.

Squared paper has possibilities, but much of it is made with large squares divided into 10 small ones for drawing graphs; therefore you cannot use the big squares for feet and the small ones for inches. In any case, you might find that this background of lines distracts your attention from the shapes you draw.

Draw with a pencil and have a good eraser ready for the inevitable alterations. An alternative is to make a basic drawing showing the room outline, with windows and doors including open and closed positions (FIG. 1-1C). If there are things in the room that must be left in position, draw them in as well (FIG. 1-1D). If any of them could be moved—even if you hope never to do so—make a pattern of the scale outline, so you can reposition it (FIG. 1-1E). This helps avoid possible errors in redrawing.

What you now have is the basic drawing of sizes and shapes you cannot alter and must accept. When you are certain you have it right, you might want to go over the vital lines in ink. You then can draw and erase the cabinets and other planned items as often as necessary, without affecting the lines of the unalterable shapes.

Another good approach is to use tracing paper for the additions. Put the paper over the permanent drawing and draw the additions (FIG. 1-1F). You can then alter them on the tracing paper, but it might be better to start again on another sheet. That way, you can try new layouts and return the old ones as often as you wish, which might be helpful if you want to discuss with others what you are proposing.

It might be useful to have separate scale outlines of the proposed additions, cut from cardboard or paper, to try in different positions. For example, you can cut a strip of the scale countertop width, then mark it the way you intend to divide the space below (FIG. 1-1G). This type of outline might be particularly handy when dealing with that possible dead area in a corner, as will be seen in the practical details later in the book.

All of the foregoing is concerned with the floor plan. You also need similar drawings of any walls you intend to work on, which probably means all of them. Treat them in the same way as the floor plan, with permanent outlines boldly marked. Pencil on other outlines or draw them on tracing paper. Remember that what projects from one wall might affect things on adjoining walls. You might have to draw a horizontal plan at a high level or up to the ceiling to see how cabinets and shelves on walls fit into each other. This is important near corners, where you must make sure that doors do not interfere with each other and that you make the best use of space.

How you draw things on the walls depends on problems of access and design (discussed later in this chapter), as well as on practical considerations (dealt with later in the book), but the methods of preparing the wall drawings are similar to those for the floor and countertop plan. Although you could do most of the work up to countertop level before finalizing the arrangements on the upper parts of the wall, you should draw what you propose, even if you have to make modifications as work progresses.

For drawing purposes it should be safe to assume that corners are square and walls are upright, but it is advisable to check. Measure and compare diagonals. Some apparently square corners might be a degree or so off. If you don't note and allow for this, you might find that what you carefully squared does not fit. However, never be tempted to alter anything that should be horizontal or vertical to conform to an inaccurate wall or other part. Countertops must be level and door openings or shelf supports vertical. If something meets an inaccurate surface, the edge should be faired to allow for it, not the whole part tilted to suit. If yours is an L-shaped room, which can make an interesting kitchen or bathroom layout, pay particular attention to the accuracy, or otherwise, of the projecting corner.

If you can curb your enthusiasm, delay actual construction for a few days, while you and others concerned study the plans. This is the period when more bright ideas to incorporate could occur. Also, you probably will be fully occupied getting and preparing materials.

ACCESS

The new kitchen or bathroom layout you plan must be usable. This might seem obvious, but it is possible to get things at an uncomfortable height, have stored items out of reach, make working surfaces too wide, or plan many parts an inconvenient size. You might want to get as much storage space in a cabinet as possible, but if that puts things out of reach or a shelf prevents you seeing and reaching them, it is bad design. The same is true of a working surface that is uncomfortably high or low. And if the edge of a wall cabinet projects too much or is too low over a worktop for you to see and reach normally, that also is bad design. To make good use of all space, some storage may have to be out of normal reach, but what the cook needs frequently should be within normal reach and he should be able to do all normal kitchen tasks at a normal stance, without being stretched or cramped.

Unfortunately, from the point of view of planning, people are not all the same size, so working sizes have to be a compromise. As you build cabinets and other items you *could* tailor the kitchen or bathroom to suit an exceptionally tall or short person, but is that wise? A number of other people will need to use the facilities, and the uncommon sizes might not suit them. Moreover, someday you might want to sell the house with its built-in furniture. Unusual sizes, particularly heights, could affect the sale.

The user of what you build will normally stand while working. If not, the person will use a high stool that requires a working height similar to that of standing. Even a freestanding kitchen table can be at standing or high-stool height. Working surfaces therefore should be at a comfortable height, most higher storage should be within easy reach while standing, and access below the worktop should be from a normal crouch position (FIG. 1-2A).

There are some fixed sizes we cannot ignore. These include range, dishwasher, refrigerator, and other equipment necessary in a kitchen. In a bathroom there are not so many critical measurements, but what you make has to relate to what is plumbed-in

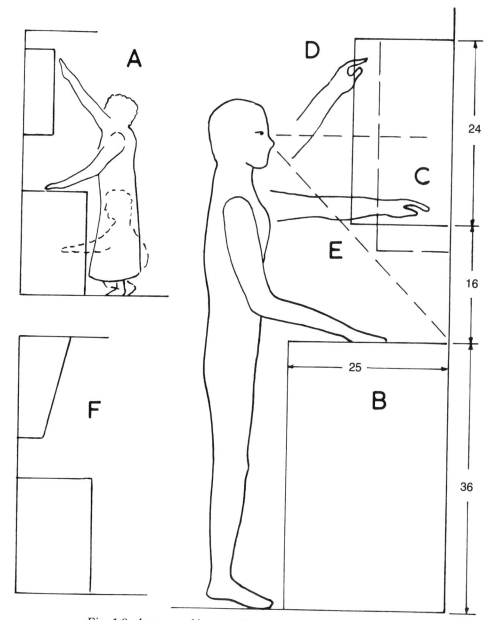

Fig. 1-2. Arrange cabinets so the cook can reach into them.

there. You might decide on sizes to suit what seem to be your needs, but if this means, for instance, that the range projects and is higher or lower than the surrounding surfaces, it will be inconvenient and look wrong.

Manufacturers are fairly consistent in certain sizes, so it is wise to conform to them. A freestanding or slide-in range has a top 36 inches above the floor. Other types of cookers may be arranged to fit in without reaching the floor, but it is advisable to conform to the 36-inch worktop height. Such equipment as dishwashers and trash compactors are sized to fit under a 36-inch-high top, often with very little clearance, so check these things at the planning stage.

A worktop should be wide enough to give plenty of working space, but not so wide to make it difficult to reach the far side. Widths need not be the same throughout a kitchen, but where you have to fit alongside or include fixed appliances, you must consider them. From back to front most ranges are 25 to 27 inches. The worktop looks better if its front edge does not project quite so far forward as the range or other equipment it adjoins, so the worktop should be 25 inches or a little less from the wall (FIG. 1-2B). This provides a good depth of storage space in the cabinets, although the back may be almost out of normal reach.

With the working surface height and width settled, you have to relate wall cabinets and shelving so that they are as useful as possible but do not interfere with use of the worktop. For convenience, irrespective of the worktop, the bottom of a cabinet or shelving should be at about the level you can reach horizontally (FIG. 1-2C) and the center at about eye level. The top of the useful storage space should then be about the same distance *above* the horizontal sight line as the bottom is below it. This will provide a comfortable height you can reach from a normal standing position (FIG. 1-2D).

To get this right in relation to the worktop depends on how far you want the cabinet to project from the wall. You should be able to see the back edge of the worktop without bending. Assuming a 45-degree view line, a wide cabinet therefore would have to be higher than a shallow cabinet (FIG. 1-2E).

Storage up to ceiling height will necessitate standing on something, so less frequently needed articles will go up there. For maximum storage capacity the shelving or cabinet could widen toward the top (FIG. 1-2F). Some actual measurements are suggested, but you should experiment with cut-out shapes or mock-ups to get the best arrangement for your actual situation.

Two wall-mounted items in a kitchen that merit consideration are a hood over a range and a microwave or normal oven at eye level. These items will project more than the usual wall cabinets. The range hood has to be about 28 inches above the range top, so you must plan your wall cabinet around and above it. Eye-level ovens are better included in wall-to-ceiling cabinets, than supported over a working surface. Be mindful that most refrigerators stand slightly forward of a 25-inch worktop, but must project higher. Allowing range and refrigerator to stand forward ensures that their doors open without restraint. Check this with any other appliance you plan to build in.

Although space is usually more restricted in bathrooms than it is in kitchens, similar access considerations apply. However, working surfaces are narrower and anything on the wall has to be shallower.

DESIGN

You might re-equip a kitchen or bathroom so that everything serves its purposes well, yet in some way feel it does not look right. Everything might be functional, but there is something lacking. Fitness for purpose can have a beauty of its own, but there is more to it than that. Certain design factors can be applied to improve appearance, usually without adding anything to the work or complicating the part involved. Much of this concerns proportion.

Some applied decoration or shaping is fine, but a kitchen is not the place for elaborate inlays and moldings or Victorian carvings and decorations. It is better to get the desired effect by proportion and with only such decoration as is needed to emphasize shape.

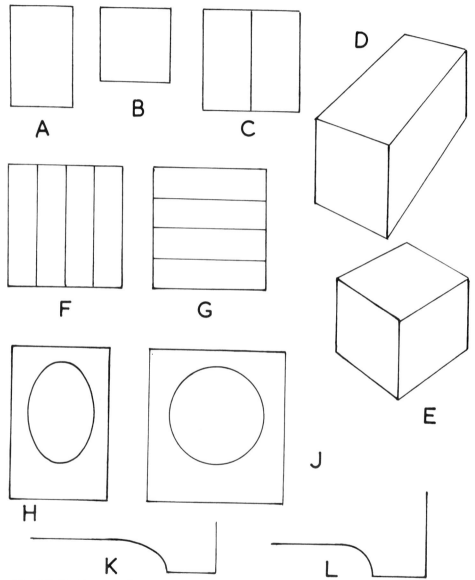

Fig. 1-3. For the most pleasing appearance, rectangles are better than squares (A-E). Vertical lines make items appear higher (F); horizontal lines make them seem wider (G). An ellipse, or part of one, is more attractive than a circle (H-L).

The basic design principles presented in the following paragraphs are applicable to anything, but here we adapt them for cabinets and similar furniture.

A square is not as attractive as a rectangle, so a door looks better higher than it is wide (FIGS. 1-3A and B). If you have a square opening to close, however, it is better—for appearance—to use a pair of doors (FIG. 1-3C).

This applies to solids as well. An island workplace looks better with all three dimensions different (FIG. 1-3D) than as a cube (FIG. 1-3E). To make something look higher,

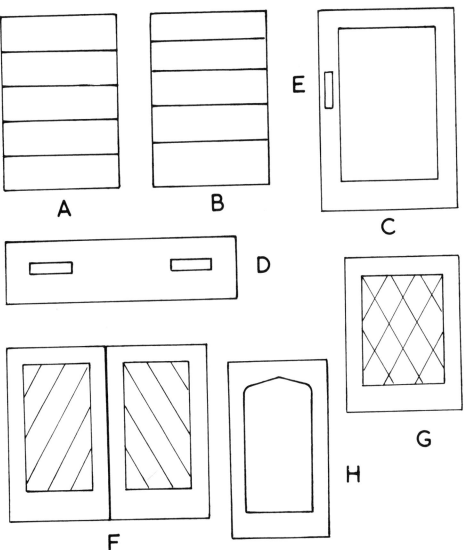

Fig. 1-4. Equal horizontal spacing makes the lower spaces seem narrower, so it is better to increase widths toward the bottom (A-D). Diagonal lines should only be complementary to the main vertical and horizontal lines (F-H).

or make a square look more rectangular, include vertical lines (FIG. 1-3F). To make an item appear wider, arrange the lines horizontally (FIG. 1-3G).

Curves do not occur in this work often, but remember that an ellipse (FIG. 1-3H) looks better than a circle (FIG. 1-3J), as in a panel in a door. This also applies to part curves—as in a cut-out edge—where an elliptical curve (FIG. 1-3K) is more pleasing than a semicircular one (FIG. 1-3L).

If you make a block of drawers all the same height, they will look narrower toward the bottom (FIG. 1-4A). Therefore, it is better to graduate the drawers' depth (FIG. 1-4B). This also applies to framed doors; with the framing the same width all around, the bottom part looks narrower. The effect is more pleasing if the bottom part is made wider (FIG. 1-4C).

As for handles, if your center drawer pulls vertically, they appear to be below the middle. It is better to place them slightly higher (FIG. 1-4D). Similarly, a door handle should be located above the middle (FIG. 1-4E).

Be sparing with diagonal lines. They should not be so prominent as to affect the squared appearance of framing. There can be diagonals in adjoining doors (FIG. 1-4F) or a diamond pattern on glass (FIG. 1-4G), but keep the lines restrained. One effective, but restrained, way to use diagonal lines attractively is in a Gothic arch form at the top of a door (FIG. 1-4H).

2

Materials

Kitchen units can be made of metal, but wood is generally better and is the only material adaptable enough to suit virtually any situation. Wood in its natural and manufactured forms makes it possible for anyone with a little woodworking ability and a few tools to construct kitchen furniture. It is therefore important to start planning the making of kitchen and bathroom cabinets by understanding what materials are suitable and available.

You could make cabinets completely from solid wood, but that would be very expensive and entail considerable skill. The result also would probably not be as good as the same unit made mainly from plywood, particleboard, or some other manufactured wood product. Solid wood expands and contracts in its width due to variations in moisture content, and in widths needed for a kitchen cabinet this could cause splits or joints to open. The other materials mentioned, however, are absolutely stable for practical purposes.

Consequently, for the main parts of cabinets and any other construction with broad panels, your best bet is plywood, with the other manufactured panels as possible alternatives. You might still need solid wood for some things, but it would be mainly in fairly narrow strips and for doors and drawer fronts for the sake of appearance.

WOOD

Wood is generally divided into softwoods and hardwoods. Softwoods come from trees such as firs and pines, which have needles and cones. Hardwoods come from broad-leafed trees. As their names suggest, hardwoods are harder and softwoods are softer, although there is great variation among the thousands of types of trees. For normal internal cabinetwork, softwood is suitable. On faces or where you have to match plywood, hardwood might be better. At points of wear, such as drawer runners or corners liable to be knocked, hardwood is a wiser choice.

When a tree is felled, it is cut into boards which are seasoned to remove much of the sap and thus to attain an acceptable moisture content. The wood might dry further, particularly in a centrally heated atmosphere, or it might take up more moisture. Either could cause warping. The amount of warping is affected by the position of the cut in the log, because shrinkage occurs in the direction of the end grain lines.

Usually, boards are made by a large number of parallel cuts (FIG. 2-1A). A board cut cut away from the center of the log will have curved end grain lines. Shrinkage along these lines will pull the wood into a dished shape (FIG. 2-1B). However, a board cut in line with the center of the tree has its grain lines across the thickness of the wood. If there is shrinkage along these lines, the board will get slightly thinner but remain flat (FIG. 2-1C). For the narrow strips needed for most parts of a cabinet, warping does not matter. But if you are buying wider pieces, examine the ends and choose wood with the grain lines across the thickness, if possible.

Wood sizes specified are as sawn. If you buy wood planed, it will be at least ⅛ inch smaller than the quoted size. For instance, wood said to be 1 inch × 2 inches might actually be little more than ¾ inch × 1¾ inches. That will not matter if you allow for it when marking out structural parts; the material will still have ample strength. Sizing discrepancy does not necessarily apply to hardwoods, which might be offered in the finished size. Sometimes hardwoods are only planed in thickness, and you have to deal with edges.

Branches cause knots in a tree trunk, all wood has knots somewhere. In forest-grown softwoods, with all the trees competing to reach the sun, most of the trunks are straight without branches. But in other woods you might have to accept knots. If they are small and obviously bonded into the wood, the knots might not matter structurally, although they could spoil appearance. If a knot has a black rim, however, it is becoming loose and will not contribute strength. In any case, avoid large knots.

Consult your lumberyard when choosing wood. For softwoods you might not have

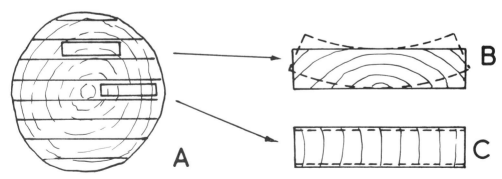

Fig. 2-1. Any tendency for a board to shrink or warp is affected by its location in the cross section of the log.

much choice, but avoid resinous woods, such as Oregon pine, which is heavier than you need and not amenable to screwing and nailing. With hardwoods, take the supplier's advice. He might have a local hardwood that is just as suitable as and much cheaper than the imported hardwood you want.

Have your detailed materials list with you. If your supplier can pick through his stock of comparatively short pieces, you might get a better deal than you would with long lengths. For instance, if you need six pieces 24 inches long, you do not need to ask for one piece 12 feet long; shorter pieces would do. If you have a table saw that will cut small sizes, it will probably be economical to buy such sections as 1-inch- × -2-inch strips when what you need are 1-inch-square strips. Just cut them down the middle. Always allow some excess length in such cases, however, as splits and damaged ends are inevitable.

PLYWOOD

Normal plywood is made from a number of veneers bonded together with glue and laid with alternate layers square to each other. This material is available in many thicknesses, but for kitchen and bathroom work the usual ones are ¼ inch, ½ inch, and ¾ inch. Some imported plywood comes in metric thicknesses; those nearest in size to what you will probably need are 6 mm, 12 mm, and 18 or 19 mm. Plywood is commonly available in sheets 48 inches × 96 inches. A lumberyard will cut these sheets, for a fee. When fitting out a kitchen, it is better to buy full sheets, however, as you will find uses for off-cuts.

The number of veneers in a particular thickness of plywood may vary. The greater the number, the stiffer the sheet (FIG. 2-2A, B). Plywood sheets have a good stiffness in all directions, but it is slightly greater in the direction of the grain of the outer plies, so it is best to cut pieces with the grain the longer way.

Softwood plywood is made from veneers cut with a broad knife from a rotating log, so a sheet might show no joints. Its grain pattern is very different from that of boards. Hardwood plywood might be cut in the same way, but face veneers could be cut in slices, so several are needed to make up the width of a sheet. This results in parallel joints, perhaps 12 inches apart and with adjoining grain patterns not always matching. However, hardwood plywood is also available with the face veneers matched, to make attractive door panels or other exposed parts. There are two approaches to this process. If the grain pattern of adjoining veneers alternate, the effect is called "book matched" (FIG. 2-2C). If the grain is all in the same direction, this is called "slip matched" (FIG. 2-2D).

There are a great many grades of plywood, and different systems are used for hardwoods and softwoods. This can be confusing, so you might have to consult your lumber supplier. It is no use asking for a particular grade if he does not stock it and it would be expensive to order. All plywoods have ample strength for making cabinets. The grades are concerned with the veneers, particularly the appearance of those on the surfaces. A poorer grade might be acceptable for inside use, but you need a surface of good appearance where it shows.

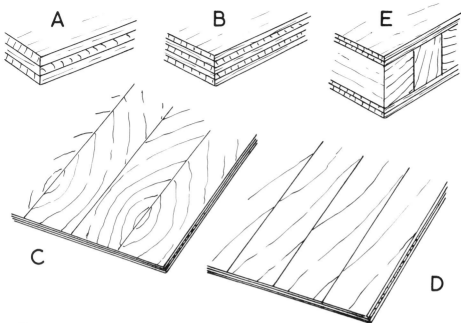

Fig. 2-2. Plywood can be made of any number of layers, and thick material can have a solid wood core (A,B,E). Decorative face veneers might be book-matched or form a continuous pattern. (C,D).

Softwood Plywood

Softwood grades usually range from A to D in descending order of quality. Opposite surfaces might both be the same grade or one might be better than the other. Grade A has a smooth surface good enough for a natural finish in kitchen work. Grade B is almost as good. Both provide a good base for a painted finish. Grade C shows flaws and could have unrepaired cracks and knot holes. Grade D has further imperfections. For cabinets—if you are not using hardwood plywood—use grade A or B where the surface will show. If the other side does not show, it could be the same grade or less.

Your supplier might mention grade N, which is an exceptional quality, better than grade A. And if he has shop grade, consider it, as it will be cheap. It will probably not meet all your specifications, but it might be good enough for some of your internal work.

Most softwood plywood has a coarse grain that does not look good under paint. Hardwood plywood is better for painting, although there are softwood plywoods available with plastic-treated surfaces that provide a good base for paint.

Hardwood Plywood

Most hardwood plywood has more veneers in a given thickness than does the equivalent softwood plywood. All hardwoods are not necessarily much harder than softwoods used for veneers, but they are stronger. For a certain strength, therefore, hardwood plywood need not be as thick as softwood plywood. Hardwood plywood surfaces are also smoother and less easily damaged than softwood plywood. Some hardwood external veneers are not distinctive, but the grain pattern of others is intended for decorative purposes with a natural finish under a clear polish.

As mentioned, hardwood plywood grades are different from those for softwood plywood. There is grade A, then grades 1 to 4 in descending order of quality. Grade A has no serious flaws and its face veneers are book-matched or slip-matched. Grade 1 is of comparable quality, but if there are joints in the face veneers, the grain pattern is not matched. Grade 2 might have exposed sound knots and is usually inferior in appearance. Grade 3 is less attractive still, but it could be used for inside parts instead of softwood plywood. Grade 4 is the most inferior type—unsuitable for cabinets, except perhaps for a back.

When making cabinets and other furniture for a kitchen or bathroom, a good general rule is to use hardwood plywood anywhere the surface shows and softwood plywood for internal work. You might have little choice among types of softwood plywood, but hardwood plywood comes in a large variety of appearances, strengths, and costs. Check what your supplier has to offer.

OTHER MATERIALS

Although ordinary plywood comes in many thicknesses, an alternative, particularly for thicker panels, is lumbercore plywood (or blockboard). This material has a core of narrow strips glued together and two veneers of the type used in other plywood on the surface (FIG. 2-2E). It is easy to work with and the extra outside thickness of veneer allows sanding to match an adjoining surface, which is difficult with most single-plywood veneers. Sheets of lumber-core plywood make rigid bases for worktops—probably better than ordinary plywood, but possibly more expensive as well.

Another manufactured board widely used in furniture is particleboard (or chipboard). As the name implies, this material consists of particles of wood bonded together with a synthetic resin under pressure and heat. The result is a board that has an unattractive surface but that is reasonably smooth, stable, and fairly rigid. Its weight is generally more than that of the equivalent plywood.

For some internal work, you can use particleboard about ¾ inch thick as it is. For face work, you can buy this material faced with a large range of surface veneers. Plain plastic surfaces in white and other colors are common, whereas other plastic surfaces have patterns, including a wood-grain effect. Some particleboard has actual wood veneer and can be used alongside solid wood parts. Many particleboard panels are supplied faced on both sides and edges. To cover cut ends, you can get strips of the same covering materials, which might be provided with heat-sensitive adhesive to enable you to simply iron them on.

Thicker and tougher plastic laminates, with a large range of patterns, are also available in sheets. They may be joined to wood or particleboard, using impact glue or other adhesives, to make a hard-wearing working surface.

Hardboard has limited use in cabinets. Some of the common grades seem little better than cardboard, but tempered hardboard is more compacted and is oil-impregnated. It is thus stronger and moisture-resistant. You can use it for drawer bottoms, dust panels between them, or backs of cabinets. Generally, however, plywood is preferable for such uses.

Medium-density fiberboard looks like grainless wood and is at least as strong as softwood. You can treat it like wood, so it might be adequate for parts of cabinets.

3
CHAPTER

Construction

The internal work in a cabinet can be as simple or advanced as you wish or feel capable of making it. In many circumstances the simplest construction will be satisfactory. For doors and other exposed parts, you can still use simple methods, if you choose the right design. But it is with these items that you can show your skill at more advanced work. Drawers can be made in several ways, from traditional dovetails to simpler joints or screwing.

Plywood does not lend itself to traditional joints. As most of an assembly will be sheets of plywood, you will have to adapt the design to suit this material's limitations. Particleboard is even more limited in its jointing possibilities. However, these drawbacks will not prevent you from making satisfactory cabinets using glue, nails, screws, and dowels. If doors are to be framed solid wood, you will have to use more advanced joints. You may show your skill there as well as in external work on shelves, wall cabinets, and other parts that show and that beautify the kitchen you are equipping.

Whenever two surfaces meet, you should put glue in the joint, even if nails or screws alone would seem adequate. Any of the usual wood glues will work, but make sure the one you choose is water-resistant. Nearly all modern glues are.

You can use nails for some parts, but screws are preferable. Nails pull parts together but only in a limited way; you can drive a large number of nails only to have ones driven earlier loosened by subsequent ones. Screws have a more positive clamping action; the upper piece of wood is squeezed against the lower one, between the screw threads and head. This ensures close contact for glued surfaces. Most glues only have very slight gap-filling qualities and are weak if not tight.

Where strips of wood are used to stiffen plywood or form joints to other pieces, you can use fine nails or pins to hold the parts while glue sets. Driving the nails at alternate angles in a dovetail fashion (FIG. 3-1A) strengthens the joint. Or use screws instead, if you wish. You can usually drive nails without drilling, but near an end where a split might develop, drill a slightly undersize hole in the top part.

SCREWS

In order to pull a joint together, a screw must have a clearance hole in the top part (FIG. 3-1B); then the head can press down. If the screw is tight in the top part, this action is defeated. You can drive fine screws into softwood without a hole in the lower part, but it is usually better to drill an undersize hole at least partway (FIG. 3-1C).

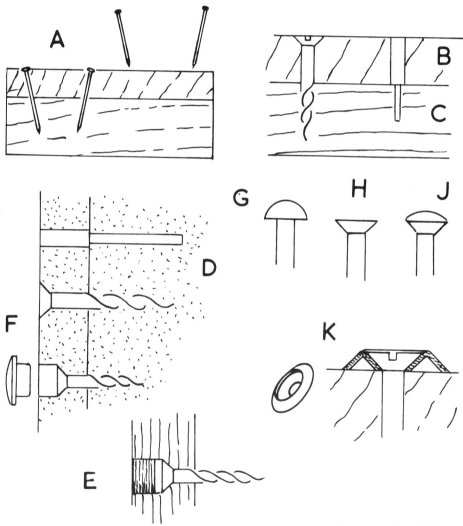

Fig. 3-1. Nails are stronger if angled (A). Screw holes should be predrilled (B-F). Several heads are available (G-K).

If you are screwing into particleboard, the undersize hole must go at least as far as the screw will penetrate, because a screw will not make its own way into this material (FIG. 3-1D). Trying to force it may cause splitting. In solid wood the size of the undersize hole is not crucial, but in particleboard try to make the hole about the same size as that of the screw at the bottom of the thread (the root diameter). This rule also applies to driving screws into the edge of plywood.

You can drive common wood screws into the edges of plywood and particleboard, but there are other screws that might prove stronger. Special particleboard screws for example, are made with sharper threads and usually with threads to the head, which may be an advantage if attaching something thin. These screws might also have two-start threads; instead of one thread wrapping around the screw, there are two, giving a finer effect and a tighter grip. Another alternative is self-tapping screws which are intended for sheet metal. These are similar to some particleboard screws but are made of harder steel.

There are places in any project where the appearance of a screw head, untreated in any way, would not be acceptable. In wood you can counterbore the screws, then glue in wood plugs and plane them level (FIG. 3-1E). This method might be acceptable in particleboard, but matching and planing this material are difficult. Instead, you could use plastic plugs, which are made in colors to match surface plastic or wood veneers on particleboard and which have very shallow heads (FIG. 3-1F). With the screws neatly spaced, the use of these plugs can be regarded as decoration, as they break up the plainness of a cabinet side. White or other plain-color plastic veneers tend to have a rather clinical appearance and thus benefit from such additions.

If you cannot avoid screws heads on the surface, brass screws are better than steel, both in resistance to corrosion and in appearance. Round-head screws (FIG. 3-1G) look better than countersunk flat heads (FIG. 3-1H). If you do not want as much projection, use an oval head (FIG. 3-1J). Another approach to making the most of the appearance of a screw which cannot be hidden is to use a cup or countersunk finishing washer (FIG. 3-1K). This gives a high-quality appearance to a flat- or oval-head screw, particularly if screw and washer are plated.

DOWELS

Dowels will provide secure and inconspicuous joints in many parts of a cabinet, whatever the material. In the simplest construction, you drill through both parts and drive in glued dowels, then cut off any surplus length (FIG. 3-2A). You should have no difficulty getting a row of holes to match, as both parts are drilled at the same time. This can be done for much internal work, where the dowel ends would not show. When you do not want the dowel ends to appear on the face, your task is slightly more complicated, as holes have to be stopped (FIG. 3-2B).

There are no rigid rules about dowel sizes and spacing, but in general you should use dowel diameters about half the thickness of the wood, plywood, or particleboard. Where there are no limitations, drill to a depth two or three times the diameter of the

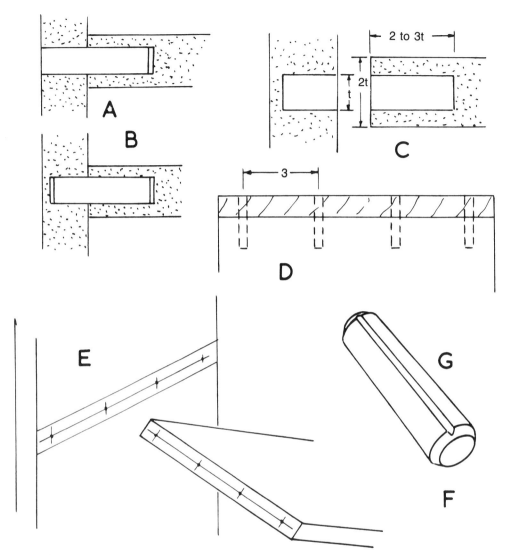

Fig. 3-2. Dowels can go through or be stopped (A-C). Accurate spacing is important (D,E). Beveled and grooved dowels (F,G) are easier to fit.

dowel. Where you have to drill into a thickness, go as deep as you can without breaking through (FIG. 3-2C).

Spacing depends on the strength needed, but in most cases dowels placed near the ends of a joint, then ⅜-inch dowels at 3-inch intervals, is an example of a reasonable arrangement (FIG. 3-2D). There are jigs for ensuring the matching of dowel holes. These have limited applications however, and you should have no difficulty in drilling accurately if you carefully mark out each position with a dot made with an awl (FIG. 3-2E).

You can buy dowels already prepared, or you can cut your own from long rods. Taper the ends so they enter easily (FIG. 3-2F); you can do this crude sharpening with a chisel. Also, saw shallow lengthwise grooves in each dowel (FIG. 3-2G) to let excess glue and air escape; otherwise the dowel will act like a piston in a cylinder and the wood will burst. To be certain that the joint pulls tight, make the combined hole length more than the length of the dowel. And when you make the joint, put glue on the meeting surfaces as well as the dowels, and use clamps or weights to squeeze the joint tight.

EDGES

Plywood and particleboard edges are unattractive and must be covered wherever exposed. How you do this depends on whether the edge will be subject to wear or simply has to *look* right. If the plywood is to be painted, you might be able to disguise an untreated edge with paint, but the alternate long-and-short grain might show through. Sealing an edge with glue first might help. In some circumstances the appearance of a rounded and well-sanded plywood edge under varnish or polish can suit a particular decor, but in most places you will want to hide it.

For veneered particleboard you can use self-adhesive strips on cut edges. These stripes are a little wider than the thickness of the boards, so you can trim them after fixing. Edges should be true, either from a fine saw or from planing. The density of particleboard and its ability to hold glue vary. To get the best surface for gluing, therefore, you might want to hand-sand an edge, using sandpaper wrapped around a wood block, to prevent rounding.

Use a hot iron to press-on the veneer strip, with a piece of paper between the iron and the strip (FIG. 3-3A). To get the right amount of heat, you might want to experiment on scrap pieces of veneer, but two or three rubs with near-maximum heat should be enough.

Leave the ironed edge to cool. There are special tools for trimming edge strips, but you can manage with a finely set small plane (FIG. 3-3B) tilted up slightly. As you near the desired size, change to fine sandpaper wrapped around a wood block (FIG. 3-3C). Remember, you are dealing with thin veneer, so proceed carefully lest you go through and expose the particleboard.

You can edge plywood in a similar way, but it is better to use solid wood, especially if wear is expected. The simplest edge is a strip glued and nailed on. For ¾-inch plywood the strip should be ½ inch thick. Let it stand above the plywood surface slightly. Use glue and fine finishing nails or pins (FIG. 3-4A); set the nails below the surface (FIG. 3-4B) and cover the heads with stopping. When the glue has set, plane the wood to match the plywood thickness. Do this carefully, so as not to cut the plywood; a hand plane held diagonally will do the job (FIG. 3-4C). Keep the plane sole flat on the plywood.

At places where wear is expected, your edge should be of thicker wood, preferably hardwood to match the plywood or maybe contrast with it. It could be wider than the thickness of the plywood—possibly 1½ inches on ¾-inch or 1-inch plywood. Fix it with counterbored screws (FIG. 3-4D). If you use cross-grained plugs from the same wood as the ends, they will finish neatly. Plane them off in the same way as the thinner strips.

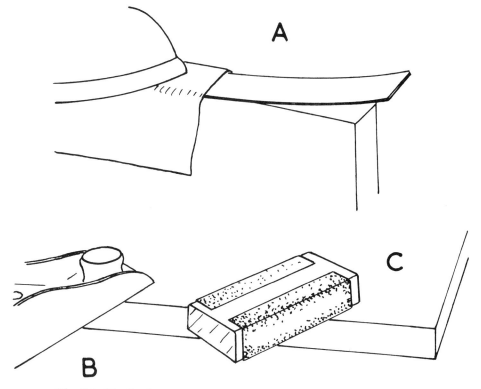

Fig. 3-3. Plastic-edge veneer can be ironed on and then trimmed level.

You can finish them by lightly sanding in the direction of the grain of the plywood, then rub a few times along the grain of the end strip.

You can put a hardwood strip along the end of a veneered particleboard panel, either matching a wood veneer or contrasting with a plastic surface. Besides protecting against wear, a varnished hardwood end gives a luxurious appearance. You could put matching strips on long edges as well.

If you want to avoid plugged screw heads or stopped nail heads on the end surface, you will have to provide better glue area than putting a strip directly against a plywood edge. This means using a tongue-and-groove joint (FIG. 3-4E). Make the tongue and groove at least ½ inch wide and about one-third the thickness of the plywood. Make the strip a little too thick and too long, so you can plane it level after the glue has set. If it suits your equipment better, make the tongue and groove the other way around. However, you cannot cut tongues and grooves in particleboard.

DRAWERS

If you examine an older piece of furniture, dating from the days before modern plywood and the heavy use of machinery in woodworking, you will see that the drawers are not only always made with dovetails but that the fronts fit within their openings, often with

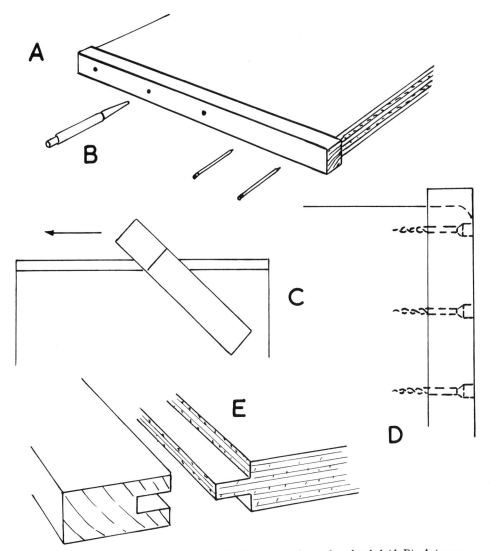

Fig. 3-4. Solid wood edging can be nailed or screwed on, then leveled (A-D). A tongue-and-groove joint could be used (E).

a fine degree of precision. Most modern drawers are made more loosely, and the gaps are hidden by the overlapping front. You could make kitchen or bathroom cabinet drawers with fronts to fit flush with their framing, but any doors in the same assembly would also have to fit flush. More likely, you will make drawers and doors to overlap completely or partially, but the drawer details can be very similar to those older ones, which were the pride of cabinetmakers.

In traditional drawer construction the bottom (now hardboard or preferably thin plywood) fits into grooves in the sides and front (FIG. 3-5A). The drawer back is above the bottom, so during assembly, the bottom can be slid in, then screwed upward into

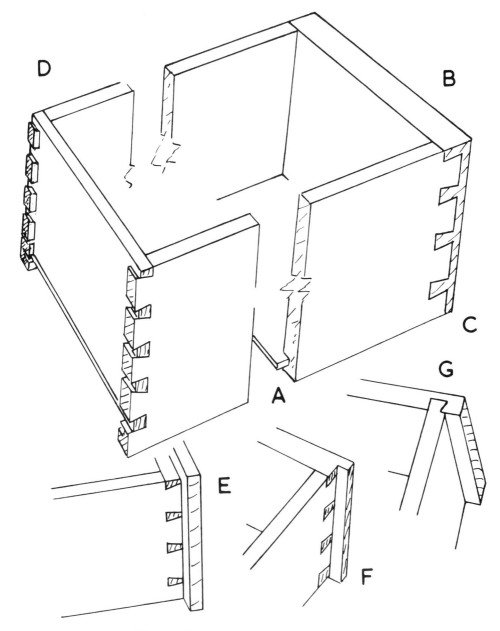

Fig. 3-5. *Dovetails are the best drawer joints.*

the back. Instead of grooves you could use rabbets and put a thin strip below the drawer bottom to hold it up. If you cannot use either of these methods, try placing square strips inside the sides and front for the bottom to rest on. At the front there could be stopped dovetails (FIG. 3-5B), the lowest of which is arranged to overlap and hide the bottom grooves (FIG. 3-5C).

The back can be held to the sides with through dovetails, but the top edge of the back extends above the groove (FIG. 3-5D). The dovetails in the sides are left long, so they project and act as stops against the back of the cabinet or against blocks on the runners. An overlapping front will act as a stop, but if the front is flush with its framing, there has to be something to stop the drawer at the back.

If you want to use hand- or machine-cut dovetails and you plan an overlapping false front, you could cut the front dovetails through, as they will be hidden. Then screw the false front from inside (FIG. 3-5E). Another option is to use thicker wood, and cut the dovetails into a rabbet (FIG. 3-5F).

If you have the equipment to cut long dovetails, you could dovetail the sides into grooves in an overlapping front (FIG. 3-5G). You would have to stop the dovetail groove, if the front is to extend above, but a groove open below would not show.

Instead of fitting the bottom into grooves in the side of the drawer, you can use grooved strips (FIG. 3-6A). This allows the sides to be of thinner wood while giving a broad bearing surface at the bottom, which is important if the drawer is to rest on bottom runners.

Instead of dovetails, you could screw the sides to the main front behind a false front. If you use a rabbet, fine screws or nails used both ways can make a strong joint (FIG. 3-6B). If a corner joint is to be covered by a false front, you can use a dado and tongue (FIG. 3-6C). Because of the short grain at the end of the side, this has to be cut and as-

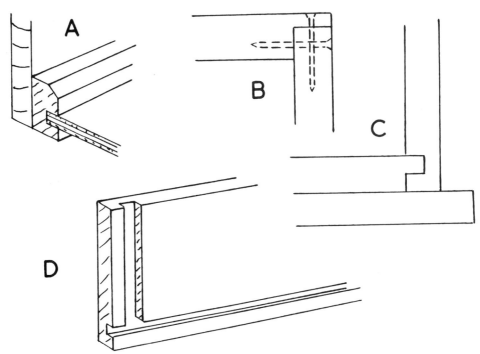

Fig. 3-6. A bottom can fit into a separate piece (A). Other joints shown are alternatives to dovetails.

sembled carefully to avoid breaking, but it finishes with enough strength. The back could fit into a groove (FIG. 3-6D) with glue and a few screws or nails.

If a drawer is to run on its bottom edges, it must have runners level with the front drawer rail (FIG. 3-7A). To ensure that the drawer does not tilt as it is pulled out, there should be a kicker above (FIG. 3-7B). In some assemblies this would be part of the runner of the next drawer above.

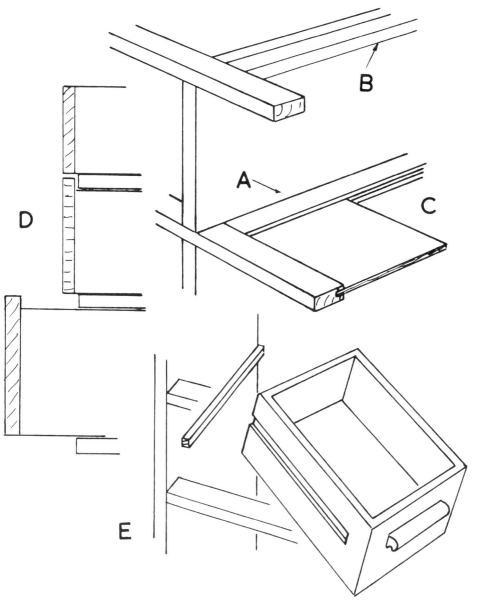

Fig. 3-7. A drawer can be controlled with strips (A-C). Drawer fronts can overlap runners (D). Grooved sides can slide on strips (E).

You can leave the space between drawers open, or you can use a thin plywood or hardboard dust panel, grooved into the runners and rails (FIG. 3-7C) or fitted on them. There need not be front drawer rails in a block of drawers; the top of each front could almost touch the one above and thereby hide the ends of the runners (FIG. 3-7D). However, where a door comes below a drawer, as it does in most cabinets, there has to be a front rail. A dust panel is also necessary, to prevent things in the cabinet from pushing up under the drawer as well to prevent dust from falling down from above.

When a drawer is supported by the lower edges of the sides on runners, it will slide without difficulty if its width is less than the length front to back. If the drawer is wide, it may not always pull straight and could catch on the skew. Keep it straight with a central guide under the bottom and inside the front. On an average-size drawer this piece might be about ¾ inch thick × 2 inches wide (FIG. 3-8A) and the groove about ½ inch × 1

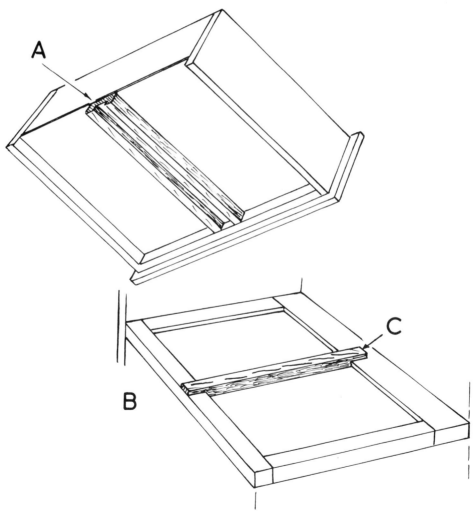

Fig. 3-8. One way of guiding a drawer is with strips underneath.

inch. The piece on the carcass should make an easy fit in the groove. Its depth depends on whether it rests on a dust panel or can be notched to go deeper between rails (FIG. 3-8B). Cut it back to clear the drawer front (FIG. 3-8C).

The drawer must be laid out to allow for this extra thickness below the bottom. Glue the grooved piece centrally under the drawer bottom. Temporarily screw the carcass strip, using oversize holes at back and front. Put the drawer in place and adjust it as necessary to bring it central; then glue down the strip. As with any new installation of this type, any wood-to-wood sliding can be eased by rubbing the parts with beeswax or candle wax.

There are other ways of supporting a drawer besides using runners underneath. One approach is to plow grooves in the sides, so each fits onto a strip (FIG. 3-7E). The sides and the strips should be a durable hardwood, to minimize wear. Related to this approach are the metal and plastic sets of drawer runners that are available. In these, rollers with minimum friction run in rails and allow heavily laden drawers to be moved with ease. Each assembly is about ½ inch thick, so the drawers have to be made that much narrower and the space hidden by the overlapping front. For many kitchen cabinet applications this drawer equipment is very convenient. The method of installation varies between makers, but in all cases only involves attachment with screws.

More specific information on drawers is provided later in the chapters dealing with the construction of cabinets to suit particular situations.

HINGES

The method you choose to hang a cabinet door depends on the type of door. (Cabinet *construction* methods are described in the next chapter). You must consider whether the door is to be flush (FIG. 3-9A), recessed (FIG. 3-9B), or overlaid entirely on the surface (FIG. 3-9C). You might also have to consider whether there is room for the door to swing as far back as you wish or if there is a wall or other obstruction that has to be cleared.

The pivot point around which the door swings has to be clear of the surface. It might be the knuckle of the hinge, although there are hidden hinges available which get the correct movement by a levering action. In recent years there have been many developments in hinge design, and it is worthwhile to inspect the stock or catalog of a specialist dealer before getting too far into making cabinets. The type of hinges you choose can affect the thicknesses of your wood or the actual arrangement of stiles (the uprights at the sides of doors).

With a flush-fitted door the hinges may be of the ordinary "butt" type, let into one or both the door and stile (FIG. 3-9D). The circle of the knuckle should stand clear of the surfaces (FIG. 3-9E), to allow the door to swing through almost 180 degrees, if necessary. The only possible problem with this method of hinging is that if the door is plywood or particleboard the screws might not grip satisfactorily to take the weight without assistance. One way to increase the grip of the thread is to put dowels in holes drilled from the inside, then let the screws go through them (FIG. 3-9F). Better yet, edge the door all around with solid wood (FIG. 3-9G), to improve appearance as well as strengthen

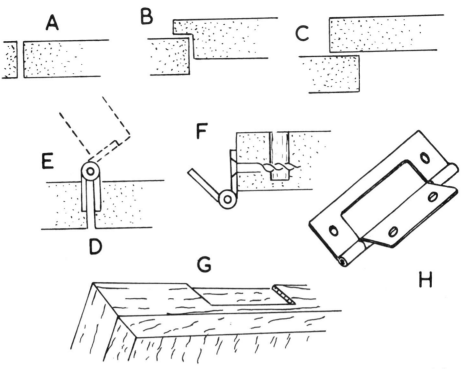

Fig. 3-9. Doors can fit flush, be notched, or fit on the surface (A-C). The position of the hinge knuckle affects the swing of the door (E-H).

the hinged edge. Flush doors that are not too heavy can use thin metal hinges where one leaf closes into the other (FIG. 3-9H). These can be used without letting in, as the thickness is no more than the gap you would leave at the edge in any case. You might want to use three of these lighter hinges where you would use two ordinary ones.

If you use an ordinary hinge for an overlaid door, the pivot point will be close to the surface and the door will not open much more than 90 degrees (FIG. 3-10A). To avoid this, use hinges with their knuckles higher. They need not reach the outside of the door but should reach at least half its thickness (FIG. 3-10B), allowing for the door edges to be beveled or rounded. Plated and bronzed hinges are available, either with decorative leaves or flanges outside (FIG. 3-10C) or narrower flanges almost in line with the knuckle (FIG. 3-10D). You can also get this type of hinge to suit a door with a lip (FIG. 3-10E). Most are intended for a rabbet ⅜ inch × ⅜ inch, so that should usually be worked as standard, but get your hinges first and measure them.

In some assemblies you might want to make a divided door or hinge one door on another. You could use two or three butt hinges, but "piano" hinges are neater and dustproof as well. This hinge is a continuous length of light butt hinge section, named after its use on piano lids. Cut it to the length of the door edges. You might have to drill it yourself. For kitchen use, brass is best.

Other hinges are intended to attach to the top and bottom edges of a door. They

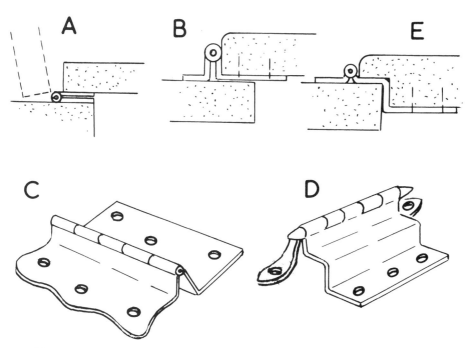

Fig. 3-10. Hinges may be cranked to facilitate fitting and the swing of the door.

do not provide any support for the upright door edge intermediately, but on the comparatively short height of a kitchen or bathroom cabinet this does not matter. One type puts the pivot point outside the surface of an overlaid door, with the hinges almost completely covered when the door is closed (FIG. 3-11A). These hinges have slot holes, so a door can be adjusted in both directions before screws are finally tightened.

With these hinges you can arrange door edges close together (FIG. 3-11B) or with a false stile between to give a flush appearance (FIG. 3-11C). The metal used might be no thicker than the clearance gap you would allow in any case, but you can cut back the stile if you wish.

From Europe comes a very different type of hinge. It has no external knuckle and is entirely concealed when the door is closed. The hinge also throws a door open so that it does not project farther than its edge, when opened to 90 degrees. This means that doors can be arranged to almost touch each other when closed, so you could have a series of doors on a long cabinet without visible stiles and with a neat, flush appearance.

These hinges have a rather complicated appearance. Designs vary, but in the basic pattern one piece goes inside the carcass and another goes on the door, with what appears to be an involved linkage between. The piece on the door is not only screwed on but has a cupped, round projection that goes in a shallow large hole drilled in the inner surface of the door (FIG. 3-12A). The part in the carcass is in the form of a base connected with the levered linkage (FIG. 3-12B).

The cupped projection on this imported hinge is 35 mm diameter, which can be treated

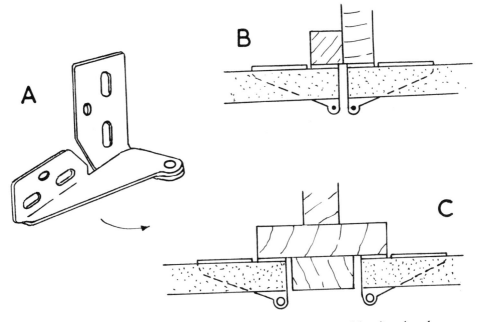

Fig. 3-11. This hinge fits at the top and bottom of a door and lets it swing clear.

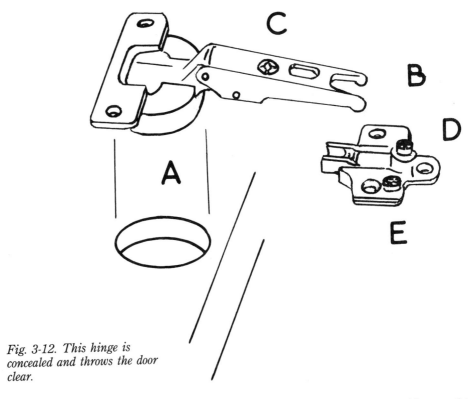

Fig. 3-12. This hinge is concealed and throws the door clear.

as 1⅜ inches. The hole needs to be about ⁹⁄₁₆ inch deep with a flat bottom, so use a Forstner or similar bit. The hinges' instructions show distances from edges and other measurements. If you are fitting many such hinges, you could make a simple jig for marking the location of holes.

The part of the hinge fitted into a hole cannot be moved, but the other part might have three screws in addition to the fixing screws (FIGS. 3-12C-E). These provide for fine adjustment of the door in relation to the carcass—allowing up-and-down, sideways, and in-and-out movement—although you should try to fit within reasonable limits initially. Some of these hinges allow opening to a little more than 90 degrees, but others will go to nearly 180 degrees.

Some concealed hinges include a spring action, strong enough to hold a door closed. This avoids the need for a catch to hold the door. For a wide door, however, it might be advisable to fit a catch—even if the spring hinges seem adequate at first—in case the springs weaken from use.

HANDLES AND CATCHES

You have to be able to pull a door open, and you might need some means of holding it closed as well. The arrangement of these functions has developed and altered considerably in recent years. Not so long ago handles were fairly bulky and quite often operated a catch inside. If yours is to be a country-style kitchen, you might want to use something of this type, but in modern kitchens opening and fastening arrangements are neater and less obvious. With spring hinges there might be no fasteners at all.

The door itself can provide a grip without an additional handle. You could bevel or hollow the door edge (FIGS. 3-13A, B) along its whole length, or rout just a short length (FIG. 3-13C). To make the grip more obvious, you could also hollow the edge (FIG. 3-13D). You can get metal strips to put on the sides of particleboard doors to achieve a similar effect.

Hollowed-edge grips are common on vertical edges, but in some cabinets they can be on the top edge. A similar grip might suit the top or bottom edge of a drawer (FIG. 3-13E). You could arrange a door grip directly below this (FIG. 3-13F), for the sake of appearance, but that would provide less leverage than an edge grip when pulling the door open. Some users might find that this needs a stronger action against a spring hinge than they expect.

A large number of wood, metal, and plastic handles are available. Select bright metal or colored plastic if you feel an otherwise plain appearance needs brightening, or choose handles that do not contrast much, if there is already enough decoration or beauty in the grain or molding of the door and drawer fronts.

Most bought handles are attached by bolts through the door or drawer front (FIG. 3-14A). Put washers under the bolt heads. If the screws are in the handle and there have to be nuts inside (FIG. 3-14B), put washers under the nuts and cut the ends off the screws so that the inside is as smooth as possible.

Some round wooden knobs have a dowel (FIG. 3-14C), instead of a bolt or screw,

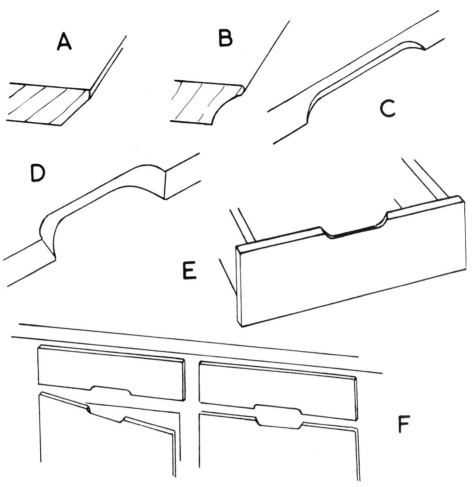

Fig. 3-13. Edges of doors and drawers can be shaped to provide a grip so that separate handles are not required.

that must be glued into a hole in the door. This knob is strongest if the dowel goes right through, but if you do not want it to show at the back and the stopped hole is too shallow to give the glue alone a good grip, you can insert a wood screw from the back (FIG. 3-14D). If you have a wood lathe available, you can turn a set of wooden knobs to your own design.

As you choose or craft handles and knobs, remember that a drawer might require two knobs if it is wide. Also, doorknobs or handles should be located high enough to grip without much stooping. And be careful that all handles in a row are level; slight differences might be more obvious than you expect.

There are advantages to long handles. If the cook is working on the counter and wants to reach to pull out a drawer or open a door without looking, he can locate a long handle with less trouble than a small handle or knob. Other ideas include making a row

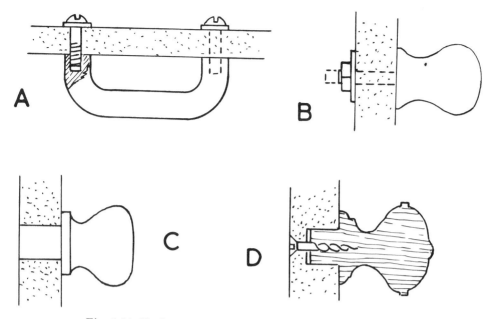

Fig. 3-14. Knobs and handles can screw on or go through.

of drawer handles full width, so they form a continuous pattern, or making the door handle half the depth of the door. Examples are shown in cabinet designs later in this book.

You can easily make wood handles by preparing a long piece and cutting it up. This ensures uniformity. Sections can vary from simple bevels (FIG. 3-15A) to more elaborate curves and hollows (FIGS. 3-15B, C). Such a symmetrical section might be used on drawers as well as doors. This might be important if you want to keep a uniform appearance between doors and drawers, but drawer pulls grip better if they are more hollow underneath, either squared or rounded (FIGS. 3-15D, E).

Cut handle-ends should be left square if they have to line up with other handles, but where they stand alone you can shape the ends similar to the section (FIGS. 3-15F, G).

Attach the handles with screws from the back. You can add a spot of color or brightness with stiff plastic or sheet metal under the handle, which also protects the door surface from soiling by prolonged handling (FIG. 3-15H).

Modern catches are simple; there is no longer any need for an action at the front to operate a catch. This might present a problem if you want to make doors childproof, however. A lock with a key is possible, but catches are available with inconspicuous outside knobs or levers, and these might suit your purpose.

Magnetic catches are simplest. One part goes on the door and the other on the stile or carcass side. The inner part might have slot holes for screws, so you can adjust the catch finely. These catches have no moving parts to go wrong and the magnet is unlikely to weaken for a very long time. Spring catches are available in several types. Most use balls or jaws on one part to grip a projection on the other part. Like magnetic catches, screws on the inner part can be adjusted in slots.

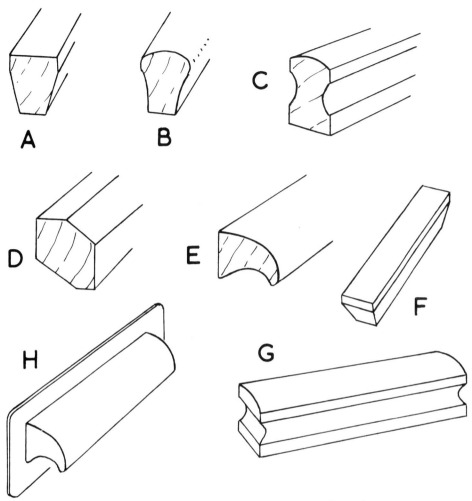

Fig. 3-15. A large variety of wood handles can be made.

For most cabinet doors and certainly if there are spring hinges, a single catch at or above the center of the edge of a door should suffice. A heavy or awkward door, however, might need two catches, arranged near the top and bottom of the edge. Exercise care in adjusting these, so the catches share the work; slight errors or a warping door could leave only one catch taking the load.

4
CHAPTER

Doors and Drawer Fronts

Cabinets and drawers should be arranged to suit convenience and practical needs. These may be the first considerations, but you also want the things you make to look as attractive as possible. Besides serving practical purposes the doors and drawer fronts are the main features that provide visual impact. Open the door of a kitchen and your first impression is likely to be the fronts below the worktop and on wall cabinets. Fortunately, the usual arrangements of storage provide a good pattern and fitness for purpose has a certain beauty, but you can do much to make the items that provide frontage make your kitchen more pleasing to the eye.

Consider all the items you are making for the kitchen as a whole, rather than treating them as a collection of individual things. For the total appearance they all relate to each other. For instance, you wouldn't want to use one door design for under the worktop and another design for wall cabinets. You also might want to think about practical problems of construction. In a fully-equipped kitchen you might have to make 30 matching doors and drawer fronts. It might be interesting and possible to make a door that involves some awkward or difficult work, but do you want to repeat that 30 times?

Another factor to consider is what equipment you have to do the work. If you have many power tools, including a router with a large variety of bits, you can do much more complicated work than if you depend on a few hand tools. Complex designs are not necessarily the most effective, in any case. There is a modern tendency towards plainness, but that can be overdone. Too stark and plain an appearance can have a clinical effect; you do not want a kitchen or bathroom to look like a laboratory. It should have a warmer and more homey feel.

Sizes, too, affect design. Cabinet doors are much smaller from room doors. If the working height is 36 inches and there is a 4-inch toe board, the effective front height is about 30 inches. The tallest doors will be near this height. If you put a drawer above the door, that may reduce it to about 20 inches high. Widths must be related to needs. You have to consider what you want to put inside or how much access you need.

Doors that are higher than they are wide look better than broad doors. If there is a matching drawer above a door, that may be considered part of the visual impact, so the door and drawer width may be considered as one when you arrange proportions. If you need a very broad opening, you could use a pair of doors meeting in the middle.

A long row of doors and drawers may look fine, especially if the pattern is broken by a range or other appliance. Or, if you would rather not have the same flat appearance along one wall, the succession of doors could be broken by something open, such as a rack or block of shelves. In addition to improving appearance, this could help the cook solve practical storage problems.

Average doors are about 20 inches × 30 inches, and drawer fronts are mostly about 10 inches × 20 inches. For these assemblies to be stiff enough to resist twisting or warping and strong enough to stand up to normal use, thickness need not be more than ⅞ inch. For the sake of appearance drawer fronts should project the same amount as nearby doors. Both may be rabbeted so the actual forward projection is small. In that case you may be able to make the total thickness of the drawer front less than that of the door, compensating to give the same projection by different depths of rabbet.

Bathroom doors and drawer fronts are usually smaller than those in a kitchen, but considerations are much the same. In both situations you can start thinking of doors as ¾ inch thick, then modify this if needed. A plywood or particleboard door should remain stiffer than a frame door, so the former would be ¾ inch thick when the latter would be ⅞ inch thick. Seasoned hardwood should hold its shape better than softwood. Store wood in conditions similar to those of the room it will be used in, especially if the room is centrally heated. This is more important with door materials than other parts. By storing wood this way for a few weeks, you can correct any subsequent shrinkage or warping before making the door or drawer frames. Movement in the wood of a finished door will then be unlikely.

PLAIN DOORS

Sheets of plywood or particleboard about ¾ inch thick should be satisfactory for doors without additional stiffening or framing. In its simplest form this door is a sheet veneered on both sides and with matching self-adhesive strips ironed on the edges (FIG. 4-1A). If the grain has an attractive pattern, possibly book-matched, the door will be sufficiently attractive in itself. If it is a plain color plastic veneer, however, you might want to break up the severity of the appearance. For this, you could use exposed decorative hinges or a handle bigger and with more contrast than might ordinarily be used. A long, varnished hardwood handle with a black plastic backing, for example, might provide sufficient contrast to a plain, pastel-shaded plastic surface.

Another way to break up plainness is to add thin strips of plain wood or moldings. A single line that continues on adjoining doors might be all that is needed (FIG. 4-1B).

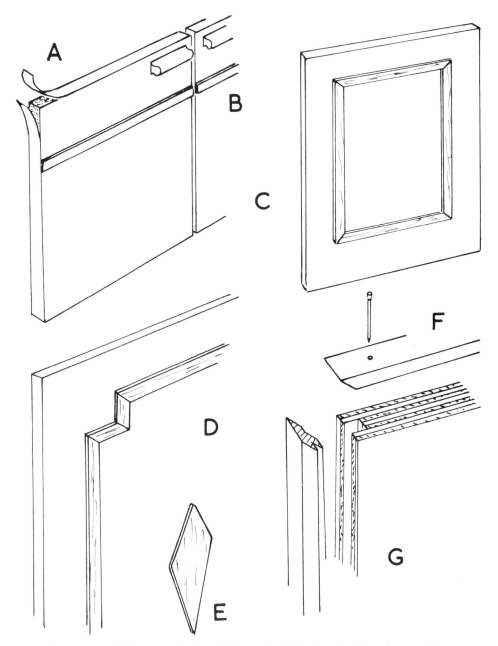

Fig. 4-1. Particleboard and plywood doors should be edged and can have surface decoration added.

Strips could be arranged to form a frame (FIG. 4-1C), maybe with different corners (FIG. 4-1D), and perhaps a motif at the center (FIG. 4-1E). However, this is a place where you should consider the work involved if you have to make a series of matching doors.

The self-adhesive strip on the door edge should stand up to reasonable use, but

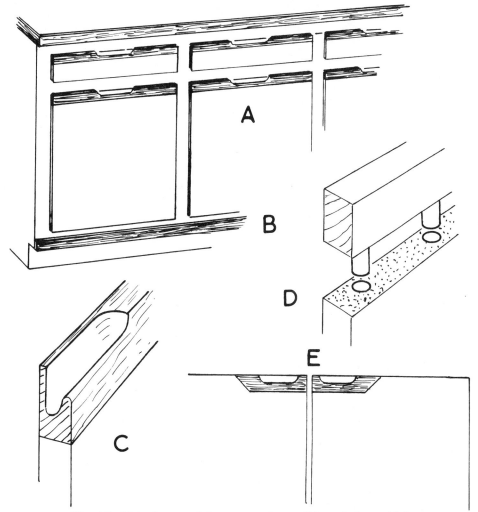

Fig. 4-2. Plain doors and drawers can have solid-wood edges added.

solid wood lips provide a more permanent coverage, particularly for plywood edges. Solid wood stands up to wear well and provides better holding for screws on hinged edges. The lips could be strips of finishing about ⅜ × ¾ inch held on with glue and fine nails with their heads sunk and stopped (FIG. 4-1F). For a stronger edge, use a tongue-and-groove joint. You could arrange this on the hinged edge only, then keep the face the same width as the other strips and mitered to them (FIG. 4-1G).

For a painted finish the color of the lips need not match the sheet surface, but if you are edging veneered plywood or particleboard, the framing might be better if contrasted with the surface. It would be difficult to get an exact match, but polished mahogany around the edges of plain plastic doors and drawers can have an elegant appearance. Try a sample first and relate it to wood edging a worktop or used elsewhere.

Plywood and particleboard sheets are sometimes available already veneered with contrasting strips. These sheets may be cut to make doors with one or more lines carried across a series of fronts. For this approach, make sure you can get enough material at one time, and be prepared to have to cut some waste to get the pattern right. Whatever you do on the front of a single sheet door, make sure there is a veneer on the back to balance the veneer on the front. It may be plain, but it gives a smooth appearance to the inside of the door *and* balances stresses due to the gluing of veneer on the front. It thereby reduces risk of the door distorting.

Another attractive way of breaking up a plain look is to have a broad wood strip across the top of doors and drawers (FIG. 4-2A) and a matching strip either at the bottoms of the doors or going across in a continuous piece below them (FIG. 4-2B). The top strip could be hollowed to provide a grip (FIG. 4-2C). You could fit the strips with counterbored and plugged screws, but dowels (FIG. 4-2D) are a better solution.

If you want to avoid a central pull on a door edge and there are no drawers above to match, a wood insert doweled in place can be put at a corner (FIG. 4-2E).

FRAMED DOORS

Cabinet doors and doors of many other types are made with frames surrounding panels. The larger ones are made that way for lightness, to avoid large pieces of thicker wood, and because they look better. There is much more scope for designing and decorating to produce pleasing results. Paneled doors have become accepted as the more normal type, so they are used extensively for cabinet doors, even when a particular door might be small enough to be made solid. Drawer fronts are even smaller, but so they will match the nearby doors they might be framed and paneled as well.

The traditional paneled door, on which many variations are based, has four sides grooved to take a panel (FIG. 4-3A). Its sides and top are the same width, but usually the bottom is deeper, for the sake of appearance. In a modern door a plain panel would be plywood; hardboard is acceptable.

The traditional way of making such a door is with mortise-and-tenon joints at the corners. You could also use dowels. For both methods, first prepare the wood with grooves to take the panel. For ¼-inch plywood, grooves ⅜ inch or ½ inch deep would be satisfactory (FIG. 4-3B). Mark out the parts, leaving the sides about ¼ inch too long at each end (FIG. 4-3C). As shown, the tenons go into the door sides about 1 inch. If the grooves for the panel are less than one-third of the wood thickness, make the mortises and tenons to that size rather than as thin as the grooves.

Cut the joints (FIG. 4-3D). Then cut the panel to a size that will allow the corner joints to be pulled tight without the panel preventing this by pressing on the bottoms of the grooves. Glue and clamp the parts together. Check squareness and see that there is twist before the glue sets. Cut off the side extensions and trim the door to size, if necessary. The simplest way to use dowels in this construction is to have two ½-inch-diameter dowels in a butt joint, then fill the end of the exposed groove at each corner (FIG. 4-3E).

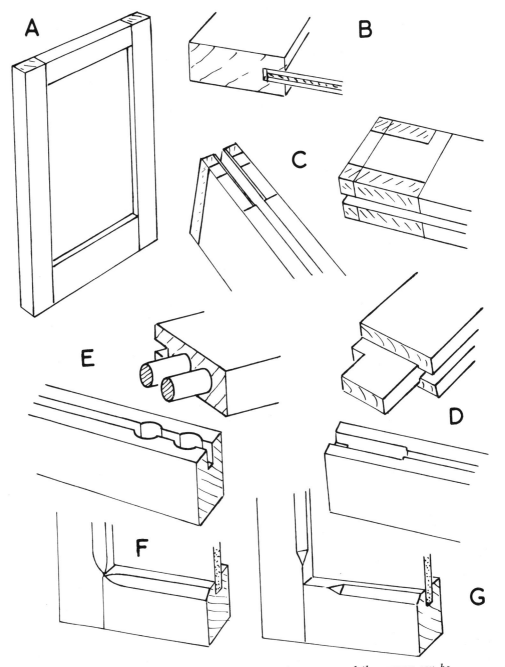

Fig. 4-3. In a paneled door the panel fits in grooves and the corners can be tenoned or doweled. Front edges can be beveled.

Appearance is improved if you bevel the inner edges of the front of the frame, either up to the corners (FIG. 4-3F) or as stopped chamfers (FIG. 4-3G). If you don't do this, at least round the edges lightly by sanding before assembly.

Drawer fronts can be made the same way. If a drawer is to match a door below it, the frame has to be the same width. Therefore, you will have to choose a size that allows there to be a panel in the drawer front, even if it is not very big.

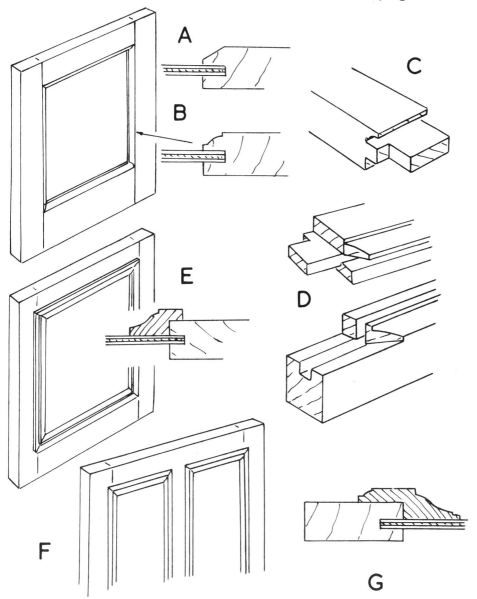

Fig. 4-4. *Molding edges affects the construction of a door. Molding can be worked in the frame or applied.*

MOLDED DOORS

The next step is to provide some molding on the edge around the panel. This could be anything from a simple bevel to a patterned section (FIGS. 4-4A and B), depending on what you can work with your equipment. There are two ways of dealing with the molding at the corners. If you have a cutter the reverse of the one used to make the molding, you can scribe the end of the tenoned part over the molding on the other part (FIG. 4-4C). Otherwise, cut back and miter the meeting corners (FIG. 4-4D).

Another way of using molding is to apply a separate length after the frame has been assembled, with square edges around the panel. Make the molding with a rabbet to fit over the frame against the panel; then shape the outside shaped over it, as with a picture frame molding section (FIG. 4-4E). The molding standing forward of the frame catches the light. It could be painted a different shade from the main parts.

If the door is fairly wide, it can be divided vertically. Putting molding around the two panels produces an interesting effect (FIG. 4-4F).

The applied molding does not have to be narrow. You can get an impressive effect by using a wide molding, but make sure its face is at least as wide as what is left exposed on the frame (FIG. 4-4G).

RAISED PANELS

In older paneled doors, made before the days of plywood, the panels were solid wood and had to be thinned to go in the grooves. This led to the development of raised or fielded panels, which were then regarded as decorative. This is still so, and you can give character to your doors by providing such raised panels. Instead of making a solid wood panel, however, you can get almost the same effect with plywood. Glue another piece of plywood centrally on the main panel (FIG. 4-5A).

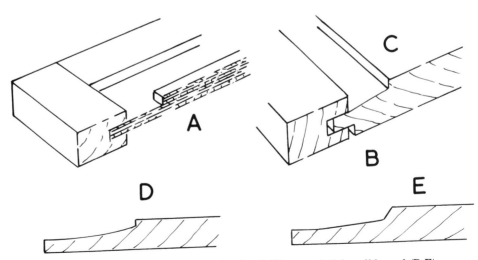

Fig. 4-5. A raised panel can be simulated (A) or worked in solid wood (B-E).

You can finish the inside surfaces of a solid wood panel level, but you must leave some room for expansion and contraction in the width (FIG. 4-5B). Make enough of the edges parallel so they fit in the slots, then slope up to the raised part (FIG. 4-5C). Normally, the edge of the center part has just a small angular section (FIG. 4-5D), but it could be thicker and angled (FIG. 4-5E). Be careful that the corner cuts make neat miters.

If you have raised panels in the doors, the drawer fronts will probably not be large enough to treat the same way, so you cannot make the drawers an exact match. With the variety of router cutters now available, however, you can work a pattern on a solid or plywood drawer front that gives an effect enough like that of a raised panel to fit into the visual scheme. The same method can be used to decorate solid wood or plywood doors.

The simplest approach is a shallow groove parallel to the edges (FIG. 4-6A). Giving

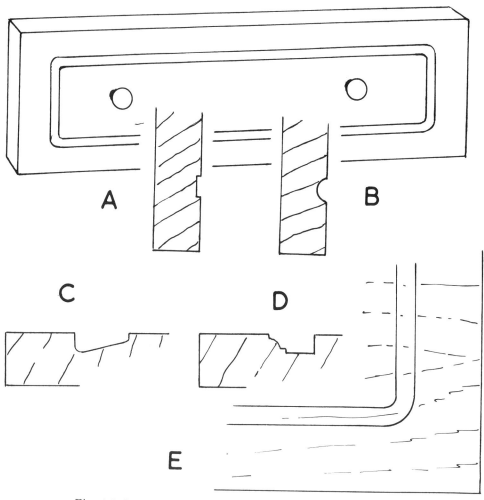

Fig. 4-6. Drawer and door fronts can be decorated with grooves.

it a curved section softens the appearance (FIG. 4-6B). You can give a wider groove a section comparable with raising a panel (FIG. 4-6C). Other sections depend on your cutters. The outer edge could be molded (FIG. 4-6D). None of these hollows can have sharp corners, unless you want to do some work on them by hand with chisel and gouge. The curve in a corner is slight and depends on the size of your router cutter (FIG. 4-6E). Appearance should be acceptable, even when related to the nearby square corners of a raised panel door.

SHAPED FRAMES

The frame parts of a door with a flat or raised panel do not have to be parallel. Some doors have very ornate shaping of the inner edges of the frame, but excessive shaping all around is inappropriate for cabinet doors in most kitchens and bathrooms. It is usually preferable to leave the sides and bottom inner edges straight and reserve any shaping for the top. You have to make a special top door rail, but otherwise construction is the same as for the other paneled doors. If you make a raised panel, the upper edge of the raised part should be parallel with the frame.

There are two ways of dealing with the groove in the top frame for the panel edge. If not much shaping is needed, you could cut a groove before doing the shaping, going deep enough to be below what will be the deepest part of the shaping, so that the panel edge can be square (FIG. 4-7A). Alternatively, you could make the groove parallel with the shaped edge and cut the panel to suit (FIG. 4-7B).

A simple and effective shape is the Gothic arch (FIG. 4-7C), with square or molded edges. There could be a rail with parallel ends and a curve in most of the width (FIG. 4-7D). You can vary the amount of curve according to the depth you make the top rail. There could also be a matching curve in the bottom rail. Curves do not have to be symmetrical within a door. And two adjoining doors can have shapes that complement each other (FIG. 4-7E).

Plain and raised are not the only types of panels. Frames have to be much the same, but you can fill them in other ways. For example, there are hardboard panels with reeded and other effects. To fit these types neatly, cut the edge level to fit the groove (FIG. 4-8A). You could use perforated hardboard (FIG. 4-8B) if you want to ventilate a space; however, the holes would let flies through, unless you put gauze behind. Another type of ventilating door has louvers. For this, you have to prepare a large number of thin section strips with rounded front edges (FIG. 4-8C), reduce the ends to slide in slots in the door sides (FIG. 4-8D), and make space to suit the amount of ventilation you want. You can plane the inner edges of the slats level after fixing, and cover them with gauze if you wish.

Many interesting fabrics, nets, and similar materials in natural or synthetic fibers can be used in panels. Stretch them over plywood or hardboard. Avoid glue on the surface, as it may show through, but a little glue at the edges pressed into the grooves should keep the cloth stretched. Remove any surplus glue inside the panel after it has set.

If you want to fit glass in a door, you must do so with the assumption that it might

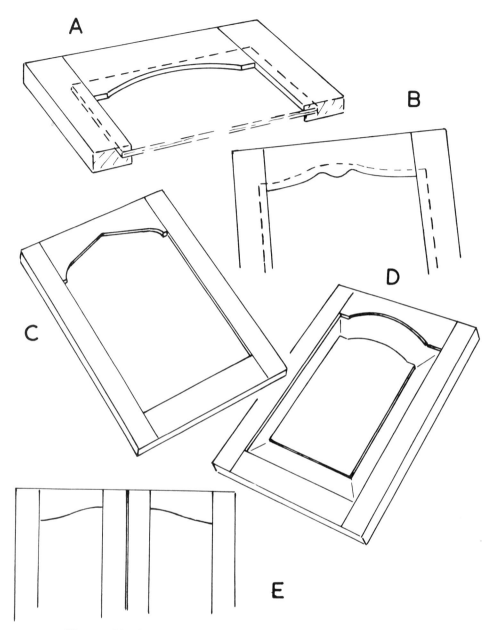

Fig. 4-7. Shaping the top of a door frame gives a distinctive appearance.

have to be replaced at some time. Therefore, it should not be let into grooves. Instead, cut rabbets in the frame parts. The glass is then held by fillets, pinned, but not glued in (FIG. 4-8E). At the corners you could cut back the frame parts and miter the front edges, as suggested for molded edges, but it is better with tenons to step the shoulders so that one is on the front and the other in the rabbet (FIG. 4-8F). If you are fitting glass

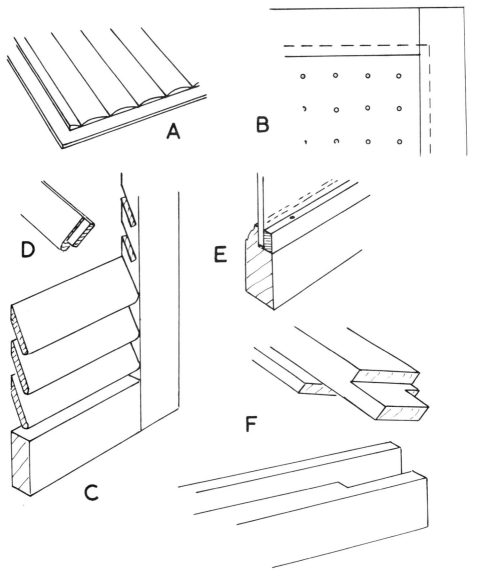

Fig. 4-8. Door panels can be reeded (A) or pierced (B). Louvers (C,D) provide ventilation. Glass or other panels can fit into rabbets (E,F).

in a lower door, it is advisable to choose toughened glass. If you want to provide a leaded effect, there are strips to fix with adhesive to make a diamond or other pattern.

The construction described in this chapter can be applied to the construction of doors used for many purposes, including kitchen cabinets. In making these doors, however, you might have to deal with edges and arrange hinges and handles. And in some cases there may have to be certain sections of wood to suit hardware or other parts. Not all doors will swing; some may have to slide or be made to lift out. Use the instructions in this chapter to make these doors, but do not make them without first ascertaining how they will fit with and relate to other parts. Usually, these doors are not made until after the cabinet carcass is made. It is easier to adapt a door to slight variations in a carcass than to fit a carcass to its door.

SLIDING DOORS

In most situations you should use hinged doors. When a door is swung open, particularly if it is able to go through almost 180 degrees, the whole of the inside of the cabinet is exposed and you have maximum view inside and clear access. But if space is restricted and a swinging door might not have room to move or would be in the way, a convenient alternative is sliding doors. Sliding doors do not project at any point in their opening and closing, so they can be used where the floor space in front of the cabinet is very restricted. This may happen more frequently in a bathroom than in a kitchen.

The main reason sliding doors are not more widely used is that they only give a view of and access to half the inside of a cabinet at a time. With both doors slid one way, half the space is hidden. You might not find this too great a problem, however, when weighed against the advantages of having doors that can be opened without projecting.

Sliding doors are also appropriate for wall cabinets, where swinging doors at head level might be unwelcome. These doors can be made of wood, and therefore opaque, or you can use glass, so cabinet contents are protected yet can be seen. This may be particularly advantageous in eye-level cabinets above a worktop.

The usual small cabinet doors in a kitchen or bathroom can slide wood on wood, but for larger and heavier doors there are metal tracks and runners. Much of this equipment might be too large and heavy for cabinet doors, so instructions here are given for wooden sliding doors only.

The simplest sliding doors are plain sheets of plywood. If you can get hardwood plywood with five plies in ¼-inch to ⅜-inch thicknesses, doors can merely run on the plywood edges. If the plies are thicker or the wood is not able to withstand much wear, you can lip the bottom edge with hardwood (FIG. 4-9A). Glue the strip and supplement it with fine nails with their heads punched below the surface.

For the bottom track, choose straight-grained wood and plow two grooves in it that will allow the doors to slide freely but not too loosely. The gap between should be no more than that needed for strength in the division (FIG. 4-9B). Sand the grooves with abrasive paper wrapped around a scrap of plywood. Rub beeswax or candle wax in the grooves but leave them otherwise untreated, even if the other parts will be painted. A groove depth of no more than ⅜ inch should be enough.

Make the top guide similar, but allow about ¼ inch for the top of the door plus an additional amount slightly more than the depth of the groove in the bottom track (FIG. 4-9C). This permits a door to be lifted into the top groove and out of the bottom one, to pull the door away (FIG. 4-9D). Gravity will keep it down in normal use, but you can always raise the door when you want maximum access.

Sliding doors function best when the width of each door in a pair is not much less

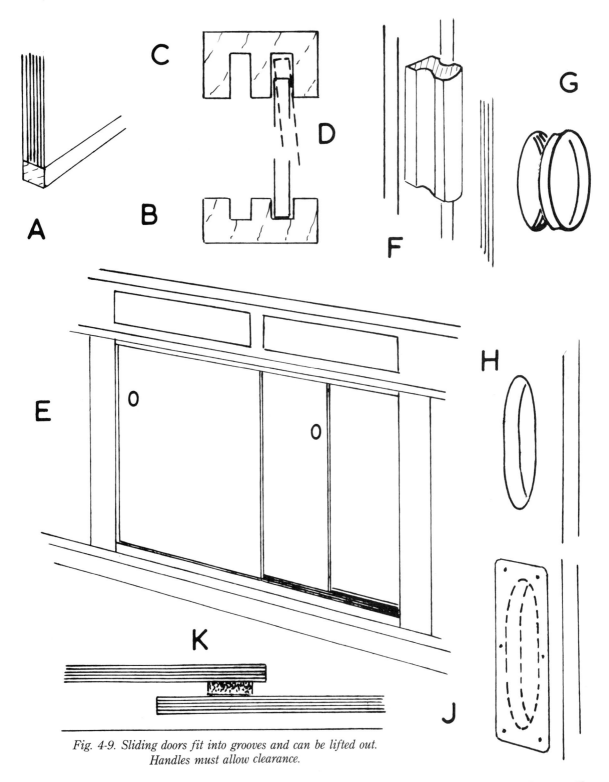

*Fig. 4-9. Sliding doors fit into grooves and can be lifted out.
Handles must allow clearance.*

than its height. A door 24 inches high, therefore, could be 20 inches wide. Tall, narrow cabinet doors do not slide easily. This means that a cabinet with sliding doors should be wider than one with a swinging door. A cabinet with two drawers or dummy fronts under a sink might be 30 inches or more wide, so the doors would be in a reasonable proportion (FIG. 4-9E). Allow a small overlap between doors, possibly 1 inch; the more overlap you allow, the less opening there will be.

The choice of handles for sliding doors is restricted, as a projecting handle on the inner door would limit movement (FIG. 4-9F). If you are dealing with a very wide cabinet, that might not matter, but ordinarily you need full movement. One solution is plastic or metal dished handles which can be fitted into holes (FIG. 4-9G). These handles don't project enough to interfere with the other door, and you can easily get your fingers into them.

A similar idea, which would be suitable for painted doors, is to make a long hole in the door (FIG. 4-9H). If the open hole would be acceptable, leave it at that, but if you want to close the back of it, tack-on sheet metal (FIG. 4-9J).

You can also get plastic and metal edgings intended to fit over plywood, with finger grooves, but most such edgings project too much to give clearance between doors. You could thicken the division in the tracks to make a gap to admit these handles, but the gap might also admit insects and dust. A pad of felt or plastic foam on the inner door will provide a barrier (FIG. 4-9K).

These sliding doors that have been discussed here are plain, which might be what you want. But if other doors in the room are paneled or otherwise decorated, you might want to do something to the plywood to reduce the contrast. One approach is to add a thin frame to the plywood to look something like nearby paneled doors (FIG. 4-10A). However, you will have to thicken the division in each guide to allow the doors to pass. Keep the framing clear of top and bottom edges, so there is still enough plywood projecting for the door to be lifted out (FIG. 4-10B).

Besides simulating a paneled door, you can include shallow half-round molding (FIG. 4-10C) or other surface decoration, provided it is not very thick. If the cabinet system is to be painted, you might get a sufficiently authentic appearance by painting an otherwise plain plywood door to look like the shaping on other doors.

Instead of trying to make a plywood door look like something else, you can use doors made like the room's swinging doors in a sliding door assembly. Make the front door with a guide strip at the bottom near the rear edge, either full length or in two pieces (FIG. 4-10D). Do the same on the top edge, but with deeper strips to allow the door to be raised into the top groove when you want to lift it out (FIG. 4-10E). Make the door high enough so that there is clearance at the bottom and the weight is taken on the guide strips, and so that there is enough clearance at the top to allow lifting. Use a close-grained hardwood for the guide strips.

Make the inner door the same way, but put the guide strips near the front edges (FIG. 4-10F). With the greater depth of door, you can make deep grips for fingers in the outer edges (FIG. 4-10G). The outer door can either stand forward of the framing (FIG.

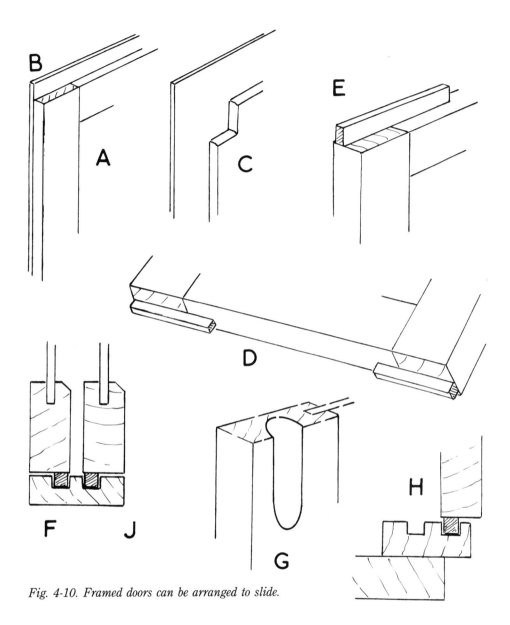

Fig. 4-10. Framed doors can be arranged to slide.

4-10H), if that is the way other doors are fitted, or you can set it back level with the framing by widening the fronts of the tracks (FIG. 4-10J).

Although all cabinets should be square and top and bottom edges parallel, this is even more important when sliding doors are fitted. Doors must slide both ways without binding. Tracks must be both parallel and straight. A thick plywood cabinet bottom with its toe board beneath should be stiff enough, but have a framing piece wide enough and stiff enough across the top to secure the top track.

5
CHAPTER

Basic Cabinets

In a modern home, kitchen and bathroom cabinets are generally built-in furniture that is sold with the house. At one time, however, most kitchen furniture was freestanding, even if it was kept against walls. Hutches and Welsh dressers are examples of units with many of the attributes of floor and wall cabinets. You can apply this freestanding approach in building cabinets, if you expect to move and want to take the furniture with you. But you are more likely to want to build-in your cabinets, and this chapter is based on that assumption.

By building-in you avoid possible movement and spaces where dirt may accumulate or things get lost. You also make the most of every bit of space. In addition, building-in enables you to allow for inaccuracies in walls, so there are no unsightly gaps. Plumbing pipes and electric wires can be more easily hidden or disguised, helping to give the whole room a neater appearance. In a bathroom, which is usually more compact than a kitchen, building-in may be the only wise method. If you have to fit around existing fittings and keep cabinets and their working tops narrow, freestanding furniture might not fit close enough and could be top-heavy.

In kitchens and bathrooms you might occasionally want to pull an apparently built-in unit away from the wall for access to something, as for maintenance. You can allow for this by making the main parts of the cabinets along a wall permanent, with one section held to the wall with a few screws in accessible positions. Therefore the unit can be moved, but still looks like part of the whole wall assembly.

There are several ways to make cabinets. What you are basically doing is providing a working surface with storage below, mostly closed by doors, although there can be drawers and open shelves. The inside may be likened to boxes standing on edge, with their openings faced forward. How you put all this together depends on several factors;

no one way is necessarily better than another. With the main constructional materials being plywood or particleboard in large pieces, the arrangement of the carcass and the way it is put together can be simple.

Cabinet units can be purchased in kits or complete with backs, sides, and ends. You can make your units in the same way, although these pieces have some redundant parts.

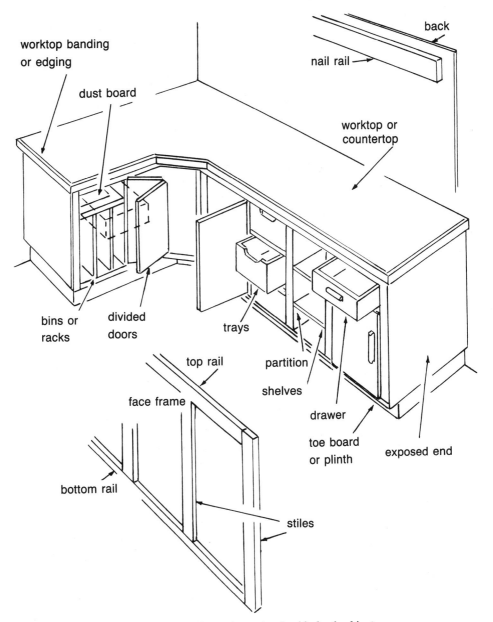

Fig. 5-1. Names of the main parts of a block of cabinets.

For example, you could just use the house wall as the back of the cabinet. And if a cabinet goes into a corner, you might decide the other wall can serve as its end. Or rather than make several units to fit against each other, you could treat the work as a whole, with single divisions where two meeting unit sides would otherwise be brought together. All these ideas eliminate some fairly large pieces of sheet material, and make capacity slightly bigger as well. Whether to build cabinets this way depends on circumstances, and you will have to decide when confronted with the actual job.

It is easier to work directly on the job and make everything there—fitting parts so as to treat the assembly as a whole and to use walls as part of the structure—than it is to prefabricate parts in a shop elsewhere. If you choose the latter approach, then it might be better to include backs and ends. That way, you can bring the complete assemblies to the room and only have to screw them in place, with the minimum of on-site fitting work.

Cabinets are usually mounted over a plinth or toe board. This structure is about 4 inches high and set back a few inches so toes can go underneath and you can stand closer to the cabinet. Work tops will vary, but they can look thick—even when they may not be—and should overhang the cabinet at front and end.

The basic cabinet parts and their names are shown in FIG. 5-1. Some of these items are called other names as well, but the names in the figure are used throughout this book.

FITTED TWO-PART CABINET

The cabinet shown in FIG. 5-2 has two compartments with doors and is to fit into the corner of a room, using the walls as the cabinet backs. To begin, lightly chalk the outline of the cabinet on the floor to see that you have the desired size and that it will not interfere with anything else in the room. Check the level of the floor within the marked area. In most homes this should be satisfactory. Check the walls within the marked area. If they are out of vertical in a 36-inch height, you will have to allow for the error. Also check any lack of squareness in the corner at a 36-inch height. The top must fit to it, but errors lower down will not matter.

If there is a baseboard within the cabinet area, you might want to remove it so that the remainder finishes at the cabinet edges. Otherwise you will have to fit cabinet parts over it. If there are pipes or wires within the cabinet area, note their location and decide how you will cut around them. As this cabinet is to be fitted directly to the walls, notching around these obstructions should be easy. Following are the basic construction steps:

• Make the exposed end as shown in FIG. 5-3A. Its height allows for 1 inch plywood on top, and it is cut back for the toe board. Because its face will show, you can leave it plain for painting or use a wood or plastic veneer. The front edge must be vertical, even if you have to shape the rear edge to suit an inaccurate wall. The top must finish horizontal.

• Fit framing strips to the end (FIG. 5-3B). They provide stiffness as well as notches and supports for lengthwise parts.

• Take the end to the corner wall and from it mark the outline there. Using these marks,

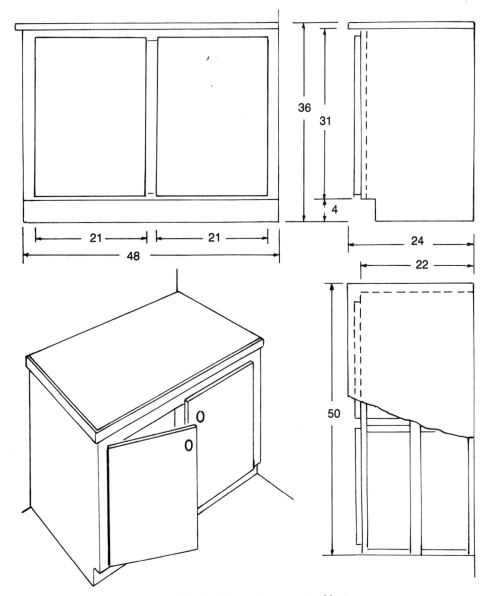

Fig. 5-2. A basic two-part cabinet.

fit matching strips to the wall for the opposite end supports (FIG. 5-3C). While doing this, sight over the end in its final position at the pieces you fit to the wall, to see that surfaces will be in line at opposite ends.

• Make the toe board (FIG. 5-3D) and a matching piece at the back.

• Join the exposed end to the wall with screws through the strip inside, and fit the toe board and its partner. Include the central piece between them (FIG. 5-3E). Parts should be joined with glue and nails set and stopped, or with screws.

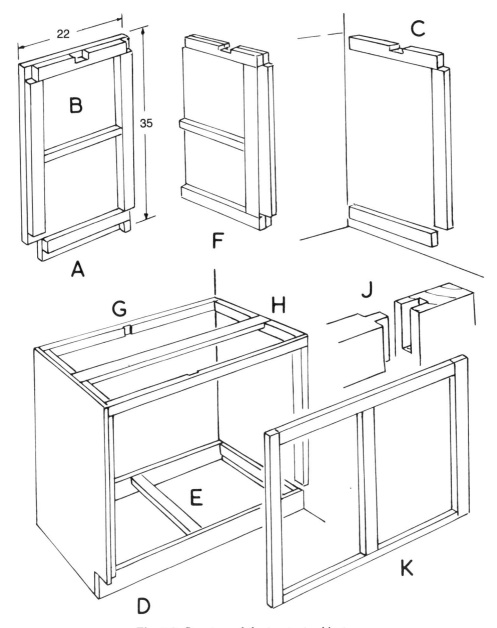

Fig. 5-3. Structure of the two-part cabinet.

• Make and fit the cabinet bottom over the toe board and other parts. Make sure its front edge is straight. An absolutely tight fit against the walls is not as important, however. Secure it to everything it crosses.
• Make the division, using the part of the end above the bottom as a guide to size (FIG.

5-3F). Frame it. The diagram allows for a shelf in one compartment, but you could put shelves in both parts or put more than one in each.

• Mark on the bottom where the division is to come. Make front and back lengthwise pieces at the top with shallow notches to steady the division (FIG. 5-3G). Fit these parts together and add another central lengthwise strip to help support the worktop (FIG. 5-3H).

• Make and fit the shelf. You can screw it down or leave it loose so it can be lifted out. Do not bring its front edge too far forward, or it will obstruct the view of things underneath.

• The front has a frame to carry the doors. This could be made with strips butted against each other and glued and nailed to the carcass parts, but it would be better if the parts met with shallow mortise-and-tenon joints (FIG. 5-3J). If the exposed parts are to be painted, you can use any wood, but if you plan to use a clear finish that will show the grain, use wood that will match the end. Arrange the strips to be the same width as the parts they cover, or a little wider. Keeping their edges level will help if you intend to fit concealed hinges. Make the frame (FIG. 5-3K) with its bottom rail matching the plywood bottom.

• Make the doors according to any of the designs described in Chapter 4. You can temporarily fit them to test their action, but save the final fitting until after the worktop has been made and fitted.

• There are several ways of making the worktop, but this example will use a piece of 1-inch plywood covered with Formica or other laminated plastic and edged with hardwood. Make the top to fit close to the wall and overhang the carcass by about 1 inch at front and end.

• It is difficult to add the laminated plastic with accurate edges with the top in position, so lay a slightly oversize piece with contact adhesive on the separate plywood top and trim the edges to size. When you are satisfied with the fit, mount the top on the carcass using screws driven upward through the framing (FIG. 5-4A).

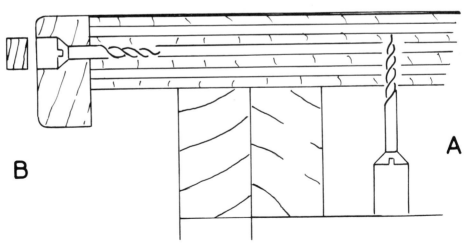

Fig. 5-4. Detail of the counter edging and how it is screwed from below.

• Edge the top with hardwood strips, mitered at the corner and projecting below the plywood. Use counterbored screws and glue. Make cross-grained plugs of the same wood to glue in the screw holes (FIG. 5-4B). Round edges and corner.

• Your choice of finish depends on your decor. You might wish to paint a light color inside before you fit the top. Whatever finish you use elsewhere, a clear finish over an attractive hardwood top edging gives the whole cabinet a rich appearance.

Materials List for Fitted Two-part Cabinet

1 exposed end	1 × 22 × 36 plywood
2 exposed end frames	1 × 2 × 32
2 exposed end frames	1 × 2 × 22
1 exposed end shelf rail	1 × 1 × 20
2 wall end rails	1 × 2 × 22
1 wall end rail	1 × 2 × 32
1 division	1 × 22 × 32 plywood
2 division frames	1 × 2 × 22
1 division frame	1 × 2 × 32
1 toe board	1 × 4 × 50
1 bottom back rail	1 × 4 × 50
1 bottom center rail	1 × 2 × 22
3 top rails	1 × 2 × 48
3 front frames	1 × 2 × 32
1 front frame	1 × 2 × 50
1 front frame	1 × 1 × 50
1 bottom	1 × 22 × 48 plywood
1 shelf	1 × 22 × 22 plywood
1 top	1 × 24 × 50 plywood
1 top edging	¾ × 1½ × 50
1 top edging	¾ × 1½ × 26
2 doors	1 × 21 × 31 plywood

ENCLOSED TWO-DRAWER CABINET

If you plan to build a cabinet completely as a unit before putting in position, you will have to make ends and a back. A cabinet built in this way should not be too large to be moved from the shop to where it is to be used. An alternative is to build several units, to be linked in position and covered by a continuous top.

The cabinet shown in FIG. 5-5 is intended to stand anywhere against a wall, but it could be adapted to fit into a corner or against an appliance. It could have full-depth doors, but as shown it has drawers above the doors and shelves between (FIG. 5-6). The carcass stands on a plinth, and the top may be fitted during construction or after the other parts are attached to the wall. Construction is mainly of 1-inch plywood, although particleboard could be used for some parts. The top is made in the same way as in fitted cabinet discussed earlier, but other forms could be used. If you use a standard-type worktop that is already surfaced, check its width before making the carcass and other parts. Following are the basic construction steps for the enclosed cabinet:

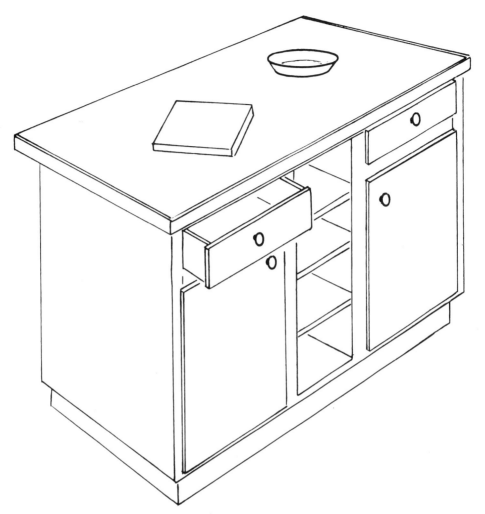

Fig. 5-5. An enclosed two-drawer cabinet.

• Make the pair of ends (FIGS. 5-6A and 5-7A). The outer face should be veneered or be suitable for painting. Rabbet the rear edges to take the back (FIG. 5-7B).

• Put strips across. Notch the top one to take three lengthwise strips that will support the worktop (FIGS. 5-6B and 5-7C). At drawer bottom level there is a 2-inch strip with a 1-inch-square strip attached to act as drawer guide and runner (FIG. 5-7D). (If your drawer-fitting method does not prevent the drawer from tilting, you could fit a similar piece on the top strip as a kicker. However, you could save that step until you fit the drawers.) Complete the ends as a pair.

• Make the pair of divisions (FIG. 5-7E), which are placed above the bottom and inside the back. On the outward surfaces fit strips across the top the same as at the ends.

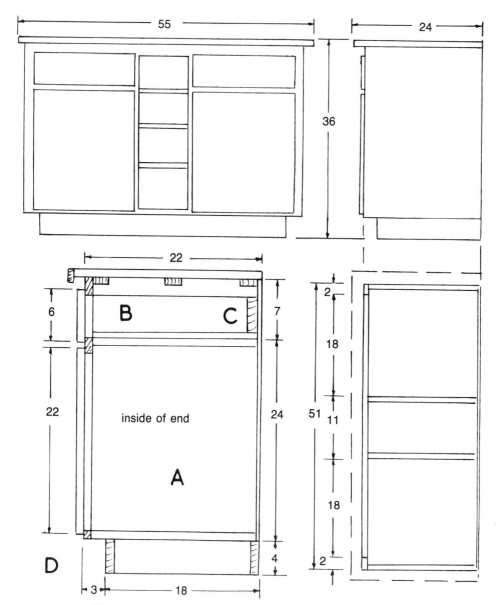

Fig. 5-6. Sizes and sections of the enclosed two-drawer cabinet.

Fit a single strip across at drawer level. Put cleats on the inner surfaces to support shelves (FIG. 5-7F).

• Make the bottom to fit between the ends. Use dowels at the ends. You could use dowels for the divisions, but it is simpler to screw up through the bottom (FIG. 5-7G).

• The three lengthwise strips at the top are the same length as the bottom. Have them and the bottom ready for assembly to the ends and divisions. Glue and clamp the dowels

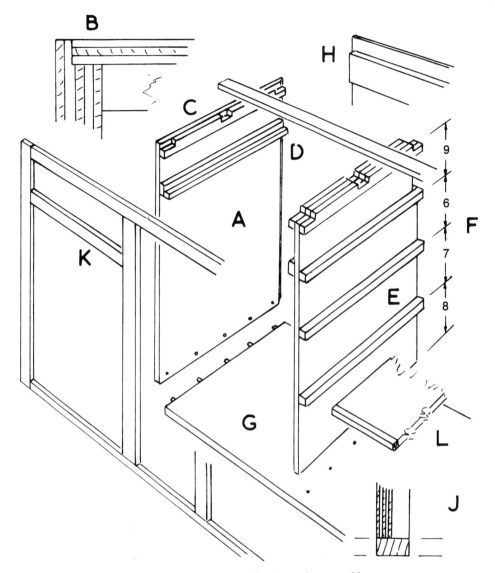

Fig. 5-7. Main parts of the enclosed two-drawer cabinet.

at the bottom, and screw the top strips in place. With the carcass face-down, compare diagonal measurements to see that the assembly is square before the glue sets.

• Make the nail rail to fit between the ends and into the notches in the divisions (FIGS. 5-6C and 5-7H). Fit the back into the rabbets and to the other parts with glue and ample screws or nails. The nail rail and back will keep the carcass in shape.

• Make the plinth as a separate unit (FIG. 5-8A). Let it stand back 3 inches from the front and ends and come level at the back (FIG. 5-6D). Miter the front corners, but have the ends overlap the back (FIG. 5-8B). You can avoid screw or nail heads outside if you fit

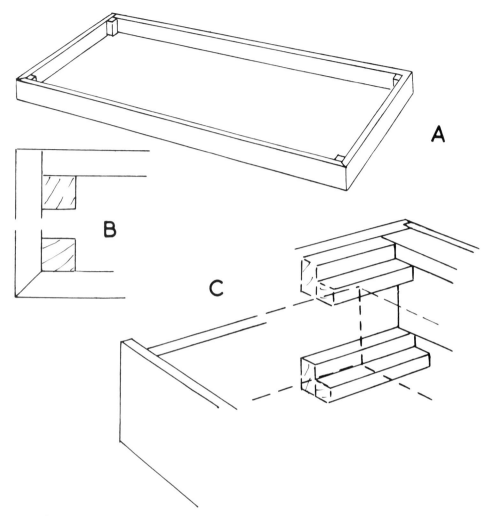

Fig. 5-8. Details of the plinth and the drawer guides for the two-drawer cabinet.

blocks inside the corners. Join the plinth to the carcass with screws downward through the bottom.

• Make a frame to fit over the front in a fashion similar to that of the fitted cabinet discussed earlier. The top rail covers the crosswise pieces. Make the bottom rail to match the carcass bottom. Fit uprights over the divisions to cover the ends of the shelf supports, but leave the ends of the drawer runners open (FIG. 5-7J). Let the rails below the drawers (FIG. 5-7K) come level with the tops of the drawer runners.

• Make the shelves with solid-wood front edging (FIG. 5-7L). Screw the shelves to their supports, with front edges level so they will come inside the front frame. Start with the bottom shelf or you may have difficulty using a screwdriver.

• Attach the front frame to the carcass. Check that the top surfaces of all parts finish level. Treat the inside of the cabinet with paint or other finish.

• You can make and fit the two drawers in any of the ways described earlier for the fitted cabinet. If you use metal side tracks, you will have to put pieces across inside ends to suit them, and you will have to make the drawers narrow enough to admit the tracks. With the carcass made as described, you can make the drawers to fit the opening and run on their bottom edges (FIG. 5-8C). The nail rail will act as a backstop, although an overlapping front will also stop the drawer. Use any of the construction methods already described. The false front can overlap ½ inch all around.

• The doors and drawer fronts should match and can be made in any of the ways described in Chapter 4. Use a ½-inch overlap all around. Fit knobs or handles to match.

• Make the top in the same way as in the fitted cabinet discussed earlier, with laminated plastic over plywood and a hardwood edging (FIG. 5-4). You may make the top completely before fitting it, but as you have room to work all around this cabinet you might prefer to fit the plywood top by screwing downward, put on the laminated plastic and trim its edges in position, and *then* add the edging at the front and ends.

• Finish the outside of the cabinet in any way you wish, but the top edging will probably look best varnished.

Materials List for Enclosed Two-drawer Cabinet

2 ends	1 × 22 × 32 plywood
4 end frames	1 × 2 × 24
2 end frames	1 × 1 × 24
2 divisions	1 × 22 × 32 plywood
6 division frames	1 × 2 × 24
6 division frames	1 × 1 × 24
1 bottom	1 × 22 × 51
3 top strips	1 × 2 × 51
1 back	½ × 32 × 51 plywood
1 nail rail	1 × 4 × 51
3 shelves	½ × 11 × 24
3 shelf edges	½ × ½ × 11
4 front frames	1 × 2 × 52
2 front frames	1 × 2 × 22
1 front frame	1 × 1 × 52
1 top	1 × 24 × 56 plywood
1 top edging	¾ × 1 × 56
2 top edgings	¾ × 1 × 26
2 doors	1 × 20 × 24 plywood
2 drawer fronts	1 × 6 × 20
4 drawer sides	⅝ × 4 × 24
2 drawer fronts	¾ × 4 × 20
2 drawer backs	⅝ × 3½ × 20
2 drawer bottoms	¼ × 18 × 24 plywood

CHAPTER

Unit Construction

One way to form an arrangement of kitchen cabinets is to make the parts as units and fit them into the available space between appliances and along walls. Worktops unite the many parts into continuous assemblies which will be indistinguishable from cabinets built completely in position. You might prefer to work in the kitchen, constructing blocks of cabinets in their final positions, but if you want to make the parts in your shop, you can bring them into the kitchen as almost complete unit sections, thus reducing the actual work done in the kitchen.

Another advantage of unit construction involves the uncertainty of how you and the cook want the cabinets, appliances, and other kitchen equipment arranged. If you have difficulty in visualizing the final appearance and the amount of space the cabinets will occupy, the construction of units allows you to try cabinets of various sorts in different parts, before finalizing positions. You are therefore unlikely to have wasted time making something that has to be scrapped or altered due to later decisions.

Unit construction entails a small amount of duplication of material, as compared with making many compartments in a single assembly, but there need not be much. Units have to be made with sides, which will be screwed to each other, so two sides are in the position where a single division would suffice in continuous construction. However, the sides are thinner. You could use plywood or particleboard about ½ inch thick for the two sides, where you would probably use ¾-inch or 1-inch material for a division in the same place.

The bottoms and backs of the units may be built-in individually, but lengthwise strips at the top to support the worktop might go through notches in several cabinet units. Shelves and other internal fittings will be included as a unit is made, stiffening each assembly and holding it square.

Toe boards could be arranged as a four-sided plinth on which the units rest, but in most cases you are better off taking the cabinet sides to the floor and cutting them back to take a long toe board that is added after you have the units in a settled position. Doors and worktops can be of any type. You should plan their arrangement, but they are not part of the units. Some front framing will hide joints between the units. Doors are a prominent feature of the whole design, and you can use anything—from plain or framed, to molded and carved—depending on your skill and the effect you want to create.

UNIT CHOICE

Standard shell units can have many different interiors. The simplest is an open compartment, which will accommodate large portable appliances or bulk packages. There could be shelves, which might be removable to enable you to convert to an open compartment. The shell unit could contain a drawer with a door underneath, or there could be a block of drawers for the full depth. You could arrange shelves without a door. There could be vertical divisions to act as bins. Instead of a door hinged at the side, you could hinge it at the bottom so the door tilts out with a trash or storage bin attached. Although most units will be a standard width, you might want at least one with a greater width and double doors. You may also need narrower units; narrow shelves and narrow

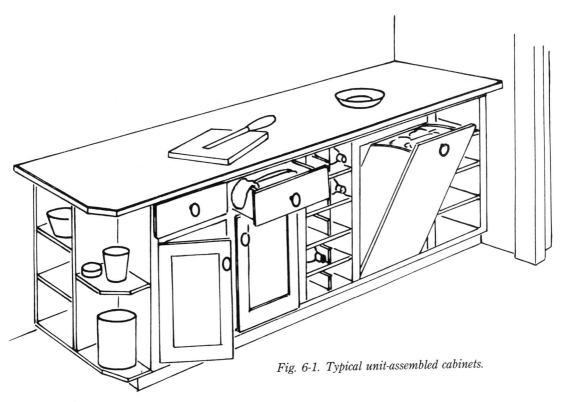

Fig. 6-1. Typical unit-assembled cabinets.

drawers are useful. Also, there could be narrower bottle racks or rails for towels to hang on in a narrow space.

You will have to consider what to do at exposed ends. Any unit can go against a wall in a corner, but if it will be exposed, something has to be done to improve its appearance. If you know a unit will come at an end, the outer side can be made with suitable veneered plywood or particleboard. Otherwise, you can add a false end with a suitable surface. If there is sufficient space, you can build-in an attractive end with a narrow shelf unit, with just open shelves or with decorative rails. What might look like an overall construction done on-site (FIG. 6-1) could actually be a collection of units, which were tried in various arrangements until you and your cook agreed on the final placement (FIG. 6-2).

Before starting to make cabinet units, consider plumbing and wiring. Backs of cabinets may have to be cut away, so decide where to do so before finally gluing and screwing on backs. It might be better to just keep the back a few inches from the wall. It would not significantly reduce the capacity of a unit and its placement away from the wall will be hidden by the worktop, which does touch the wall.

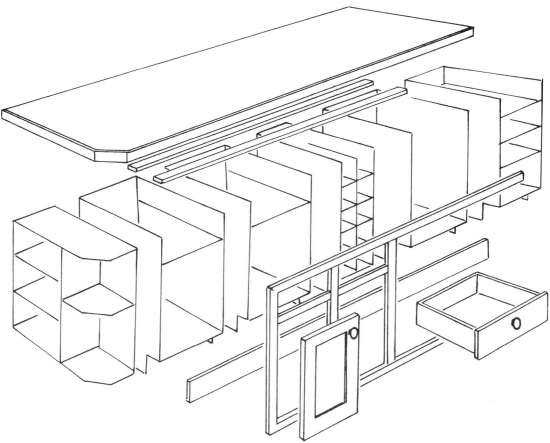

Fig. 6-2. Layout of the cabinets and top of the assembly shown in Fig. 6-1.

You might also have to consider such things as sinks and built-in ranges, which have to be let into a worktop and project below. What you make to fit underneath may not take the unit form, but although lengthwise sizes will differ, other sizes can match your standard units. For items needing space under the worktop you may have to include dummy drawer fronts or otherwise disguise the depth you allow at the front. As top drawers will form a continuous line in the appearance of the cabinet fronts, you should see what allowance has to be made under a sink or hot plate, as this will determine the depth of matching drawers.

UNIT SIZES

Before planning units, consider the worktop and its relation to any appliances that will either fit under it or against it. If you use a stock section of surfaced worktop, the unit sizes will have to relate to it. You might have restrictions in the kitchen as to how far cabinets can project from the wall. Also, there could be something already in the room that has to be matched. If you are starting with an empty room, planning is easier, but even then you have to relate unit sizes to other items of fixed size. If possible, have all the appliances, hardware, and other items being bought in ready, so you can arrange your measurements to suit. You can alter the units in the planning stage, but you cannot alter many of the things they have to match. You will be making a large number of units to match each other, and it would be frustrating if they do not then match a dishwasher, range, or something else that is unalterable.

The key parts on which the sizes of many other items are based are the sides of the units (FIG. 6-3A). All units must have matching sides, with square corners and identical measurements. Errors may creep in if you use a tape rule or other measuring device to individually mark out parts that have to be made the same. Instead, mark a stick with all the important sizes (FIG. 6-3B) and measure everything against that.

If you have a table saw with suitable guides, cut all the unit ends at one time, to produce pieces exactly the same size. If you have to cut pieces individually, use the first side you made as a pattern for the others and check squareness at all stages. It is better to prepare at one time all parts that have to match than to make one complete unit before cutting panels for another.

SHELL CONSTRUCTION

The sides and bottom of a unit shell can be ½-inch plywood, with the back ¼-inch plywood and solid wood strips ¾-inch square. Glue and nail or screw all parts.

You can rabbet the sides to take the back plywood (FIG. 6-3C), although any that will not be exposed can be lapped (FIG. 6-3D). If you are planning a false piece at a visible end, it will not matter if the back is lapped there. If you want to inset the back to clear wiring or plumbing, you can use supporting fillets (FIG. 6-3E).

The front edges of the sides will be covered by strips after assembly. The bottom reaches the front edges of the sides, but then the door overhangs, so cover the plies with a solid wood strip (FIG. 6-3F). Following are the basic construction steps for the shell:

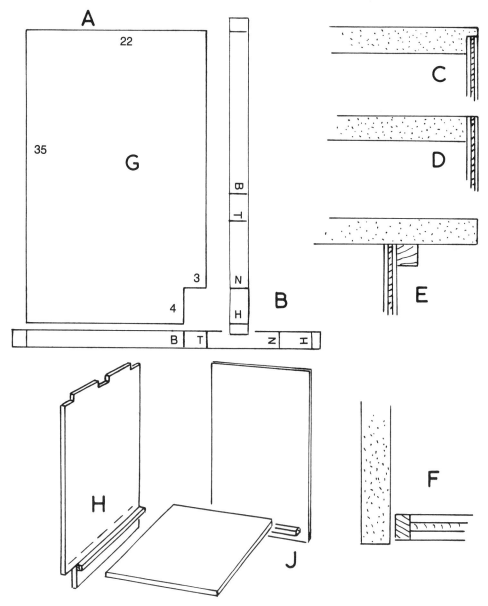

Fig. 6-3. Laying-out units and some assembly details.

- Cut all the sides (FIG. 6-3G). Notch the top edges to take the 1-inch × 2-inch strips that will go through all units. Put strips across to support the bottoms (FIG. 6-3H).
- Adopt a standard width for the shells; 20 inches would be suitable. Edge the bottom and cut it to suit.
- Make the back to match. It need not reach the floor, but it should go far enough to accommodate a strip to support the bottom (FIG. 6-3J).

• Assemble a pair of sides, the bottom, and the back. If there is any tendency for the open top corners to spring out of square, lightly nail a temporary piece of scrap wood across.

• That completes the shell, which is all you will need if this is to be a cabinet without internal additions (FIG. 6-4A). Make as many shells as you need, up to this stage.

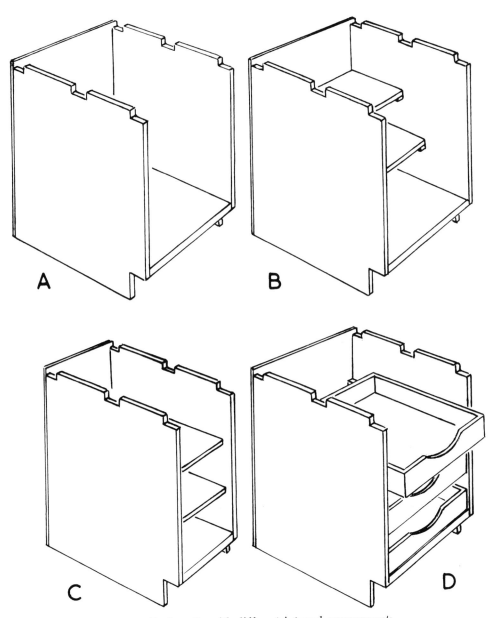

Fig. 6-4. Basic units with different internal arrangements.

CABINET WITH SHELVES

Shelves inside a cabinet provide stiffness as well as squareness, even when not screwed down. However, do not include too many shelves in a cabinet with a door, and do not bring fixed shelves too far forward or it will be difficult to see or reach to the back. One shelf, to about three-quarters of the width, or two of different widths should be enough (FIG. 6-4B). Unless a cabinet is very wide, ½-inch plywood should be stiff enough for normal shelves. Following are some tips for adding shelves to your cabinet shell:

• A simple shelf rests on cleats (FIG. 6-5A). Round the front edge of the shelf. Cut the cleats back about 1 inch and bevel the ends at the front. A strip across near the front will help the shelf resist bending under a heavy load (FIG. 6-5B).

• Another way of stiffening and hiding the cleats is to carry the stiffening piece across at the front (FIG. 6-5C).

• If you want the shelf to be able to be lifted out, but to resist sliding forward, put blocks on the cleats (FIG. 6-5D).

• If a loose shelf is mounted by one of the first two methods mentioned above and it

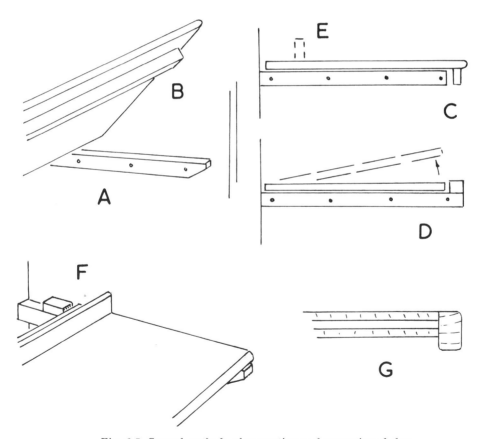

Fig. 6-5. Several methods of supporting and arranging shelves.

is difficult to reach things at the back, you can convert the assembly to something like a tray. Simply put a strip across near the back (FIG. 6-5E). If the shelf is pulled forward, this strip will keep things from falling off the back.

• You could make a unit with shelves, but without a door (FIG. 6-4C). Remember, however, the difficulty of reaching to the back if the shelves are too close. Two shelves at the usual depth will be enough, if they are to go to the back. However, if the items you want to put on the shelves do not need to go all the way back, you can either bring the cabinet back forward or put stops on the shelves or their supports (FIG. 6-5F). For shelves that will be exposed at the front, you should not only hide the plies with a solid wood strip but extend it down a little to provide stiffness (FIG. 6-5G).

SLIDING TRAYS

Trays for storage come between shelves and drawers in design. You can put most things that would go on a shelf in a tray. Each tray rests on runners and can be pulled right out, so you can lift it and its contents out and onto the workshop. Trays do not take up the full depth of a drawer in a similar place. A tray is a box, with a hollowed front to provide a grip (FIG. 6-6A). FIGURE 6-4D shows the basic shell fitted with trays to the front, but they could also be set back a little behind a door. If you make the space between trays about the same as their design, that should be satisfactory. Following are some tips to adding trays to your cabinet:

• In its simplest form, the corners of a tray are nailed and a plywood or hardboard bottom is nailed on (FIG. 6-6B).
• The best construction is with dovetailed corners and the plywood bottom in grooves (FIG. 6-6C).
• Rabbeted corners allow the bottom grooves to be hidden, and you can glue and drive thin nails both ways (FIG. 6-6D).
• Round the top edges, particularly around the hollowed grip.
• Fit bearers in the shell to act as runners, but bring them to the fronts of the trays, or nearly there, to prevent tipping (FIG. 6-6E). The lowest tray slides on the cabinet bottom.
• If you want to have trays that do not go all the way to the back of the cabinet, put stop blocks on the runners (FIG. 6-6F).

CABINET WITH DRAWERS

Although many kitchen items can be stored behind doors, you need drawers for cutlery and other smaller things. Multiple cabinets along a wall should have a few single drawers above doors and probably a block of several drawers from the toe board up to the worktop. For some items the drawers should be as wide as the cupboards, but you may find a narrower block of drawers will accommodate many smaller and longer things. If you make a drawer block 10 inches wide in a 20-inch-wide shell, you will have better adjustment in overall length as you plan the assembly of a row of cabinet shells.

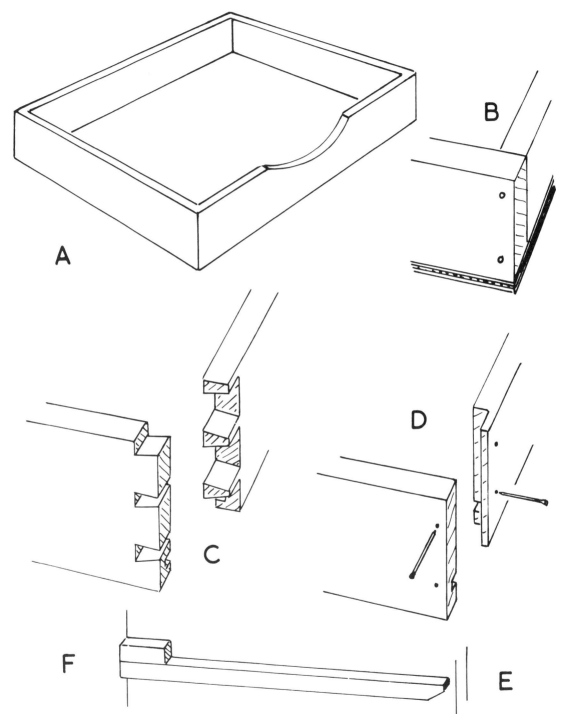

Fig. 6-6. Different ways of joining the corners of a tray.

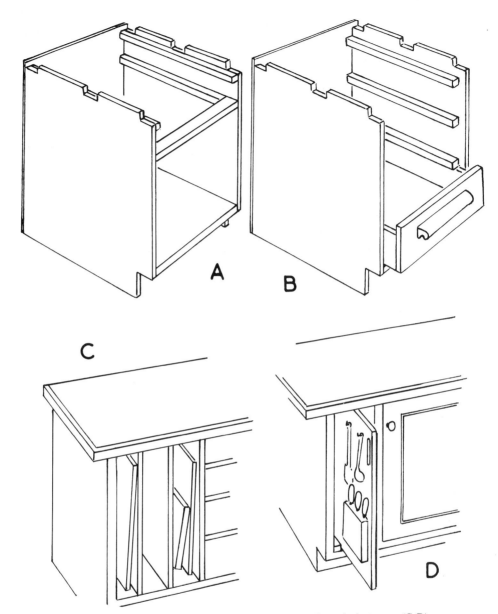

Fig. 6-7. Drawer arrangements (A,B) and vertical storage (C,D).

For a shell with a drawer above a door (FIG. 6-7A), relate the drawer rail position to the dummy front under a sink or to other drawers or sliding parts nearby, so these items follow at matching heights even if they are not adjoining. If a block of drawers comes between shells with full-depth doors, you will not need to match heights, but if the block comes next to a drawer over a door, you might wish to make the top drawers the same depth. In general, a block of drawers looks best if the drawer depths are graduated from small at the top to deeper at the bottom (FIG. 6-7B). This usually suits storage needs better than drawers all of the same depth. It also obviates the need to make the drawers interchangeable, which can be difficult if your shop facilities are limited. Following are some hints for adding drawers to your cabinet shell:

• There should be a rail below a drawer above a door (FIG. 6-8A). You can locate it with dowels, which can go right through (FIG. 6-8B) unless you are working on an exposed end which will not be covered. Two ⅜-inch dowels into a 1-inch × 2-inch strip would be satisfactory.

• If you are using metal or plastic runners on the sides of the drawers, they may provide all the support needed. However, it is usually worthwhile putting wooden runners under the drawer (FIG. 6-8C).

• Although there need be nothing between the drawer bottom and the cupboard, it is better to seal it off with a dust board. One type has a piece of ½-inch plywood fitted

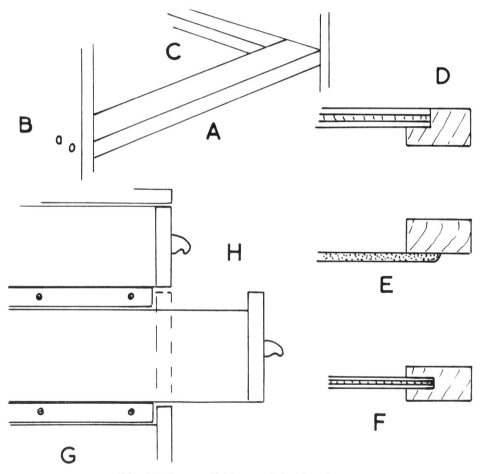

Fig. 6-8. Drawer divisions and dust boards.

like a shelf and into a rabbet in the front strip (FIG. 6-8D). The drawer slides on it, taking the place of bottom runners.

• Another type of dust board is a piece of hardboard or thin plywood under the other strips (FIG. 6-8E). If you want to follow traditional construction, let the piece into grooves (FIG. 6-8F).

• Make the drawer by any of the methods described earlier, but you might want to delay making and fitting drawers until the units have been brought together and all parts are fitted except the worktop. That way, you can see inside and obtain an exact fit, with the drawer front matching the door below it.

• You could make a block of drawers with front rails and dust boards in the way described above. This might be advisable if you need to have a uniform appearance on the front. For the greatest drawer capacity, omit rails on the front. If you use metal or plastic runners on the sides of the drawers, there should be no more gap between drawer sides than is needed to provide working clearance.

• If the drawers are to be supported along their bottom edges by wooden runners, screw the runners to the unit sides (FIG. 6-8G). Whichever method of support you use, make sure that the heights of opposite sides match, because you do not have front rails to ensure that drawers hang horizontally.

• Make each drawer, except the top one, with its front extending high enough to hide the ends of the runners above (FIG. 6-8H). How far you bring the drawer fronts forward depends on how you will be finishing the assembled front. You will probably have a front frame, and the drawer fronts should be the same thickness as that if they are to be flush. If they need to have overlapping fronts to match other parts, you could lengthen the drawer and make the front to overlap the frame at its sides, or you could complete the drawer with a flush front and add a false front to match other parts in front of it.

VERTICAL STORAGE

Pastry boards and other large, flat items too big to be stored flat may be stood on edge. Your cabinets should provide at least one compartment, open to the front to suit this storage method.

All you will need is a unit with one or two vertical divisions (FIG. 6-7C). And to accommodate tools that can hang or fit into slots, you could add a vertical panel arranged to pull forward (FIG. 6-7D). Following are some tips for these vertical storage approaches:

• Make the vertical divisions from ¾-inch plywood or particleboard, with solid-wood front edging (FIG. 6-9A). The divisions need not come to the front edge of the unit. If the solid-wood edging is made wide enough, it can be hollowed for hand access (FIG. 6-9B).

• At the bottom use dowels or screws driven upward (FIG. 6-9C).

• Although the tops of divisions may be held by the lengthwise pieces in the final assembly, you should include extra strips across (FIG. 6-9D) to hold the divisions and the shell in shape until you connect this with other units.

• Make a pull-out board (for cook's tools that hang or knives to fit into slots) in a similar

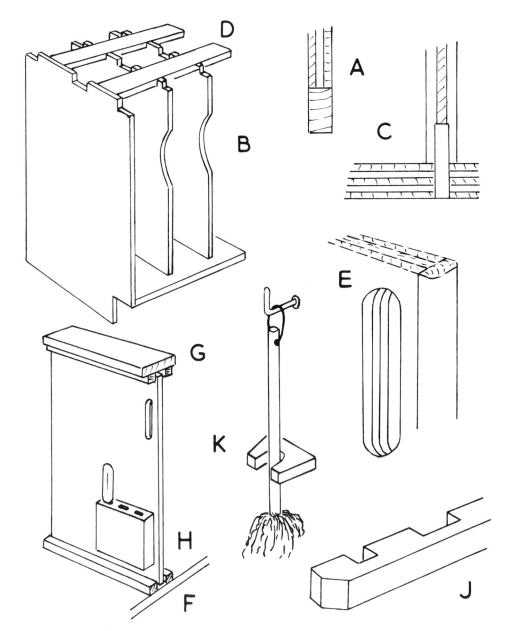

Fig. 6-9. Construction and arrangement of vertical storage.

way to the divisions, but cut a hand hole at the front (FIG. 6-9E). This could be in a wide solid-wood edging, securely attached to the plywood, or you could use a narrow solid-wood front edge and make the hand hole entirely in the plywood. In either case, round the edges of the hole carefully.

• At the bottom, put two strips across as guides (FIG. 6-9F). At the top you will need an inverted trough to serve the same purpose, but allow for the depth of the front framing which will be added during final assembly. Put the guide strips on a piece deep enough to provide clearance.

• The pull-out board does not have to be a close fit at top or bottom. Its weight is taken by the bottom edge, which should slide easily enough, but you can get a light sliding door track that will provide an easier movement.

• What you put on this board depends on the cook's needs. For many kitchen tools, hooks may be sufficient. Spring clips can hold other items.

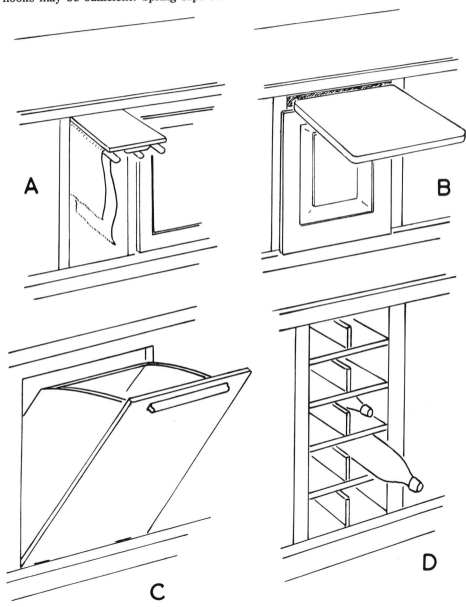

Fig. 6-10. Special built-in storage arrangements.

• Knife blades should be protected, so they might go into a row of slots in solid or built-up wood (FIG. 6-9H). Other items might fit into slots or notches (FIG. 6-9J). Use notched blocks to restrain hanging items which might swing excessively as you move the board in or out (FIG. 6-9K).

CLOTH-HANGING COMPARTMENT

Cloths may be stored folded in a drawer, but when they are brought into use, they need to be hung. A suitable solution is a compartment similar to that for vertical storage, but with top rails, preferably made so they will slide forward (FIG. 6-10A). You can get metal rails for this purpose. They have a track to be screwed in from above. The instructions that follow, however, are for a *wood* assembly that serves the same purpose.

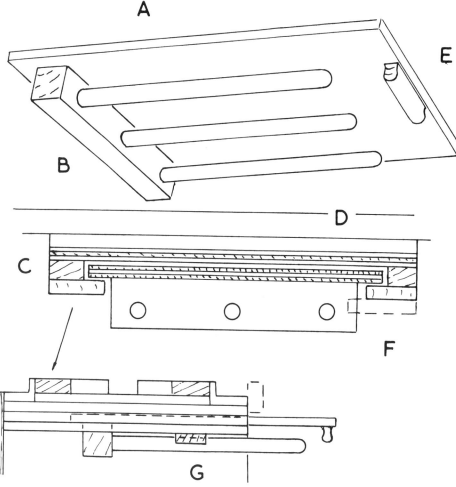

Fig. 6-11. Construction of sliding cloth-hanging rails.

- Make the top rail assembly from ½-inch plywood (FIG. 6-11A). Sizes provided in the figure are only for purposes of an example and might have to be changed to suit your unit.
- Use ¾-inch dowel rods. Round the forward ends and fit the other ends into holes in a 2-inch-square block (FIG. 6-11B).
- Put strips across the top of the unit in the same way as in the vertical storage unit discussed earlier.
- Make a support for the sliding rail assembly, with guides to fit each side (FIG. 6-11C). This has to be attached to the strips across the unit but held far enough down to allow the sliding part to pass under the cabinet top front rail when the units are joined together (FIG. 6-11D).
- Put a handle under the front edge of the slide (FIG. 6-11E). However, you might wish to delay making and fitting this handle until final assembly.
- If you want to prevent the slide from being pulled all the way out, screw pieces under the guides to come against the block when the rail assembly has come out as far as necessary (FIGS. 6-11F, G). Use screws without glue, so you can remove the stops if you need to service the parts.

BREADBOARD SLIDE

Instead of storing a bread or cutting board vertically, you can build-in a board under the worktop, to be pulled out like a drawer and lifted onto the worktop surface. This assembly is most conveniently arranged above a door (FIG. 6-10B). You can use a purchased cutting board, but if you make you own you can size it to precisely fit your unit. It need not go to the back; there can be stops on its bearers. Following are the basic steps for constructing this assembly:

- The board can be a piece of thick plywood or plastic-veneered particleboard or several solid-wood boards glued together with cleated ends. A good board should be made in the butcher block manner, with hardwood strips about 1¼ inch square (FIG. 6-12A). This would be stout enough to use for chopping as well as for normal cutting and food preparation. Round the corners and make a hollow for fingers under the front edge.
- Put top runners across the unit sides, with the lower edges level with the final depth of the front top rail (after the units are assembled) (FIG. 6-12B).
- Allow sufficient depth for the board to fit easily and put a front rail across (FIG. 6-12C). Its ends can be screwed or doweled.
- Put lower runners behind this rail (FIG. 6-12D). If the board is not to go all the way to the back of the cabinet, put stops on the bearers.
- The door below will fit in the same way as it would below a drawer.
- If you arrange the board to project far enough forward to come fairly close to the front of the finished worktop, the hollow for pulling should be clear of the top of the door. If not, you may have to hollow the top edge of the door to provide enough clearance.

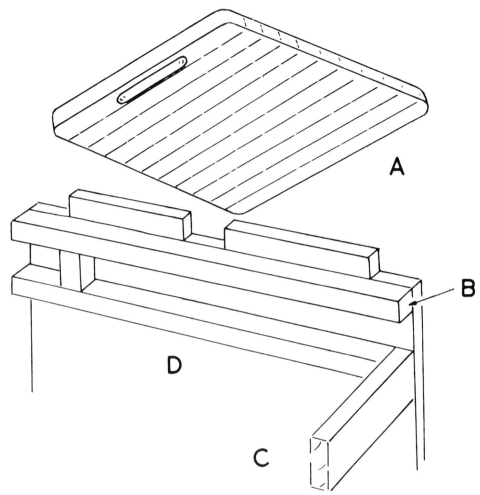

Fig. 6-12. Details of a sliding, laminated breadboard.

TILT BIN

Many types of waste containers can be mounted inside a normal door. With a suitable liner, that is probably the best way of dealing with trash. Instead of having the door hinge at one side, however, you could hinge it at the bottom and tilt it forward. Or, instead of hinges at the bottom, you could make the door lift off as well as swing out. The assembly might carry a bought plastic or metal container secured with brackets, or you could make a wooden bin of larger capacity (FIG. 6-10C). Following are the basic steps for constructing such an assembly:

• To make a door that pivots at the bottom so it can be lifted off, put a rail across the bottom of the unit (FIG. 6-13A) with its outer edge level with where the inside of the door will be.

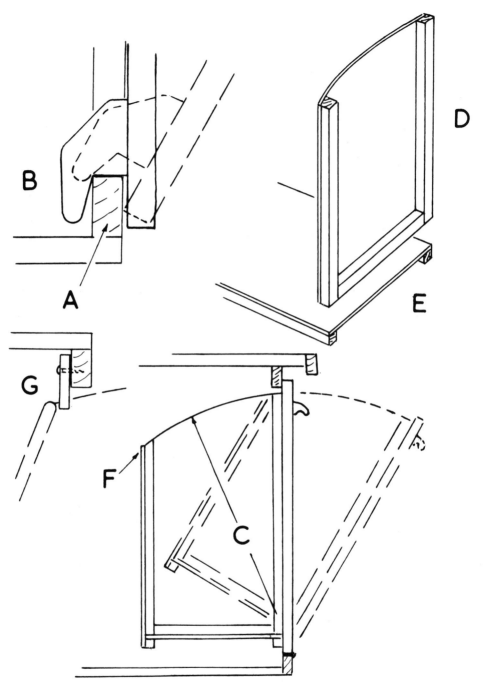

Fig. 6-13. Constructional details of a tilt bin.

- Make two brackets about 1 inch thick to fit loosely over the rail, and attach them to the door a few inches in from its edges. The weight of the door is taken by the tops of the notches. Taper each notch so the door can swing forward (FIG. 6-13B).
- Almost certainly, the weight of the bin attached to the inside of the door will be enough to keep it closed. However, you could provide a fastener at the top, to guarantee against unintentional opening.
- A bin made of plywood can be almost any size. If it is intended for trash, you could make it to suit one of the largest plastic liners. If the bin is for storing food in bulk, you might measure the packages you hope to stow there. The bin could go almost to the back of the cabinet, so it can occupy nearly all the available volume. With a narrower bin there will be space behind for other things, but they will not be easy to reach unless you remove the bin. Whatever the bin's size, its top must have a curve with its center at the pivot point, so it can clear the top rail (FIG. 6-13C).
- Make the bin sides framed outside (FIG. 6-13D), with an overall width that will pass easily inside the unit.
- Fit the bottom with a framing strip to go against the door and another strip to take the back (FIG. 6-13E).
- If you are using ½-inch plywood, the top edge of the back (FIG. 6-13F) should be stiff enough, but if you think it necessary, add a stiffening strip there.
- Join the parts together and to the door. Made this way, the bin interior is smooth. Round the top edges.
- If the bottom of the door is held with hinges, you might want to occasionally pull the door as far as the floor, for cleaning out. If the bottom pivot is on brackets to lift off, you will have to bring the door far enough forward for the back of the bin to clear the top rail as the whole thing is lifted out. At other times you might want to tilt to a lesser extent. A simple way to limit movement while allowing further tilt when necessary is to put two strips of wood on screws at the top, as turnbuttons (FIG. 6-13G). These will stop the back when they are down, but if you turn them up, you can tilt the assembly any amount.

BOTTLE RACK

Wine is best stored horizontally, and other bottled drinks can be stored the same way. To store bottles in this way under a counter or worktop, a suitable rack need not take up very much width (FIG. 6-10D). Check the sizes of the types of bottles you expect to store, but make your rack with plenty of clearance. Fortunately, the range of sizes of common bottled drinks is not great. Perhaps the safest approach is to base the rack on the biggest bottles you find.

The sizes suggested in FIG. 6-14A can serve as a guide. All of the parts could be ½-inch or ¾-inch plywood or veneered particleboard. Cover the front edges with matching veneer or solid wood. Pulling bottles in and out can be hard on the front edges, so protect them, preferably with solid wood. Construction of a bottle rack is very similar to making a block of shelves, as you will see in the following steps:

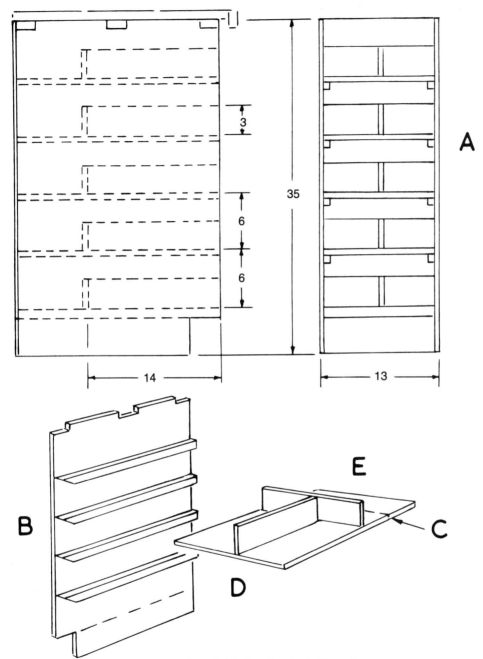

Fig. 6-14. Details of a bottle rack.

- Mark divisions on a pair of unit sides and put in shelf bearers (FIG. 6-14B).
- Make the shelves to fit. Although the bottles will not go right to the back of the cabinet, the shelves could, or they may be cut off (FIG. 6-14C).
- Make lengthwise divisions to stand slightly higher than half the height between shelves. Make them as long as your longest bottle (FIG. 6-14D).
- Put stop pieces across (FIG. 6-14E), and glue and screw or nail upward through each shelf.
- Screw downward into the bearer at each front corner of a shelf. You can then remove a shelf easily if you ever need to make alterations.

WIDE UNIT

So far as possible, units should be narrower than they are high. For units of normal height, then, try to keep compartments narrower than 24 inches. Apart from other considerations, this gives the doors a pleasing proportion and the front appearance of multiple cabinets is attractive.

Doors wider than they are high do not look right; they also swing out too far and they are more likely to sag or develop strained hinges. So if you want to include a wide unit in your layout, it should have double doors (FIG. 6-15A). Such a need may arise under a sink or other wide appliance set into the worktop. Such a large compartment provides

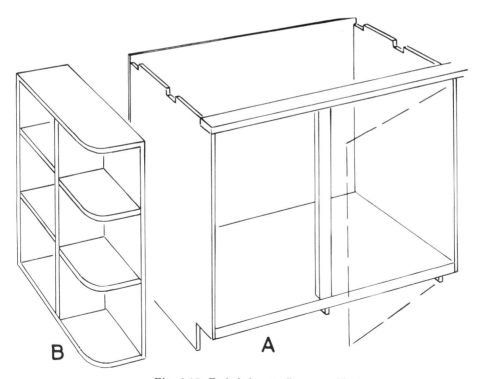

Fig. 6-15. End shelves to fit on a cabinet.

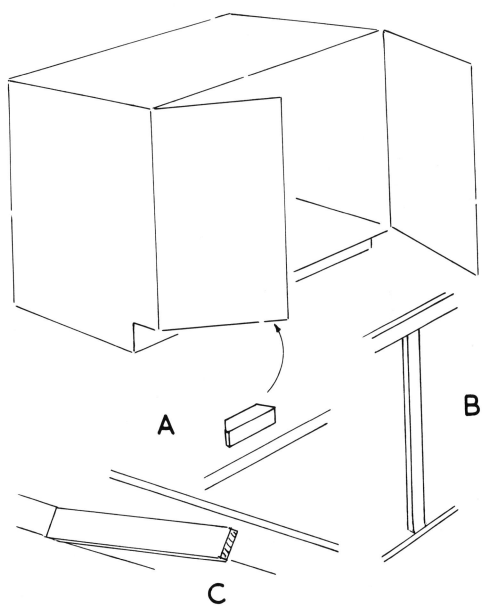

Fig. 6-16. Doorstops (A,B) and a bottom support (C).

good access to plumbing or other work. Following are some tips for working with wide units:

• If the unit is to be less than twice the width of a standard unit, you can make it in the same way as a standard unit but to the greater width.

• There should be doorstops at top and bottom (FIG. 6-16A). These may carry spring or magnetic catches, so choose the size of block to suit. If you wish to lock the compartment, you could put bolts at the top and bottom of one door and a catch or lock on the other door.

• For a wider double unit, you would be wise to have an upright at the front for the doors to close against (FIG. 6-16B). It can be doweled into the bottom and may be doweled at the top as well, but this arrangement depends on whether the doors will close against the unit or be over a frame, with the upright as part of the front frame.

• In a wide unit, you might want to provide extra support under the bottom. Put a piece centrally underneath with its front edge in position to take the toe board (FIG. 6-16C), and screw it down through the bottom plywood.

END SHELVES

Carrying cabinets to the end under the worktop along a particular wall might give the storage capacity you need. There is a certain plainness about such an end, however, and its appearance can be greatly improved by building a block of shelves on it. These can be anything from straight, narrow shelves to fairly elaborate ones (FIG. 6-15B). You could simply add the shelves to the outside of the end cabinet, but as we are dealing with unit construction, the instructions provided here are for a shelf unit to be joined onto the next cabinet unit.

Be careful to avoid too much projection. The worktop marks the outer limits. So keep everything on the shelf unit well within that outline. Avoid sharp angles which legs may knock against. Even if you do not fully round the outer corners, soften their angles with bevels. The worktop may have a matching bevel, although not cut back as far.

The instructions below are for a fairly elaborate shelf unit. This approach can be modified in many ways to suit your needs, but you can still use these instructions as a basic guide (FIG. 6-17A). As one face of each part and both faces of the division will show, choose suitably veneered ¾-inch plywood or particleboard and cover the edges with matching veneer or solid wood. Join all parts with dowels; in most places ¼-inch dowels at about 3-inch intervals should be satisfactory. At the division the dowels will have to go into stopped holes, but in other places where their ends will not show, they can go right through. Following are the basic steps for constructing end shelves:

• Make the unit side the same as that of the other units (FIGS. 6-3G and 6-17B). On it, lay out the positions of the other parts.
• Make the top and bottom to fit against the side (FIG. 6-17C).
• Make the back (FIG. 6-17D) and the division (FIG. 6-17E) the same as each other, to fit inside top, bottom, and side.
• Mark the positions of the shelves and prepare all the parts made so far for doweling to each other.
• Cut the front shelves with curves to match the bottom (FIG. 6-17F) and the other shelves to fit between back and division.
• Check that all dowel holes are clear, and have sufficient dowels ready. If you have

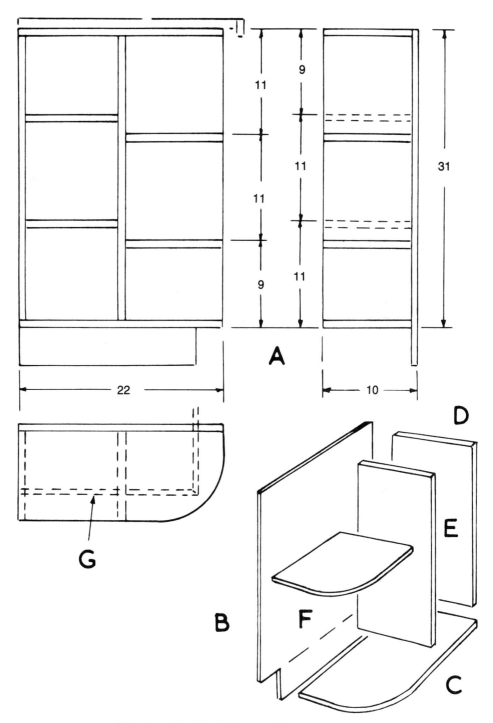

Fig. 6-17. Details of the end shelves.

marked out accurately, the parts should assemble correctly, but check squareness as you progress.

• When the unit is assembled, carry the toe board under the shelf unit and put another piece mitered to it underneath (FIG. 6-17G). You can avoid screws through the bottom of the shelf unit by using a strip inside the toe board and screwing upward.

UNIT ASSEMBLY

The units described in this chapter are basic. You might wish to elaborate on them to add to their usefulness, but appearance will be mainly due to the doors and framing at the front as well as the worktop and its edging.

When you have experimented with unit locations and settled on final positions, screw the units to each other. The purpose of this is mainly to get the units truly lined up, and there will not be much load on these screws. Two screws at each place might be enough, therefore, although you might need more where gaps will not otherwise close. See that front and top surfaces match. If necessary, do a little hand planing of edges. Screw through the backs to the wall. A few screws near the tops of some units should be sufficient.

Fit the toe boards, using solid wood or plywood. You could make the board continuous, but this is an opportunity to use up odd pieces where they will not show.

Screw lengthwise strips into the top notches. Short pieces could be joined in notches. Drill for a few screws that will be driven upward into the worktop.

The front arrangement will depend on the types of doors you have chosen and on the location of open bins and shelves. Basically, however, there should be a front strip going the whole length, attached to the front top lengthwise strip and to the unit edges. Fit matching vertical strips over the joined unit edges; also you might want to put a facing strip along the front edges of the bottoms. All of these visible pieces should be of wood that matches the doors.

Before fitting the worktop, deal with any final internal fitting. You will probably have to ease drawers and other slides, and you might have to screw down shelves. Such jobs would be much more difficult once the worktop has been secured. The worktop can be thick plywood with a laminated plastic top and a solid-wood edge, or any of the other tops described elsewhere in this book.

7

Dealing with Corners

A kitchen cabinet might form straight lines, but in most cases you will have to deal with a corner in the counter-and-cabinet assembly. Usually this is an internal corner, but in an L-shaped room or where a wall projects into the room, you will have to work with an external angle. In both cases the problem is how to get at the storage space within the angle. Of course, if there is already as much storage capacity as you need along the walls, the corner could remain empty and inaccessible. Most kitchens, however, need all the storage space you can provide them.

Assuming the usual widths of worktop and cabinets, there will be a minimum of 24 inches square at the corner (FIG. 7-1A). You can make one double-length cabinet to overlap a standard one in the other direction (FIG. 7-1B). It will be a long reach to get at anything stored at the corner of the wide cabinet in this arrangement, but it is a workable solution. In such an arrangement, remember that you cannot arrange the doors to open so they do not interfere with each other, whichever side you hinge (FIG. 7-1C). You must open one or the other.

Another solution is to use standard cabinets and cover the corner space with a section of worktop that lifts off to give access to the corner square (FIG. 7-1D). Because the weight of worktops could make this lift difficult for some people, this arrangement might be best for storing something bulky that is only required occasionally.

You could also make the corner assembly with doors each way only about half width, hinged together in the corner (FIG. 7-1E). A full-length piano hinge would be suitable. One door is hinged to the cabinet in the normal way, and the other folds on the first, swinging back to provide good access diagonally to the corner (FIG. 7-1F).

Yet another answer is to use doors of standard width both ways at the corner, but no divisions (FIG. 7-1G). This approach would leave a fairly large area of top without vertical

89

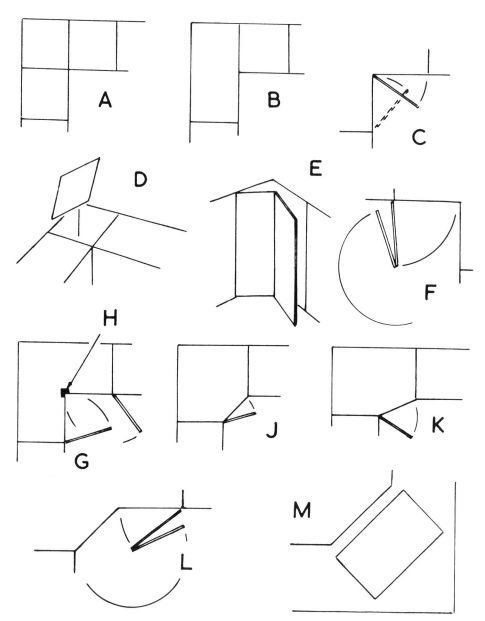

Fig. 7-1. Various ways of dealing with cabinets and their doors in corners.

support, if you want maximum access. Horizontal supports might be adequate, however, and you could put a post where the doors meet (FIG. 7-1H). That may prevent very wide things from being put in the corner compartment, but you will still have as much doorway width as the other cabinets.

Another way of providing corner access is to use a diagonal door (FIG. 7-1J). You must then carefully decide what width of door you need, because too wide a door might

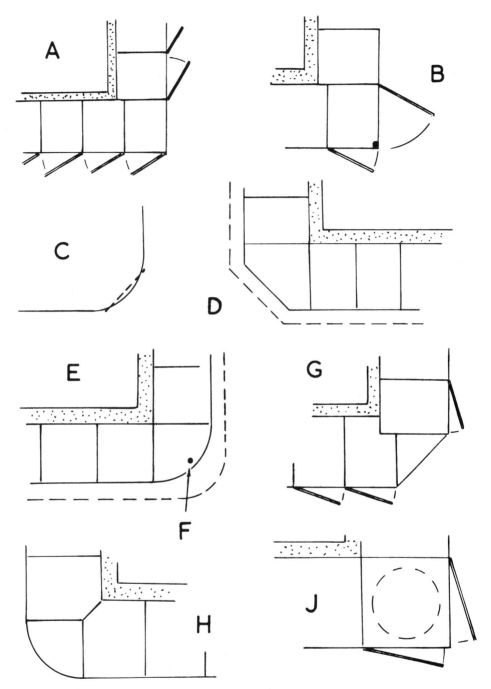

Fig. 7-2. *Various arrangements of cabinets at an external corner.*

come farther into the room than you wish. On the other hand, too narrow a door can make reaching fully into the corner difficult. Corners are sometimes used for a storage carousel or Lazy Susan. If that is what you want, you must relate the door width to it. The cut across a corner does not have to be at 45 degrees, but that is the usual angle. Making it more acute allows you to fit a wider door (FIG. 7-1K). Further access can be obtained by hinging one door to another, in a way similar to that of a sharp corner (FIG. 7-1L). In such a case you might have to provide a post for vertical support.

The worktop must overlap a diagonal door by as much as it does at the sides. Check that this does not take up too much of the standing area. Bringing the diagonal edge further forward also makes the extreme corner harder to reach. That may not matter, as you can fill the corner with racks or bins on the top or store large items there without using up valuable working space.

Yet another way of using corner space is to put a sink or range there (FIG. 7-1M). You can set a sink back from the diagonal edge so that the cut across need not be great. You can fit an inset range unit the same way, but the average range would involve a fairly wide diagonal cut. Will your kitchen allow you to take that much? There may not be much storage space left underneath, but the arrangement could still allow you to fit a door.

An external angle is a smaller problem. Compartments one way can overlap those the other way (FIG. 7-2A); the side of one compartment will be in line with the doors the other way. Or you could have doors both ways, meeting on a corner post (FIG. 7-2B).

In many kitchens a rounded or diagonal corner (FIG. 7-2C) is favored over a square corner because it is less hazardous for anyone moving about. You could use a corner unit with a diagonal door, cut back to far enough under the top overhang (FIG. 7-2D).

Instead of an enclosed compartment you might use the external corner for open shelves (FIG. 7-2E). If the adjoining cabinet sides meet at the wall corner, however, the shelves might be too wide to leave unsupported and you might need a post, preferably turned (FIG. 7-2F). Another way to deal with that problem is to bring the angle of the shelves forward, either by setting the corner of one cabinet into the other (FIG. 7-2G) or mitering the sides of both of them (FIG. 7-2H). This gives you shelves of a more reasonable size that should not need a post. The corner space under the worktop could be left open for storing a stool there or decorating with a potted plant.

An external corner is also an ideal place for a storage carousel, with doors to open away from it (FIG. 7-2J). Its contents will be much more accessible than those of a carousel put in an internal corner.

OVERLAPPED CORNER

A corner with one long unit behind the cabinets (FIG. 7-1B) is easy to arrange. If the corner is far out of square you will have to cut the cabinets to fit against each other, but slight errors do not matter at cabinet level because they will be hidden by the top, which will be carefully fitted. Whether you make the cabinets as units or in continuous lengths built in position, the work at the corner is the same.

Make the long compartment with end and back to overlap the other cabinet and have a doorway wide enough to reach into easily. For the sake of appearance you might want to allow for a door the same width as the others in the row, but it might be better to make it wider. The cabinet that meets this long unit can be of standard construction, except for some modifications detailed here. Following are the basic steps to constructing this overlapped corner:

• Allow for the front framing on the long unit to meet the framing on the other cabinet (FIG. 7-3A). You could put a post under the front top piece. And if you move it a few inches toward the end from the opening, it will be out of the way when anyone reaches inside (FIG. 7-3B).
• Complete the long unit with normal framing for the door (FIG. 7-3C), so it will fit closely

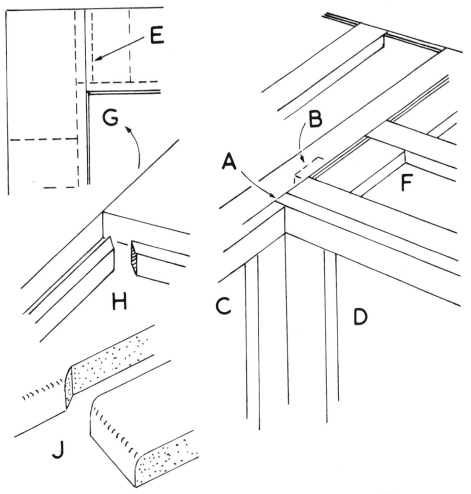

Fig. 7-3. Constructional details of overlapped corner cabinets.

to the framing the other way. You might wish to save final fitting of the upright part until assembling in position to get a close fit, particularly if the corner of the room is slightly out of square. Continue the top and bottom framing to the end wall, but the part that will come against the other cabinet need not have a plywood facing, as the other cabinet will provide that.

• To give as much clearance as possible to the doors, which will come fairly close in the corner, make the end upright of the meeting cabinet wider (FIG. 7-3D); if normal framing is 2 inches wide, this could be 4 inches. The end compartment could be that much wider if you want door widths to match.

• The worktop overlapping the cabinets needs a joint a short distance to one side of the point at which the cabinets meet. To support this, put pieces across between the lengthwise strips (FIGS. 7-3E, F) wide enough to give at least 1-inch bearing under the short top piece.

• If the top is thick plywood covered with laminated plastic, fit this and trim the end to get as close a fit as possible. Fix it with glue and screws from below.

• Miter the meeting ends of the wood edging (FIGS. 7-3G, H). If you use a prepared top with its own shaped edge, you will have to cut back and miter the longest meeting part (FIG. 7-3J), which can be difficult with some materials. Experiment with a scrap piece.

• You can hinge the doors on either side of their openings. Experiment with scrap wood first to see which arrangement gives the access that best suits your needs. You will have some interference whichever way the doors are hung (FIG. 7-1C). Another option is to use double hinged doors, as described later.

TOP-ACCESS CORNER

Arranging a corner with a square of worktop to lift out (FIG. 7-1D) can give you a roomy bin with good access, provided you are prepared to lift the countertop and whatever is inside. The meeting cabinets in this arrangement can have standard ends, except for slight modifications. Following are the basic steps in constructing a top-access corner.

• Make the cabinets with normal closed ends. Bring them together in the corner, and either miter the toe boards or fit a square block where they meet.

• If there are three lengthwise strips each way on the tops, stop the center ones at the plywood or particleboard ends (FIG. 7-4A). Continue the other strips through to the opposite walls (FIG. 7-4B). Use halving joints (FIG. 7-4C) where the strips meet or cross.

• Make plywood backs for the bin (FIG. 7-4D); they can go to the floor. A few screws into the wall will be all the fixing they need. If you do not want to use the kitchen floor as a bottom, you can use a piece of plywood.

• The level of the top strips is important if the lift-off top is to rest without wobbling. Sight along to see that the strips follow on the lines of the top edges of the cabinets. Try a flat piece of thick plywood or particleboard over the square opening before finally screwing the top strips to the wall.

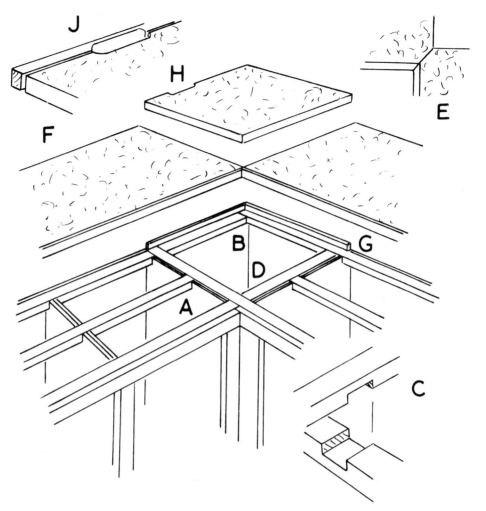

Fig. 7-4. Constructional details of a corner with top access.

- Fit the front framing in the same way as described for the overlapped corner discussed earlier, with one upright wider than the other to help give door clearance.
- Cut the two main tops to meet at their inner corners. With the usual small overhang, you should only need to miter the wood edging, but if you have a wide overhang you might have to continue the miter a short distance into the top material (FIG. 7-4E). The ends of the main tops should finish over the unit ends or be just a short distance along the extended top strips.
- You could fit the lift-off top right to the wall, but it might scratch wall covering as it is moved. Instead, put a wood strip not more than ¾-inch thick against each wall (FIGS. 7-4F, G), then cut the top to fit inside.

- To be able to grip the top, cut a hollow in the edge at a convenient place. It will be helpful to hollow the wood as well (FIGS. 7-4H, J).
- Front framing and doors may be made as described for the overlapped corner discussed earlier.

CORNER UNIT

Instead of filling a corner by extending the cabinets along each wall, you can join them with a unit that follows the lines of the adjoining cabinets but that is built as a separate item. The unit can have doors both ways to provide good access (FIG. 7-5A). If you want these doors to match the widths of other doors (probably about 20 inches), you should build-in a corner post, which adds strength and stiffness and which also acts as a doorstop. But if you keep the doorways narrow, you can avoid having an intrusive post (FIG. 7-5B).

Sections of wood can match those of other cabinets. For most of the structure you can use 1-inch- × -2-inch strips of plywood or particleboard. Make sure that sizes match and front frames will line up with similar adjacent frames. Following are the basic steps for constructing this corner unit:

- Make two end frames the same as you would for standard units, but you do not need to notch the top edges. The pair of top pieces are better let into strips across the inner surface (FIG. 7-5C).
- Make the two backs and the bottom, which sets the sizes for the assembly (FIG. 7-5D). Fit cleats on the ends and backs to support the bottom. Or prepare the unit for dowels between the ends and the bottom.
- Using the bottom as a guide to sizes, make the top pieces to form a frame, with halving joints where they cross and meet (FIG. 7-5E).
- Assemble the parts made so far. For the toe board, put cleats under the bottom in line with the positions on the ends. Attach the toe boards. They need not be mitered where they meet; let one extend and bring the other to it.
- Make two front frames. Do this in position, if you wish, but have one piece wider than the other at the corner (FIG. 7-5F). Join these to form the corner post.
- If you are making a corner unit without a post, make the frames without the inner uprights. You will still have to provide doorstops at top and bottom, however (FIG. 7-5G).
- Hinge the doors to the outer corners of the unit (FIGS. 7-1G, H). You could use the folding doors, described next.

FOLDING DOORS

Hinging one door to another allows you to swing them clear and thus provide more room than single doors in some circumstances. As mentioned earlier, they are useful for corner cabinets. But there are several practical considerations if the doors are to function successfully.

The two doors can be the same width, but it is better for the door that swings on

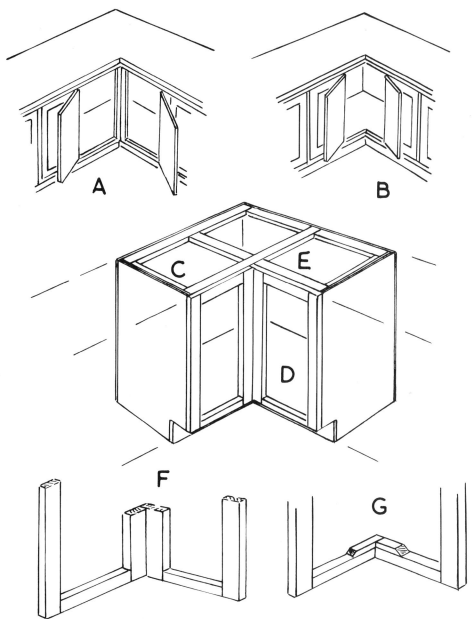

Fig. 7-5. Layout and construction of a corner unit.

the other to be slightly narrower (FIG. 7-6A). If wider, it can limit movement (FIG. 7-6B).

With ordinary hinges the knuckles must be clear of the surfaces (FIG. 7-6C), so the second door will fold flat on the first (FIG. 7-6D) and the combination will swing slightly more than 90 degrees. But if you use a hinge that brings the knuckle outside the outer edge of the door (FIG. 7-6E) the combination will swing much farther—to almost 180

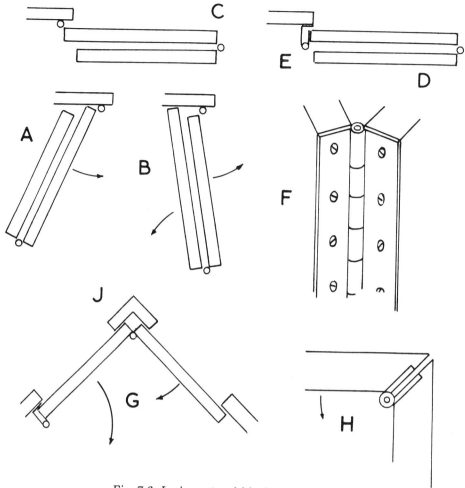

Fig. 7-6. Laying out and hinging folding doors.

degrees if there are no obstructions. Between the doors you could use ordinary hinges, but a continuous piano hinge is better. It extends the whole length of the door edges and makes a seal there (FIG. 7-6F).

Doors that fold against each other cannot have projecting handles, so grips should be provided by handles fitting flush or by notched edges. You only need to grip the second door, as it can be used to pull back the first. A double-hinged arrangement is most appropriate to doors on the surface, but you can arrange a more limited action with doors flush with their frames.

When the doors joined together form a corner (FIG. 7-6G), the placement of the knuckle on the outside means that there will be a gap between square-edged doors. You could cut mitered edges on the doors (FIG. 7-6H), but that would require shorter screws. If the doors are thick enough, that might not matter. If the doors close against stops or a post, the square edges will fit satisfactorily (FIG. 7-6J).

Spring or magnetic catches for each door will keep the pair closed firmly and also allow you to open the second door when you do not need to open both.

DIAGONAL CORNER UNIT

Arranging cabinets that meet at a corner with a door set diagonally (FIG. 7-1J) is an attractive option, both in appearance and in convenience. Usually the door will be at a

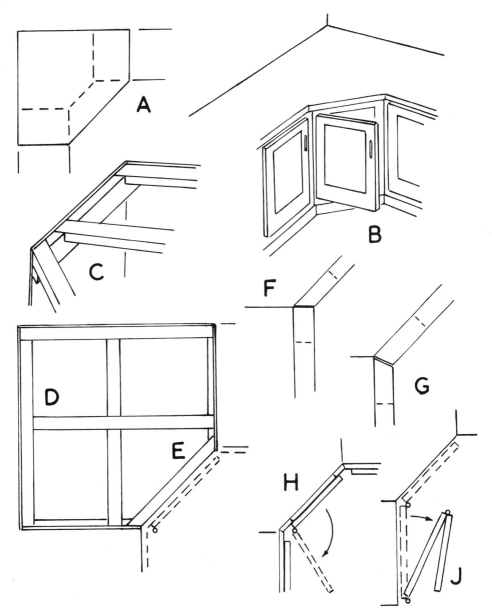

Fig. 7-7. A diagonal corner unit and different arrangements of doors.

45-degree angle, but making it at a different angle (FIG. 7-1K) will not affect construction. You have to decide how wide a doorway you want. Making it very wide provides good access but brings the diagonal edge farther into the room (FIG. 7-7A). The space inside is greater, but the far corner—on top as well as inside—becomes difficult to reach. A door width of 15 inches is about the practical minimum, but 20 inches would be better (FIG. 7-7B).

Construction of this unit is very similar to that of the square corner unit (FIG. 7-5). To make sure the design is correct, set out the shape on the plywood that will form the bottom and try it in position. The corner unit sides have to meet the sides of the other cabinets, but you can move them on your layout until the diagonal measurement is as desired. Following are the basic steps for constructing this unit:

- Make two ends the same as you would for standard units, but you do not need to notch the top edges. The top pieces are better let into strips on the inner surfaces. On each strip one top piece is at the back, the diagonal piece fits into the front notch, and another top piece is placed a short distance behind it (FIG. 7-7C).
- Make two backs and cut the bottom to size. Fit cleats on the ends and back to support the bottom, or prepare the ends for dowels.
- Make the top framing, with the bottom as a guide to sizes. Using halving joints where the parts meet or cross (FIG. 7-7D).
- The diagonal piece at the top (FIG. 7-7E) should match the edge of the bottom, so the doorway is kept square.
- Assemble the parts made so far. Put cleats under the bottom to locate the toe boards. The side pieces of the toe board may extend past the diagonal section, which can be beveled to fit against them.
- You will have to relate the diagonal front frame to the front frames of the side cabinets. If these are to remain square, you will have to bevel the door frame edges to 45 degrees (FIG. 7-7F). Better yet, miter the joints at $22\frac{1}{2}$ degrees (FIG. 7-7G). The top and bottom parts of the frame should follow on the lines of the corresponding parts on adjoining cabinets, but the upright parts should be wide enough to allow the door to swing back easily (FIG. 7-7H). However, making them too wide restricts access.
- For a single door, use hinges that allow it to swing back against the next cabinet door. Projecting handles on both doors would stop the diagonal door from going all the way back, so use sunk handles or notch the edges of the doors.
- One way to get the diagonal door out of the way is to hinge it to the next door (FIG. 7-7J). If the diagonal door is narrower than the other one, it will fold back on it. If wider, you can still use this method, but the open doors will have to be kept almost in line. If the diagonal part is so wide that you need to fit double doors, they can still be hinged to adjoining doors. Opening both sides will give wide clear access to the side and corner units.
- Joints in the top will probably be best made where this unit meets the side units. Widen the tops of the unit ends to give a good bearing. Arrange the top on the corner

unit to match any pattern in the side tops, but if the pattern cannot be matched both ways, set the corner unit top pattern diagonally.

EXTERNAL CORNERS

The various options for dealing with external corners are shown in FIG. 7-2. You can have enclosed units all the way, or the corner can be filled with shelves or provide other storage arrangements. Constructional details are very similar to those for cabinets meeting at an internal corner.

In both cases it has been assumed that the corners are square, but other angles can be dealt with in a similar way and cabinet arrangements around or in such corners can be quite attractive. If the angle is much more acute than 90 degrees, the storage space in an internal angle may not be enough to bother about access, while an acute *external* angle will probably require you to cut back the cabinets. Carrying them to meet might result in too sharp a point or a very rounded cut-back curved top.

SQUARE CORNER

The simplest way to deal with an external square corner is to make standard cabinets and let them overlap (FIG. 7-2A). The end overlapping unit should have suitable surfaced plywood for the exposed side.

Another way of dealing with this corner is to have the overlapping cabinets finish about 6 inches short of the corner, so you can include some shelves (FIG. 7-8A). If the shelves are narrow, they will get sufficient support from screws, but you could add solid (FIG. 7-8B) or turned (FIG. 7-8C) supports near the corner. Wider shelves could accommodate cookbooks, but some of these books are very wide, so the shelves would definitely need supports.

Instead of or behind the shelves, you could include space for boards (FIGS. 7-8D and 6-7C). Together, these two assemblies might occupy as much space as a unit with a door.

If you want to use the corner for enclosed storage, you might alter an end unit so it is closed at its narrow front and has a door on its wide side. For more open access you can have doors both ways (FIG. 7-2B). The doors should meet on a square post (FIG. 7-9A), which can fit into the front framing with dowels at the top (FIG. 7-9B) and bottom (FIG. 7-9C). For neatness, let one door edge overlap the other (FIG. 7-9D). This will not affect the opening of either door.

If you fit one or more shelves into this unit, you can rest them on cleats on the panels and notch the corners into the post (FIG. 7-9E). Hollowing the edge of an upper shelf will allow you to see a little more of what is on the shelf below (FIG. 7-9F).

A corner compartment with doors both ways need not be the same size as other compartments. For example, making it square (FIG. 7-2J), might be better for some items and could accommodate a storage carousel, with maximum access, because of the twin doors.

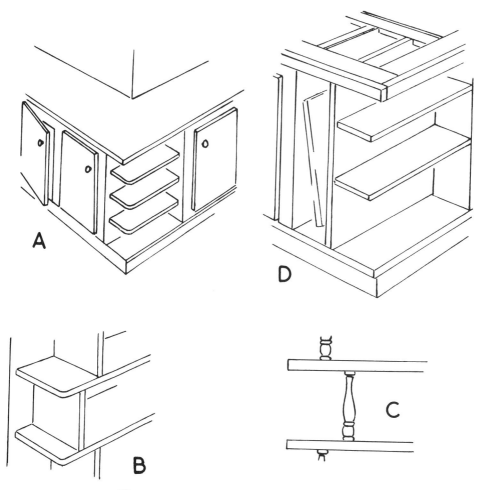

Fig. 7-8. Shelves at an external square corner.

LARGE SHELF CORNER

If two standard cabinets meet at a corner, the square that results has sides equal to the depth of the cabinets. If the top is continued over this, the floor area below can be used for storage without further treatment. This might be a good place for bulky items such as tall stools and steps or any large food containers that would not fit in a cabinet. In most kitchens, however, it is better to enclose the space, as already described, or to put shelves there.

You must decide if the top is to finish with a square corner, be beveled, or have a rounded corner. A sharp angle allows maximum work space on top, but in some places the sharp corner might be hazardous. Rounding depends on how the edge of the counter

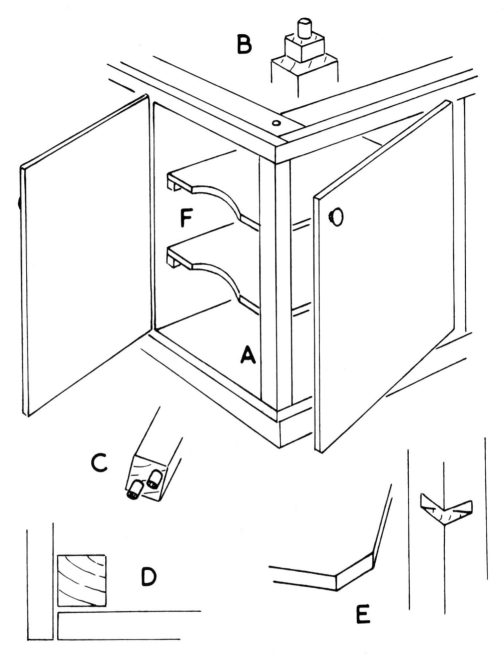

Fig. 7-9. A cabinet with two doors at an external corner.

is finished. Some edgings could not be curved without difficulty. It might be easier to cut straight across the corner and miter the point at which the edging pieces meet.

You must also decide whether to put a bottom on the corner section or leave the kitchen floor exposed. Adding a bottom helps preserve the continuity of appearance, but you get a little more storage space by using the floor. In addition, anything really heavy can slide in and out without being lifted.

You can arrange shelves to suit your needs. One may be enough, but two—giving clearance between shelves of about 10 inches—is the usual choice (FIG. 7-10A). Following are the basic steps to this corner treatment:

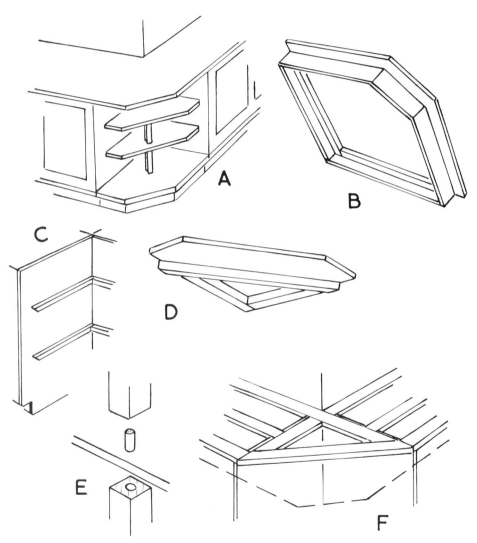

Fig. 7-10. The arrangement of a large shelf at an external corner.

- You could build a bottom to match the cabinets and connect it with cleats to the adjoining ends, but it is probably better made as a unit, which could be left loose or screwed in place. Decide on the outline of the top and make the corner bottom with a similar outline. Use the same plywood as the cabinet bottoms, and edge with solid wood. Make toe boards and rear supports. You can avoid screws down through the bottom by using cleats inside (FIG. 7-10B).

- Set back the shelves a few inches and put cleats in place (FIG. 7-10C). Make the shelves with outlines to match the top and bottom. Plywood or particleboard ¾ inch thick should be suitable, with solid wood or veneer edging. The diagonal length is long enough to make stiffness a consideration. Depending on what you put on the shelves, in time they may sag. You could put a diagonal support under each shelf (FIG. 7-10D), but that would reduce the height of things put on the bottom and on the lower shelf. Alternatively, you could use pillars, which might be square or turned. Use dowels for these pillars, with one long dowel at each point where pillars meet (FIG. 7-10E).

- To support the worktop, continue the inner lengthwise pieces over the cabinets. Cut off the others. A diagonal piece should then provide enough support for the top plywood, if all parts are glued and screwed to the cabinet sides (FIG. 7-10F).

- If the pattern allows, continue the top from one side and bring the top from the other direction to it. If there is a prominent pattern, you are better off stopping the side panels opposite the wall corner and putting another piece diagonally across. Continue edging from the sides and miter a strip across the diagonal corner. If you want to round the edges of the top and shelves, follow the relevant instructions in the next section.

SMALL SHELF CORNER

The shelves in the preceding example might occupy more of the corner than you wish. If you would prefer to use more of the under-counter space for enclosed cabinets, you can reduce the size of shelving. To do that, however, you have to fit one cabinet into another (FIG. 7-2G) or miter two meeting cabinets (FIG. 7-2H).

Fitting one cabinet into another is the easier of the two options. But if you decide on mitered cabinets, you must cut the corners at 45 degrees; fit plywood across with beveled cleats, either to both cabinets as units or to one only; and then close up the cut parts of the other cabinet. The following instructions are for the other approach: fitting one cabinet into another.

- Make one cabinet complete and without alterations.

- Decide how much area you wish to leave for shelves; then prepare the parts of the other cabinet cut away to fit around that area (FIG. 7-11A). Put cleats on the places where the parts meet (FIG. 7-11B); some of these can be added as you bring the parts together, but those under the bottom will have to be put in place first.

- Decide on the shape of the top. In this example it is rounded (FIG. 7-11C), but it could have a straight beveled corner, as in the preceding example.

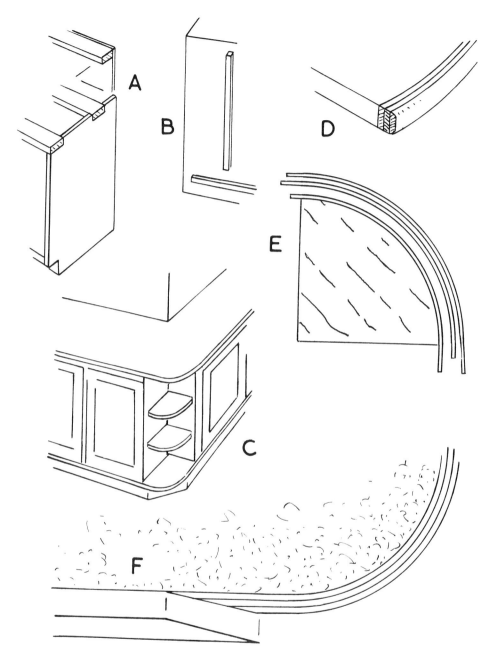

Fig. 7-11. Dealing with curved edges on an external corner.

- You could fit a bottom to the unit, similar but smaller than the one described in the preceding section, or leave the floor uncovered.

- The shelves will be much smaller than those in the preceding example and therefore will not need diagonal supports or posts. Put cleats on the cabinet sides to support them.

- If the front of a shelf is to be rounded, you might cover it with veneer bent and glued on. Or make a stronger and better-looking edge by laminating solid-wood strips. Use pieces not more than ⅛ inch thick. Three pieces will then make a solid edge, which you can give a curved or other cross section (FIG. 7-11D). Use strips slightly wider than the thickness of a shelf. Working with one piece at a time, bend, glue, and secure it with pins (FIG. 7-11E). When the glue has set, plane and sand the edges level with the shelf. Trim the ends and work the edge to whatever section you choose.

- You can make the curved edging to the corner in a similar way, but the laminations must make up the same thickness as the straight parts and they are best continued a short distance on the straight edges, then spliced to the solid parts. Do the work in position after the laminated plastic has been fitted to the plywood, but before fitting any of the straight edging. Bend and fit sufficiently wide laminations long enough to go about 6 inches along the straight edges. Cut the ends of the laminations to a long angle; 3 inches for a thickness of ½ inch would be satisfactory. Bevel the ends of the straight edging to match (FIG. 7-11F).

- When all these pieces have been fitted, trim the curved section to match the straight parts.

- It would not be very difficult to make a laminated section of toe board, working around a scrap wood pattern, but it would be simpler to put a straight diagonal piece across under the bottom, where it would be out of the way and barely visible.

CHAPTER

Cabinet Ends

If cabinets along one wall reach another wall, there is no problem at the end because it is hidden in the corner. This also applies to a counter that goes around an internal or external corner. But if cabinets finish partway along a wall or alongside a door, you have an opportunity to arrange the end in a decorative and useful way. You could leave it as merely the flat side of the last unit, or you could add simple shelves (FIG. 6-15). But because this is usually a fairly prominent place, the room's appearance demands that you do something more.

If the cabinets finish near a room door, you might be able to improve the layout *and* increase work space by extending the cabinet outward a short distance, with more useful and decorative space below. (Such an extension could not, however, go as far as becoming a table or breakfast bar, which would probably be at a changed level (see Chapter 11).

In another place, you could increase the height of the end compartment, either by a small amount or almost to the ceiling, adding to storage capacity although reducing worktop area.

LEDGED SHELVES

Open shelves are useful, but items can get knocked off them, particularly if the shelves are crowded. This applies whether the shelf has a square corner, is beveled, or is rounded. A simple solution to this problem is to put narrow strips around the edge. They could be mitered (FIG. 8-1A), but leaving gaps is simpler and allows easier cleaning (FIG. 8-1B). The easy way out when you have to deal with a curved corner is to leave it open (FIG. 8-1C), but if it is a big curve, that would leave too large a gap.

You can laminate a curved strip, using the same wood as the straight strips—at least

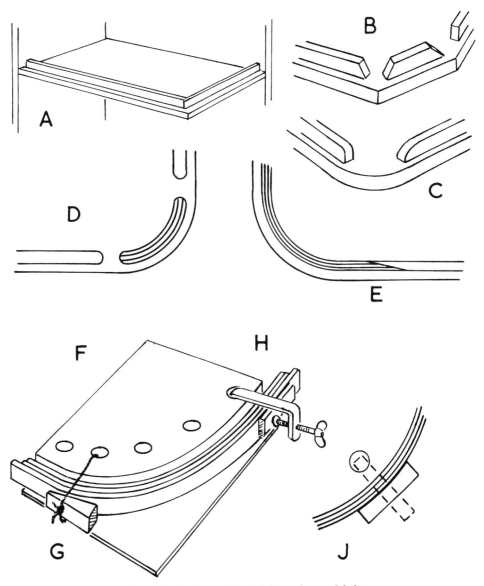

Fig. 8-1. Shelves with straight and curved ledges.

three pieces to make up the thickness. The more pieces you have in the thickness, the easier it is to bend them and get a true shape. The laminated part may stand alone, with gaps (FIG. 8-1D), or be spliced to the straight strips (FIG. 8-1E).

To make the curved part, you need a scrap-wood former shaped to match the inside curve of the laminated strip. Its thickness must be more than the depth of the strips, which should be a little more than the final size, to allow for truing. The former could be on a piece of plywood, which would help keep the strips in line, but that is not essential. Drill several holes through the former (FIG. 8-1F).

Either grease the former or put paper where the strips will come, to prevent glue from sticking to it. Use strips longer than the finished size; glue them and bend them to shape. Clamping can be done with cord and wedges (FIG. 8-1G) or you can use small C clamps (FIG. 8-1H). In both cases, spread the pressure with wood pads, preferably shaped to the outside curve the strip will match (FIG. 8-1J).

When the glue has set, plane the edges level and work the top edge to match the straight stripes. If they are to form a continuous piece, splice the straight parts of the laminated corner to the solid pieces. In a ⅜-inch thickness, a length of 2 inches would make a good slice.

RAILED SHELVES

Rails up to 3 inches high are better than ledges at holding articles on a shelf. They allow you to put things on the shelf easily, and even when it is packed with mixed and unattractive packages, the decorative rail provides an interesting visual facing.

The rail could be on square posts (FIG. 8-2A), dowel rods (FIG. 8-2B), or turned spindles (FIG. 8-2C). The bottoms of the supports could be directly on the shelf (FIG. 8-2D), but the assembly will look better with a lower rail matching the upper one (FIG. 8-2E).

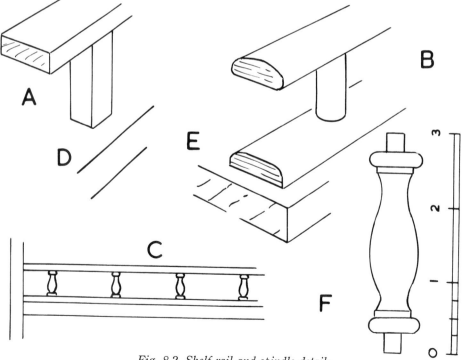

Fig. 8-2. Shelf rail and spindle details.

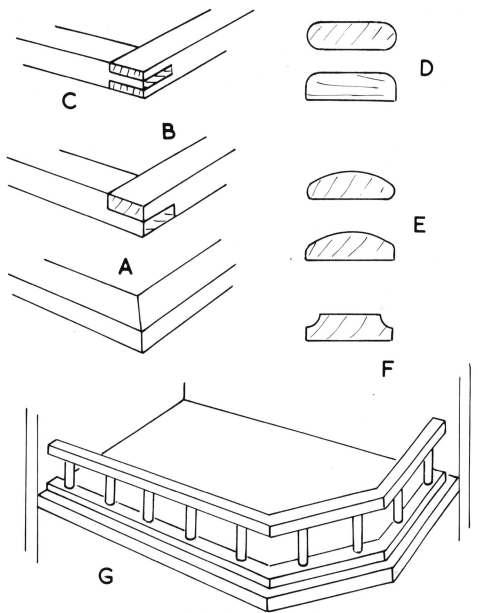

Fig. 8-3. Shelf rail construction and sections.

If you have the use of a lathe you can turn your own spindles with dowel ends, but you can also buy then ready-made. FIGURE 8-2F shows a suggested design. The dowel rods could fit into holes, while square posts could be tenoned or be used with dowels. For neatness, keep whatever you use to not much more than ½ inch across with spindles about 4 inches apart.

If the shelf has a square front corner, you could miter the rail on the shelf (FIG. 8-3A), but the top rail would be better halved (FIG. 8-3B) or open tenoned (FIG. 8-3C). Rails will usually be about ¾ inch wide and not more than ⅝ inch deep, so cut and fit the corner joints carefully. If you let ends extend a little before gluing, they can be planed and sanded level afterwards. The exposed joint details may then be regarded as decoration.

You can leave the top rail square or you can round it (FIG. 8-3D), give it an upper elliptical section (FIG. 8-3E), or molded it if you have a suitable small router (FIG. 8-3F). Shape the upper edge of the bottom rail to match the top one. The bottom rail can just butt against the cabinet back and end, but the top rail is better joined with a tenon or dowel.

If the shelf has a beveled corner, construction of rails is similar, but you will have to cut corner joints to match the bevel. If possible, space the spindles so the gaps are the same all around, with those at the angles equally spaced about the joint (FIG. 8-3G).

If a shelf has a curved front corner, you could laminate the railing vertically as shown previously (FIGS. 8-1F–J). However, it is preferable to laminate horizontally—dealing with a rail as a whole—unless it is very long and splicing would be possible. Laminating horizontally involves putting together several thin pieces with their grains different ways and joints staggered, thus avoiding the weakness of short grain that would be inevitable if you cut a curved rail from one thickness.

Use three or, preferably, four pieces to make up the total thickness of rail (about ½ inch). Draw the complete rail on a piece of plywood or hardboard as a guide (FIG. 8-4A). Make up each layer with pieces of wood wider than eventually needed, with the grain on each going in the direction of the straight parts or in the general direction of the curve. Arrange the joints in each layer at different places, so when the whole assembly is glued up they will be staggered. FIGURE 8-4B shows a suggested arrangement of a layer. So long as you arrange the joints in one layer so they are away from those in the next layers, it does not matter how you cut the wood. Make sure there is enough width to mark and cut the final shape.

Glue the pieces. Putting weights on the boards will provide clamping. When the glue has set, draw and cut the final outline. Round or mold the strip, treating it as a single, continuous piece (FIG. 8-4C). For rails on several shelves, make them at the same time, working through the stages on each one so they will match. Arrange spindle spaces on the curves in the same way as on the straight parts (FIG. 8-4D).

ANGLED END CABINET

If you plan to angle the end of a row of cabinets into the room, you will have to weigh your needs against the loss of floor space. If there will still be plenty of space to move around, a small projection into the room can be attractive and useful. It will mark a positive end to a countertop as well as give you extra working and storage space. It might enable you to provide storage space that would be difficult to obtain in a straight row of compartments.

There are many ways to arrange the projection, but the example in FIGS. 8-5 and

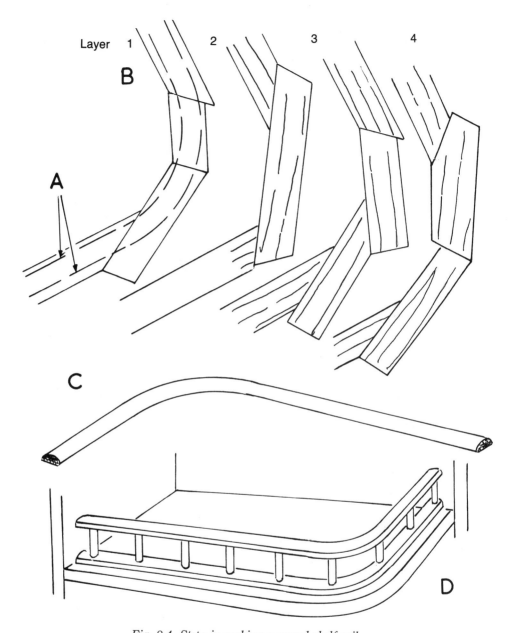

Fig. 8-4. Steps in making a curved shelf rail.

8-6 assumes that the countertop will extend about 24 inches and be 22 inches wide, with the existing worktop reaching 24 inches from the wall. The extension has a cupboard with a door at the end, bookcase-type shelves facing both ways, and a shelf at the end (FIG. 8-5). From these instructions it should be easy to adapt an angled cabinet to suit your needs.

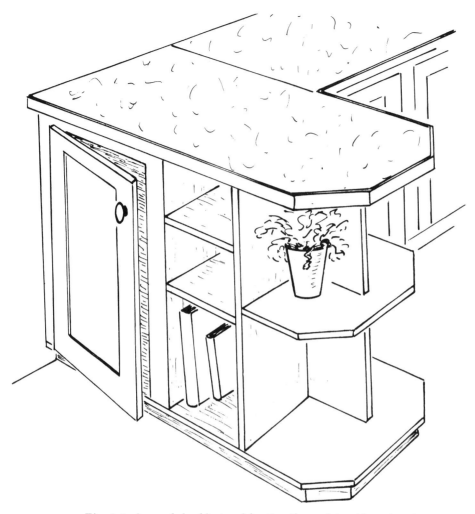

Fig. 8-5. An angled cabinet end is attractive and provides extra storage.

As drawn (FIG. 8-6), the toe board, top, and cupboard width are matched to the adjoining cabinet. The shelves are at different heights and the division is off-center, so you can provide here for large cookbooks that are difficult to store elsewhere. At the end there is a single shelf at about half height, which is supported and divided by a vertical piece. The top and shelves have corner bevels, but they could be square or rounded to match tops elsewhere in the kitchen.

All panels and shelves could be ¾-inch plywood. Exposed surfaces should have a suitable veneer or may be painted, but exposed plywood *edges* should be covered with solid wood strips. Where the heads will not show, some parts may be screwed, such as underneath and against the wall or other cabinet. Elsewhere you can use ⅜-inch dowels spaced about 4 inches apart. Following are the basic steps for constructing an angled cabinet end.

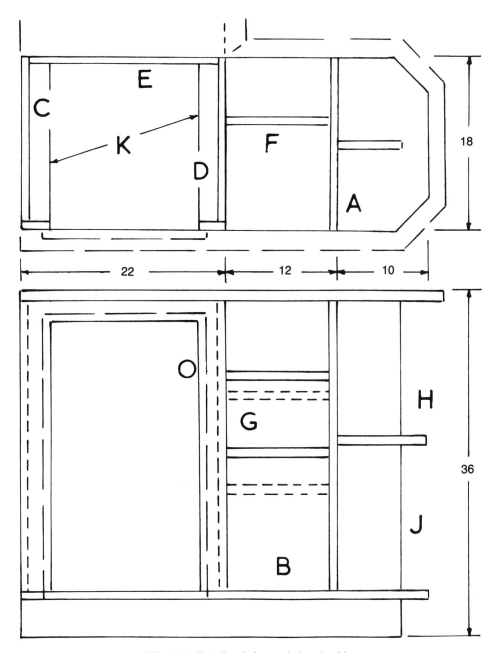

Fig. 8-6. Details of the angled end cabinet.

- Start by making the main division (FIGS. 8-6A and 8-7A) and the bottom (FIGS. 8-6B and 8-7B). Edge them with solid wood and mark on them the positions of other parts. These are the key pieces, from which sizes of other parts can be determined.
- The two cupboard sides (FIGS. 8-6C, D and 8-7C, D) have 3-inch vertical strips to take

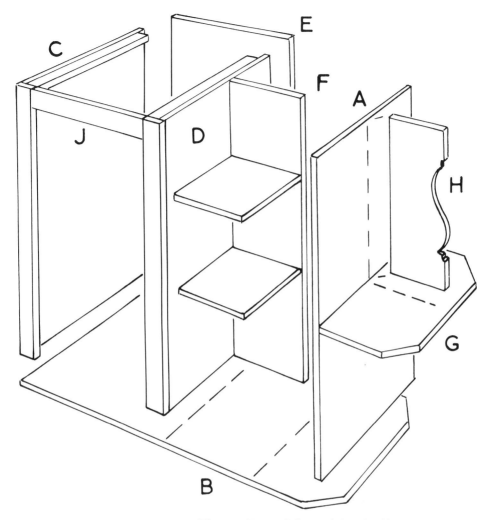

Fig. 8-7. Parts of the angled end cabinet.

the door. Their overall height and width should be the same as those of the main division.

• Make the cupboard back (FIGS. 8-6E and 8-7E) to fit between the cupboard sides. The total width should match the end of the next cabinet.

• With the bottom markings as a size guide, make the shelf division (FIGS. 8-6F and 8-7F). Make shelves to fit each side of it. Two are suggested for each side (FIG. 8-6G), with one deep, wide compartment for large books.

• The front shelf (FIGS. 8-6H and 8-7G) should have bevels that will be parallel with the bevels on the countertop and bottom.)

• Make front uprights parallel pieces (FIG. 8-6J), or shape the exposed edges (FIG. 8-7H).

• Mark and drill for screws and dowels.

• Assemble the cupboard parts first. Arrange a top bar over the doorway (FIG. 8-7J) and put two strips inside (FIG. 8-6K) to take screws into the top. Mount this cupboard on the bottom.

• Dowel the shelves to the shelf division, and screw through the cupboard side.

• Put the front shelf and its uprights on the main division, then dowel that to the shelf division and shelves. Screw into all these parts through the bottom.

• Add toe boards to match the other cabinets, using cleats inside to avoid having to drive screws downward through the bottom. You could put the toe boards square across at the front or make beveled corners to match the bottom.

• Treat the top as part of the angled unit. Cut the worktop on the adjoining cabinet level with its side, so the new top can close tightly against it. The tops should match in amount of overhang and type of edging. Cut the new top back where it meets the other top, to allow the correct overhang, and miter the meeting edgings. You may have to thicken the cupboard back and the other cabinet side, to allow for glue and screws.

• Toward the front, arrange dowels from the edges of the main division and other upright parts into the top plywood.

• Make the door to match other doors. It can overlap the framing and edge of the bottom and can be hinged either side. There should be ample clearance if it hinges at the wall side.

Materials List for Angled Cabinet End

1 main division	18 × 32 × ¾ plywood
1 bottom	18 × 46 × ¾ plywood
2 cupboard sides	18 × 32 × ¾ plywood
2 cupboard sides	1 × 3 × 32
1 doorway top	1 × 2 × 18
2 cupboard top strips	1 × 2 × 18
1 cupboard back	21 × 32 × ¾ plywood
1 shelf division	12 × 32 × ¾ plywood
2 shelves	12 × 12 × ¾ plywood
2 shelves	8 × 12 × ¾ plywood
1 front shelf	10 × 20 × ¾ plywood
2 front uprights	8 × 16 × ¾ plywood
1 toe board	¾ × 4 × 44
2 toe boards	¾ × 4 × 24
1 top	22 × 44 × 1 plywood
Edging	to match adjoining
1 door	to match others nearby

RAISED END CABINET

Another way of making a positive and decorative cabinet end is to build a higher and deeper compartment there. This could be simply closed with a door, or you could combine drawers with a cupboard or make the whole thing a block of drawers. What you do depends on your needs. Do not arrange drawers so high that it is difficult to see or reach into them. You can continue design features into the enlarged end, but you probably cannot continue door or drawer lines.

The example in FIG. 8-8 has a full-depth door and a removable tray. It is 6 inches

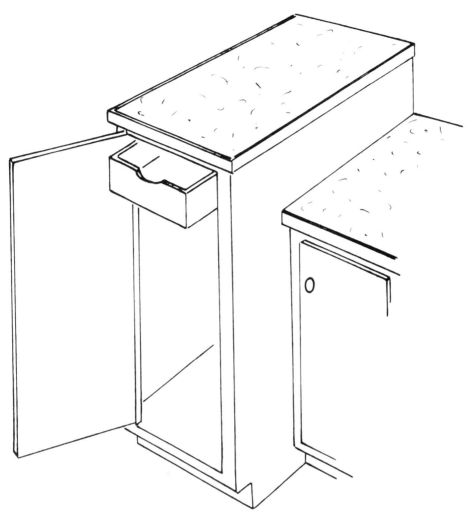

Fig. 8-8. A raised end cabinet makes a positive finish to a countertop.

higher and 6 inches deeper than the adjoining cabinet. Therefore, the top is not too high to be used when standing, and the cabinet can store wider and taller items. The top can be a place to put food or packages, away from the main counter work space.

Build this assembly as a unit to fit against the end of a normal cabinet that has its top finished level with its side. Panels can be ¾-inch plywood or particleboard, with a suitable veneer on exposed surfaces. Parts are screwed where the heads will not show and doweled elsewhere. Doors and top should match adjoining cabinets.

FIGURE 8-9 shows suggested dimensions. Following are the basic steps of construction:

• Make the pair of sides (FIG. 8-9A), with notched strips for the three top crosspieces.

The exposed side (FIG. 8-10A) stops above the toe-board line whereas, the inner side (FIG. 8-10B) continues behind the toe board to the floor, to match the bottom of the adjoining cabinet.

• Make the back (FIG. 8-10C) and bottom (FIG. 8-10D) to fit between the sides.

• Make the top crosspieces (FIGS. 8-9B and 8-10E) the same length as the bottom.

• Drill for screws and dowels, then assemble the parts made so far. Placing the back and bottom between the sides should keep the assembly square, but check that there is no twist in the open front.

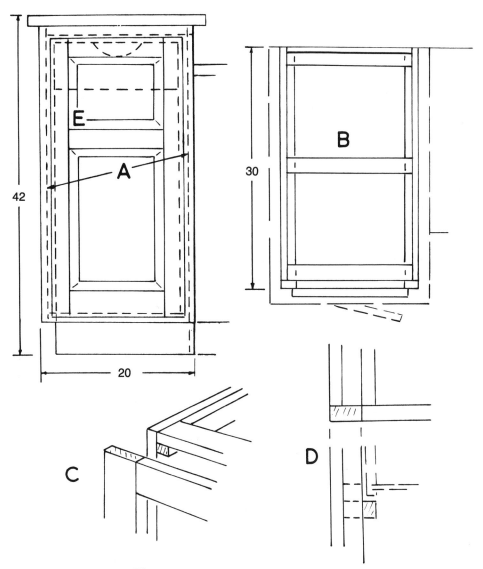

Fig. 8-9. Details of the raised end cabinet.

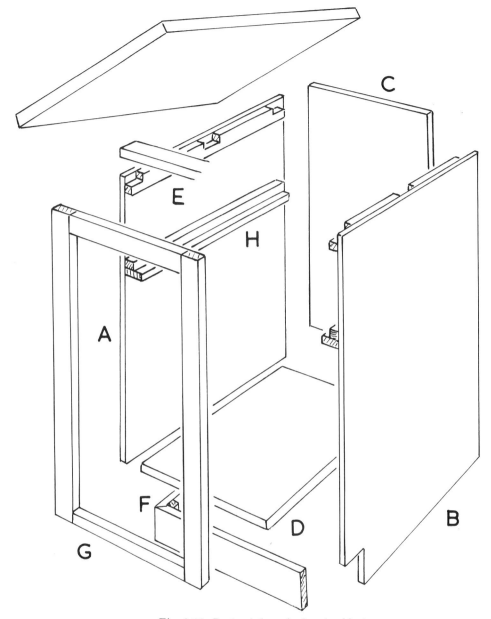

Fig. 8-10. Parts of the raised end cabinet.

• Fit toe boards under the end and across the front, with a mitered corner (FIG. 8-10F).

• Make a frame to cover the front. It should be 2 inches wide at the sides and top and of a thickness to match the plywood at the bottom (FIGS. 8-9C and 8-10G).

• The bearers for the tray should have guides level with the edges of the front frame but should then extend about ¾ inch past that point (FIGS. 8-9D and 8-10H). You could fit any number of trays and shelves, but remember to leave room for taller items.

- Make each tray like an open box, with a hollowed front to provide a grip (FIG. 6-6).
- Make the top in the same way as the adjoining cabinet: level at the back and overhanging the same amount at the sides and front. Fit matching edging. You could also fit a tiled top (see chapter 9). To avoid having to cut tiles, get the tiles first and then arrange the size of the cabinet and its top to accommodate whole tiles.
- Make the door to match those near it. If they are paneled, however, this taller door might look better with a dividing rail across it (FIG. 8-9E).

Materials List for Raised End Cabinet

1 side	30 × 42 × ¾ plywood
1 side	30 × 38 × ¾ plywood
1 back	19 × 38 × ¾ plywood
1 bottom	19 × 30 × ¾ plywood
3 top strips	1 × 2 × 19
2 top supports	1 × 2 × 30
2 tray guides	1 × 1¼ × 30
2 tray bearers	1 × 2 × 30
2 front frames	1 × 2 × 38
1 front frame	1 × 2 × 20
1 front frame	1 × 1 × 20
1 toe board	1 × 4 × 30
1 toe board	1 × 4 × 20
2 tray sides	⅝ × 6 × 30
2 tray sides	⅝ × 6 × 20
1 tray bottom	20 × 30 × ¼ plywood
1 top	24 × 34 × 1 plywood

Door and top to match adjoining cabinet

TALL END CABINET

A cabinet that reaches almost to the ceiling can provide good capacity and close the end of a normal countertop, possibly as a barrier between areas or as a stop near a doorway. If you include shelves on one or both sides, you improve the appearance and you gain even more storage space. The cabinet could also have wall cabinets against its inner side.

The end cabinet could project farther forward than the room's standard cabinets, but the design shown in FIG. 8-11 has its front in line with the other cabinets. Its height is divided at 60 inches from the floor, and the door above that hinges at the top, to give good access to the upper compartment. No posts or corner supports are shown for the shelves, which will probably be stiff enough attached to back and sides, but you could add turned or square posts. The shelves could be left plain or have rails (FIGS. 8-1 to 8-4).

The method of construction should be similar to that of the cabinets alongside. The example in FIG. 8-1 comes against a cabinet 36 inches high and 24 inches from the wall. The cupboard alone is 24 inches wide and with shelves it needs 34 inches of wall space (FIG. 8-12).

The panels may be ¾-inch plywood or particleboard, with suitable veneers on ex-

Fig. 8-11. This tall end cabinet with shelves increases storage capacity.

posed faces. The shelves should be veneered on both surfaces and suitably edged with veneer or solid wood. You can screw most parts, but use dowels where screw heads would show. The top is shown with a molding, which you could buy or make with a router. Or you could have a plain wood edge at the top. The extending molding is more appropriate to a top above sight level.

The carcass is like an open-front box, with a frame over it and doors overlapping it. The front frame should finish in line with the adjoining cabinet front, and the toe board should be of a size to follow through. Following are the basic steps of construction:

• Make the side that comes alongside the adjacent cabinet (FIGS. 8-12A and 8-13A). Check that its bottom parts will fit against the other cabinet's side. Add the cleats (FIG. 8-12A).
• Make the bottom (FIG. 8-13B). It fits inside the first side, but under the second and below the back, extending to form the bottom shelf. Use the bottom and first side as size guides for other parts.

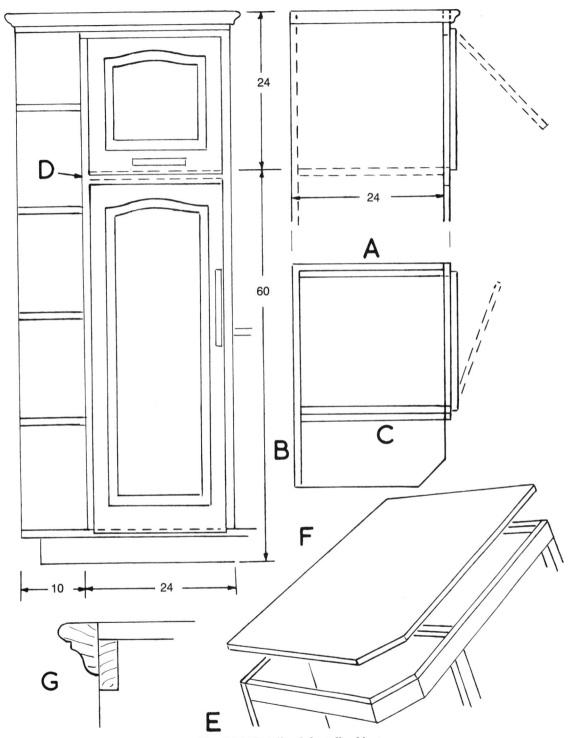

Fig. 8-12. Details of the tall cabinet.

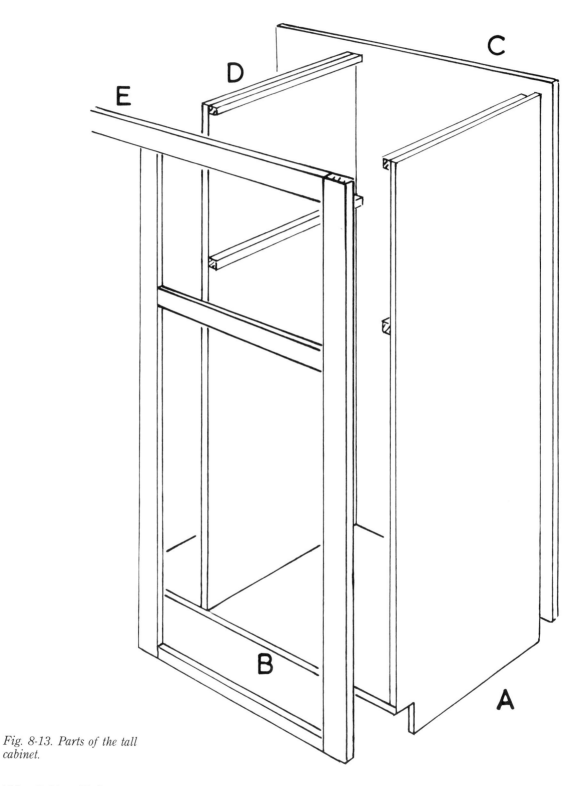

Fig. 8-13. Parts of the tall cabinet.

- Make the back (FIGS. 8-12B and 8-13C), to extend from inside the first side and to the end of the bottom.
- The second side (FIGS. 8-12C and 8-13D) comes above the bottom and inside the back, but it should have the same cleats across as the first side.
- Prepare the shelves. FIGURES 8-11 and 8-12 show them with beveled front corners, but you could make them rounded or square. Make ledges or rails if required, as described earlier in this chapter. Prepare the shelves, back, and side for dowels. Join the shelves to the side.
- Make the division (FIG. 8-12D) to fit on its cleats.
- Assemble all the parts made so far. Check squareness, but the division and shelves should prevent the front from twisting.
- Prepare the front frame (FIG. 8-13E). Deepen the top rail to allow for hinging the top door and for molding. It extends over the shelves and will be shaped to match them (FIG. 8-12E).
- Cover the top with a board (FIG. 8-12F). To it, attach the top frame and extensions around the shelf cover. Put molding around the outer edge (FIG. 8-12G).
- Make the doors to match those on the other cabinets. Hinge the top one on its upper edge. A long handle there would be better than a knob. You can use a strut pivoting on a screw in the side of the opening to hold the door out to about 45 degrees.
- Carry a toe board from the other cabinets to go under the tall cabinet, and shape it under the bottom to match the end angle.

Materials List for Tall End Cabinet

1 side	24 × 84 × ¾ plywood
1 side	24 × 80 × ¾ plywood
1 bottom	24 × 36 × ¾ plywood
1 top	24 × 36 × ¾ plywood
4 shelves	10 × 26 × ¾ plywood
1 back	34 × 84 × ¾ plywood
4 cleats	26 × 1 × 1
2 front frames	84 × 2 × 1
1 front frame	24 × 2 × 1
1 front frame	24 × 1 × 1
1 front frame	34 × 3 × 1
1 end frame	30 × 3 × 1
1 molding	38 × 1½
2 moldings	30 × 1½
2 toe boards	36 × 4 × 1

Doors to match adjoining cabinets

TALL CABINET WITH OVEN

Including an oven in a floor-standing range is a good and long-standing idea, but the cook usually has to stoop to reach the oven. This can be avoided by arranging the oven at eye level. If you are equipping a kitchen completely, the cook will probably want a separate raised oven. This calls for a tall cabinet. If you plan to make the tall end cabinet discussed in the preceding section, you can make this to match it, probably for location at the end of another counter.

Ovens vary in size and ventilation requirements. The makers recommend how much air space to leave, which affects the size of the cabinet and the space you leave for the oven. Therefore, you must settle on the choice of oven before starting on the cabinet.

The cabinet suggested in FIG. 8-14 is designed around a single, average-size oven. As the amount of cabinet space taken by the oven is the most important variable, measure your oven and modify the cabinet sizes to fit it. You can arrange the height to suit the user, but be careful not to locate the oven too high. The cook should be able to look into the top of the oven with little effort; having to bend a little to look into the lower part is no problem.

This cabinet in FIG. 8-14 is made mostly of ¾-inch plywood with framing of 1-inch-×-2-inch strips, including the front framing. The unit has storage space below and above the oven, which can be closed with doors. FIGURE 8-15 shows sizes to suit an oven that will fit in an opening 26 inches square, so modify these instructions accordingly

Fig. 8-14. A tall cabinet to take an eye-level oven.

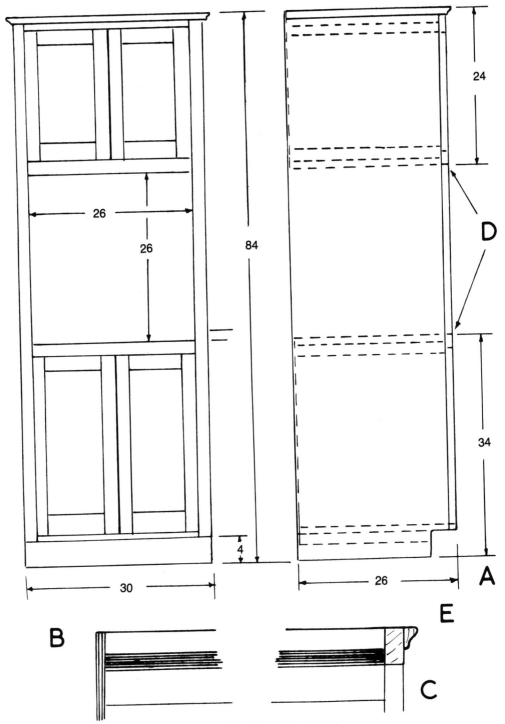

Fig. 8-15. Details of the cabinet to take an oven.

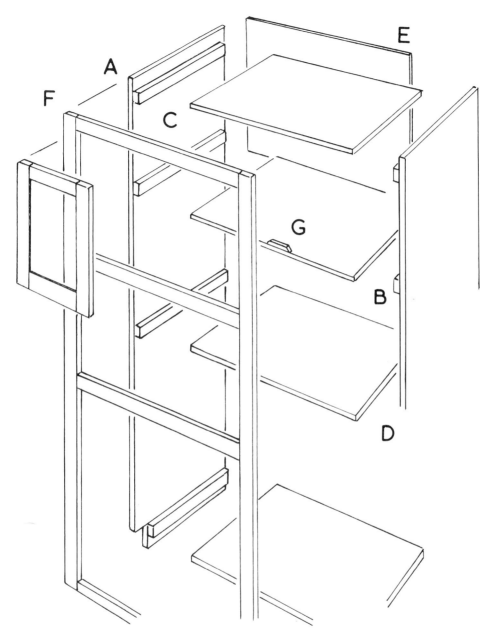

Fig. 8-16. Parts of the tall cabinet to take an oven.

when you have measured your oven. The example has double-paneled doors above and below, fitted flush in the frames, but you could substitute doors to match those on other cabinets. The cupboards have backs, but the oven space is left open for ventilation. Check your oven's instructions to determine these requirements.

The two sides are the same (FIGS. 8-15A and 8-16A). Cleats across go under the shelves, except at the opening, where they are above the shelf to leave the oven space free of obstructions (FIG. 8-16B). The top will be fitted a short distance down so there is a ledge around it to prevent anything put there from falling off (FIGS. 8-15B and 8-16C). See that the toe board will match the height of the adjoining cabinet, even if it will stand forward of it. Allow for the backs fitting into rabbets or being held by fillets inside.

The four shelves are all the same (FIG. 8-16D), although you could increase the thickness of the bottom one to 1 inch. Have the backs ready (FIG. 8-16E), then assemble all the parts made so far. They should hold together squarely, but check that there is no twist at the front edges.

Make the front frame (FIG. 8-16F) to match the outline. The bottom of the top rail should be level with the underside of that shelf (FIG. 8-15C). The rails above and below the oven opening should be level with the opening's edges (FIG. 8-15D). The bottom rail should match the shelf edge.

Fit the frame to the cabinet. Add a toe board if the size does not allow an adjoining toe board to continue through.

The suggested doors are framed, with plywood panels, and shown fitted flush with the cabinet frame, using hinges on the uprights. Fit stops at top and bottom where the door meet (FIG. 8-16G). If you make doors that fit on the surface of the frame, the stops will have to be on the frame.

You could leave the top of the cabinet as it is. However, you could add a large molding—as on the tall end cabinet discussed previously—or you could add a small molding (FIG. 8-15E) or even a plain strip, to provide a pattern above eye level.

Materials List for Tall Cabinet with Oven

2 sides	$25 \times 85 \times \frac{3}{4}$ plywood
3 shelves	$25 \times 30 \times \frac{3}{4}$ plywood
1 bottom	$25 \times 30 \times 1$ plywood
1 back	$24 \times 30 \times \frac{1}{2}$ plywood
1 back	$30 \times 32 \times \frac{1}{2}$ plywood
8 cleats	$1 \times 2 \times 26$
2 front frames	$1 \times 2 \times 84$
3 front frames	$1 \times 2 \times 30$
1 front frame	$1 \times 1 \times 30$
4 door sides	$1 \times 2 \times 24$
4 door sides	$1 \times 2 \times 30$
8 door rails	$1 \times 2 \times 12$
2 door panels	$11 \times 22 \times \frac{1}{4}$ plywood
2 door panels	$11 \times 28 \times \frac{1}{4}$ plywood
1 toe board	$1 \times 4 \times 32$

CHAPTER

Countertops

The worktop or counter is the area that accommodates the equipment, dishes, and other things associated with the preparation of food. It also forms a prominent part of the general appearance of the kitchen. In constructing countertops, you have to provide a surface that will stand up to a considerable amount of use, yet look good and match the cabinets and other items in the kitchen.

One advantage of equipping a kitchen yourself is that you do not have to conform to standard sizes. If you want a wide top, you can make it that way. Realistically, however, the top should be narrower at one place to allow passage or more floor space. If two tops meet at a corner they can be different widths, and a diagonal section across a corner will certainly be wider. If you are dealing with a room, or part of one, which is not square, you will definitely have to work with nonstandard sizes.

Although nonstandard tops might be attractive, you have to fit them against ranges and other appliances, most of which are now made to come against a top 36 inches from the floor and 25 to 26 inches wide. In general, unless a particular situation demands otherwise, you should work to standard sizes. If you intend to buy manufactured tops you will *have* to, or else allow for cutting them down. Greater widths will also involve joints, which in many materials might be difficult to make.

In the early days all cooks worked on plain wood. But counter materials have developed in recent years, so you now have more choices. By far the most commonly used material is a plastic laminate, but if you want to be different you can use ceramics, marble, or other materials. You also do not have to use the same tops all around a kitchen, but for the sake of appearance you need to coordinate colors.

PLANNING

Countertops are in such prominent positions and form such a large part of a room's visual impact that they have to be as near perfect as you can get them. You can inconspicuously make some alterations to the cabinets below to correct a mistake or arrange a modification, but you can do little to the top. There is no way you can add a few more inches, for instance, without it showing. Therefore, know ahead of time what sinks, ranges, and other appliances will have to be fitted in. If possible, get them in advance, but if not, be certain of what you are getting and measure them carefully.

Visualize your worktops at an early stage in planning a kitchen layout, even though you might not make them until after the cabinets have been made. In particular, consider where there will be a change of counter type that involves different thicknesses. You might have to make some cabinet parts lower to allow for a greater total thickness in a section of the top.

WOOD WORKTOPS

If you are equipping a kitchen in a country style, your counters should be wood—that is, if they are to be traditional. Laminated plastic in most modern patterns would not look right. However, you can get laminates with a wood appearance that are hard to distinguish from the real thing.

Plain board tops were used in the early days, and they are not unknown in some of the best modern kitchens. A top-class chef or cook might still prefer a top made up of wide boards. But he has someone else to scrub it! Also, wood can now be treated to provide a fairly durable surface, if you want to avoid scrubbing, but you will have to resurface it every year or so.

If there is space in the kitchen for a table or island unit, your cook might like a top made of plain wood, to work on in the traditional way. The wood should be close-grained and preferably of a light color, so it looks hygienic. Sycamore would be suitable. Do not use softwood. If possible, get wood with the grain lines on the end through the thickness, showing that the board was cut radically (FIG. 2-1C). A table top made with boards cut this way is unlikely to warp or expand and contract enough to matter in the width.

To conform to the best tradition, glue the boards together. Then fit cleats across the ends with tongue-and-groove joints (FIG. 9-1A). If the assembly allows, fit the top to its framing with buttons in grooves (FIG. 9-1B). This will allow for slight movement of the top; fixing it down rigidly runs a risk of splitting or cracking.

Old-time carpenters did not have the benefits of the fully waterproof, strong glues available today. They used butcher-block construction but had to depend on dowels and metal connections. You can use the same technique, but depending only on glue, simplifies construction.

A butcher-block top should not be too thin, or there could be difficulty in keeping it flat. It should not be much thinner than 1½ inches. You can then use widths of about 2 inches, although random widths look attractive. If you have to make up lengths, you

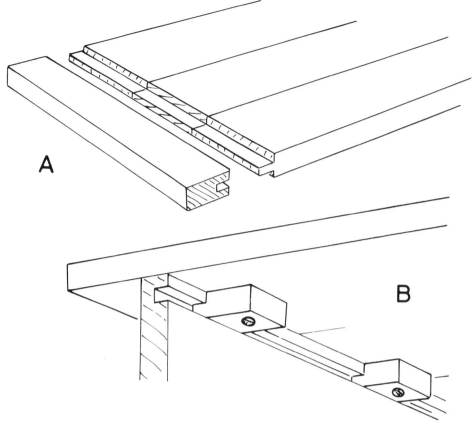

Fig. 9-1. A solid wood top with a cleat end (A). Buttons allow for expansion and contraction (B).

can use simple butt joints, which should be staggered, preferably with full-length pieces between (FIG. 9-2A). To ensure accuracy and a minimum amount of leveling of surfaces later, join the pieces in pairs first, then join pairs (FIG. 9-2B), and so on until you have made up the width. The whole process may take longer this way, but you can more easily get parts level when clamping.

If an end of the butcher-block top is exposed, do not fit a cleat or other extra crosspiece. Instead, carefully finish the end, as the finished grain will appear quite attractive. Another traditional way to finish an end is to let a strip into a groove (FIG. 9-2C). A wood strip of a contrasting color can be attractive.

Cabinet units of standard height suit tops about 1-inch thick. If you make a thicker butcher-block top, the extra height may not matter, but if the surface has to match a different standard top or come against an appliance, you may have to lower the cabinets.

A butcher-block top looks best if its construction is obvious and of full thickness, but for a countertop with an edging, you could work on a plywood base (FIG. 9-2D). To maintain the standard thickness, you could use ½-inch strips on ½-inch plywood. The assembly will be stronger, however, if the total thickness is more—1½ inches, for example—particularly if the cook expects to do much chopping or hitting on it.

A butcher-block worktop strip looks good with an edging of a contrasting wood, either narrow and molded or wider and rounded. Mitered and taken around an end, this approach can be very attractive (FIG. 9-2E).

You can use a surface finish of varnish or lacquer on a wood top, but it has to be able to withstand abrasion, impact, and the effects of liquid heat. You will have to watch for any breakdown of the surface finish and be prepared to renew it before dirt and liquids have penetrated the grain.

A better idea is to use a penetrating finish, such as Watco oil, or teak oil. Apply several coats of it. It could be colored, if you wish, but the natural oil will darken with age. Follow this with a wax finish. At first, apply wax every few days, then lengthen the intervals until you are waxing once a month, depending on the work load the surface has to withstand. Another good treatment is vegetable oil (which is used for cooking), with frequent rubs after the initial soaking.

Your cook might want a wood countertop for only a short distance, with laminated plastic or some other, more durable top adjoining. In such a case, you might leave the wood top bare, as periodic scrubbing of only a few feet may be acceptable.

You could tile the wall immediately above a wood countertop, but you could easily make a wood splash-back. It could be of the same wood as the surface, although it would look better if made of the same wood as the edging, particularly if carried around a corner. If you are fitting the counter to a really straight wall, the splash-back could fit behind the top (FIG. 9-2F), but if there are defects in the wall surface, you can more easily get the necessary close fit by placing the splash-back on top (FIG. 9-2G). The tiles above should cover any slight unevenness. You can then finish the splash-back to match the worktop.

LAMINATED PLASTIC COUNTERS

Plastic development in modern times has produced a countertop material that will stand up to hard kitchen or bathroom use, and maintain its attractive appearance. This is laminated plastic or plastic-laminate, perhaps best known under the trade name Formica. The plastic used is melamine, which has a good resistance to all liquids and other kitchen substances and can withstand wear and abrasion for a long time. This is the most popular countertop material.

Laminated plastic is made from a large number of paper layers, with the top one carrying a pattern. The result is saturated with the plastic and subjected to high pressure and heat. An extra layer of melamine is added to the top, to produce a stiff, hard board about ¹⁄₁₆ inch thick. The pattern can be almost anything, including pictures, futuristic color patterns, and other designs inappropriate for a kitchen. For your worktop however, you can choose from a large range of marblelike and other passive patterns or imitations of wood grain or other natural materials. The choice of pattern does not affect the characteristics and durability of the working surface because the pattern is beneath a transparent protective coating.

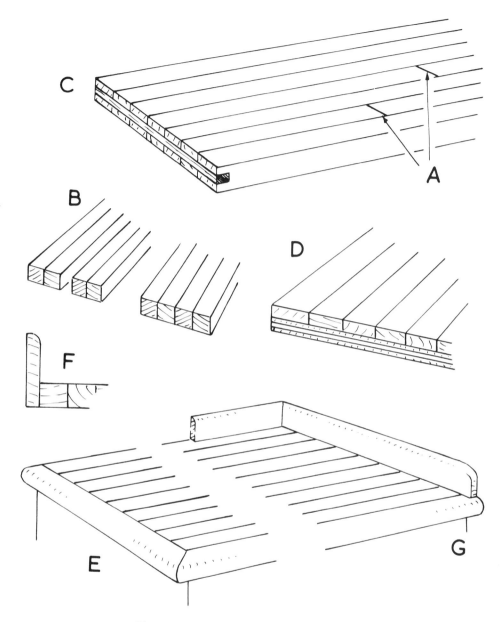

Fig. 9-2. Construction of a laminated worktop.

Laminated plastic is available in several grades and sizes. The standard grade should suit all kitchen applications. Sizes of sheets vary between makers, but you can get widths beginning at 24 inches and lengths from 6 to 12 feet. Besides the smooth surface commonly available, laminated plastic also comes in textured surfaces. These might have nonslip advantages, but some are not so easy to keep clean.

Post-Formed Counters

You can attach sheet laminated plastic to your own plywood or particleboard, but many remodelers use post-formed counters. In these tops, the plastic comes already bonded to high-density particleboard. This is done under heat and pressure, thus enabling shaping.

The simplest already-covered top has just the front edge rounded (FIG. 9-3A). An-

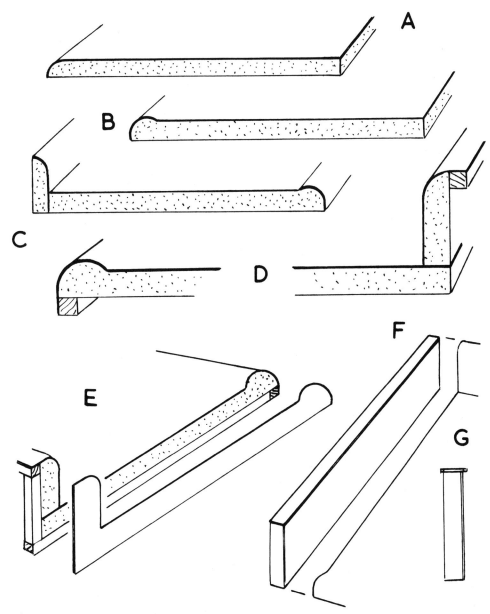

Fig. 9-3. Sections of laminated plastic countertops.

other type has a raised nosing (FIG. 9-3B). You can also get it with a splash-back included (FIG. 9-3C), with the laminated plastic in one width shaped over the nosing and the splash-back.

The particleboard used for these countertops can be about 1 inch thick, with a flat underside, or thinner with the edge thickness increased. If a splash-back is included, that may also be thickened (FIG. 9-3D).

When cutting a post-formed counter to length, you must guard against chipping the plastic surface. It helps to apply masking tape, mark the cut line on that, and then saw through. A sharp, fine circular saw will make the cut. If you use a hand saw, it should have at least 12 teeth per inch—a tenon saw rather than a panel saw—and cut at a fairly flat angle. Support the counter close to the cut, as it must not be allowed to vibrate while being cut. You can hand-plane the edges, with the cutting edge skewed away from the upper surface. Hand-sanding an edge with coarse abrasive paper over a wood block will furnish the best surface for taking adhesive, but be careful to avoid rounding the edge.

You can finish a ready-made counter with a piece of laminated plastic to cover the open end. This may have to be fitted with contact adhesive, or it may be precoated with an adhesive and only needs to be rubbed down with an electric iron over a piece of paper. Where the counter has thickened edges, you will have to glue-in strips to make up the same thickness across the end, before adding the end cover piece (FIG. 9-3E).

If you want a splash-back at the other end where the counter fits in the corner, you will have to make it from flat particleboard and pieces of matching sheet laminated plastic (FIG. 9-3F). Cut the end of the counter to the same angle as the corner it has to fit, but make it shorter by enough to fit the splash-back you will make.

Cut a piece of high-density particleboard to cover the end of the countertop. Its edges cannot be rounded to match the counter edges. Fasten a piece of laminated plastic to the surface and trim its edges. Cut strips slightly too wide to cover the top (FIG. 9-3G) and front edges. Attach the front piece first and level its edges; then do the same with the top piece. If the end wall is out of true, you can let the top strip of plastic overhang a little and match it edge to the wall by filing. Extensive overhang is inadvisable.

You can level the edges of this short piece with a small, sharp, block plane. Hold it at an angle so it takes a slicing cut away from the surface, with the plane sole tilted a little so you do not cut the adjoining surface. You can finish the edge by lightly sanding with abrasive paper around a block of wood, or by one of the methods suggested below for dealing with edges of self-made worktops.

Prepare the end splash-back with holes for screws into the counter end. Four should be enough. Drill to the screw core diameter in the counter end. Put some caulking compound in the joint before you tighten the screws.

Self-made Countertops

To make your own countertop with a laminated plastic surface, start with 1-inch plywood or high-density particleboard. If the particleboard is not at least 1 inch thick, thicken the front edge to give a deeper and more attractive appearance. You can finish the front edge with more of the same plastic (FIG. 9-4A) or have a narrow (FIG. 9-4B) or wide (FIG. 9-4C) wood edge. Plywood may be thickened in the same way.

At the back the edge can come against the wall, to be tiled later. You could make a splash-back, which can be thickened in the same way as the front (FIG. 9-4D), with its top edge covered with plastic (FIG. 9-4E) or with a strip to match the front edge (FIG. 9-4F).

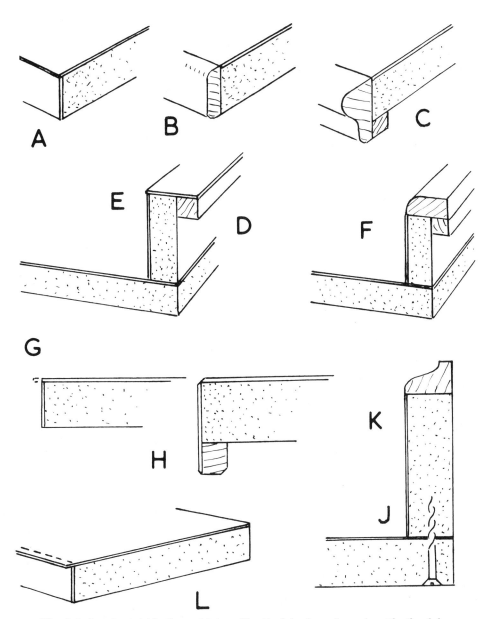

Fig. 9-4. Laminated plastic worktops with splash-backs and wood or plastic edging.

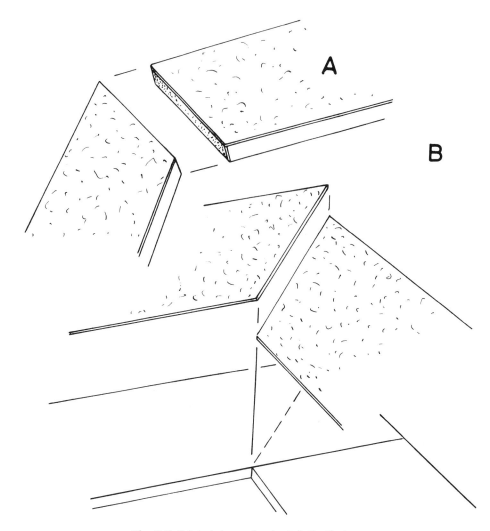

Fig. 9-5. Joints between laminated plastic tops.

Although you cannot use the heat-and-pressure method of a post-formed counter, you can attach laminated plastic to the counter with contact adhesive. Follow the maker's instructions exactly.

Where the plastic and its base must finish exactly level, leave up to ⅛-inch overhang of plastic to true after fitting. Where precision is not so important, as at the back which is covered with a splash-back, you can fit the edge by eye. With help if necessary, lower the laminate plastic (having first coated it and the base with adhesive) by curving it upward, so you can fit one end or edge and lower the sheet progressively. That way you will not trap air bubbles. Some adhesives allow you a little tolerance for sliding into position, but do not expect much. Use all the pressure you can as you fit the laminate, but once surfaces are close, there should be no risk of them parting.

You can true an edge by manual planing and sanding—as described earlier for the end splash-back—or you can use a router, which should have a plastic-laminate bit and be controlled by a ball bearing. A solid pilot may burn the surface.

If you plan to have wood edges, you only have to cover the top counter surface, but if you plan to put plastic-laminate on one or more edges, do them first. You can cut these narrow strips on a table saw with a veneer blade. As you cut, hold the plastic down firmly with wood. If the plastic vibrates as you feed it in, the surface will probably chip. Make the strips slightly too wide, then trim them to match the base after fitting. The top surface will go over a narrow edge strip (FIG. 9-4G). When you true its overlapping edge, either use a special bevel plastic-laminate bit or hand-sand the sharpness off. Do this under the bottom edge as well, including the inner edge of the wood, so there is nothing sharp or rough when the cook slides a hand along (FIG. 9-4H).

If you want one, the splash-back can sand about 4 inches high and be screwed on over caulking compound (FIG. 9-4J). If it is to have a wood top, you only have to cover the front with plastic (FIG. 9-4K). However, if you plan to have a plastic-covered top surface, do the narrow edge first and take the other piece over it (FIG. 9-4L) in the same way as for the broad surface.

For joints in a countertop, you have a choice of two techniques. You can cut the plastic and its base to the miter or to whatever the joint is to be, and bring them together (FIG. 9-5A). You can make the base parts to join in a different place than the joints of the plastic (FIG. 9-5B). In the other method, you must lay at least one of the pieces of laminated plastic in position after the cabinets and tops have been assembled. This ensures a level joint and with care should bring the top surface close. The first method enables you to lay and trim the plastic away from the job, then put the parts together. There must be a broad bearing surface below where the parts meet, and it is difficult getting the joint really close. Much depends on the actual circumstances, but the second method is usually more likely to give you the best results.

STONE COUNTERTOPS

Laminated plastic might be the worktop material for most situations, but as an alternative or in addition to wood, you might consider marble or slate. In the days before refrigeration these and other stones were welcome in the kitchen because they were cool. Dairies had large expanses of marble on which to cool containers. Marble was a favorite of the Victorians for wash stands and bathrooms. It still has a place in a bathroom if you want something different from plastic. However, you can get laminated plastic that simulates marble, if you want the easy way out.

New slate or marble suitable for countertops can be prohibitively expensive, but much can be salvaged from old furniture and buildings. You may have to pay an expert to cut and prepare the material, but either stone can be made into a countertop. Most cooks would not want it all over, but a section of marble or slate is ideal for pastry rolling and certain other food preparation processes.

In a bathroom you might want the stone to have a rounded front edge, but in a kitchen it could have a wood front edge as part of a wood box in which the stone rests.

Stone is heavy, so the structure below it needs to be strong. A marble top on a table or island cabinet needs strong legs and a rigid construction that cannot wobble. If you choose not to surround the stone with wood, you can expect it to almost stay put under its own weight. To ensure against movement, however, drill and plug underneath for at least two screws upward through frame part.

TILED COUNTERTOPS

Like stone, ceramic tiles can provide a cool surface. A traditional, fully tiled counter is laid on a reinforced mortar base and is really a job for a specialist, but you should be able to lay tiles over plywood to a satisfactory effect. Doing it yourself, however, will preclude your having the tiled shaped front and set-in sink that an expert might arrange.

You will probably not want a fully tiled counter, but a tiled section makes an interesting change from the sometimes clinical appearance of a large expanse of plastic top. The tiles might match those on an adjoining wall or a row used as a splash-back. You could also mix designs or colors.

Tiles are available in many qualities. Some which are intended only to be decorative and mounted on a wall, might not have surfaces that can stand up to wear. For counters, buy tiles described as impervious or fully vitrified, which means they will absorb very little water.

Tiles come in many sizes as well. You can cut them, but it is easier to arrange the layout to use whole tiles as much as possible. In any case, try not to require anything less than half a tile. Very small tiles are inappropriate for counters; about 6 inches square is a reasonable size. The tile supplier should be able to provide a suitable mastic, on which to lay the tiles, and a grout material that has an admix to make it resistant to water and other liquids.

Treat the top to be tiled as a box (FIG. 9-6). Use a 1-inch piece of plywood to provide stiffness. If the finished tiled top has to line up with another top, you might have to lower the supports to bring the tiles level, as the total thickness will be about 1½ inches.

Put a strip of wood at the back (FIG. 9-6A) and bring the front edging to the same height (FIG. 9-6B). The finished wood height should be a little below the tile height. If you have to use cut tiles, arrange them towards the back or side, so there are full tiles at the front where they are most obvious.

Allow for the recommended width of grout line—probably between ¹⁄₁₆ and ⅛ inch— when planning the layout of tiles. For a small area you can set the tiles by eye, but to get a really uniform spacing, use strips of veneer (or something similar) in the gaps (FIG. 9-6C) and check across with a straightedge.

Coat the bottom of the box with mastic, remove the spacers, and lay in the tiles. Work-in the grout paste, making sure you press it all the way down and completely fill the gaps, including around the outer edges. Wipe off surplus paste and press the grout

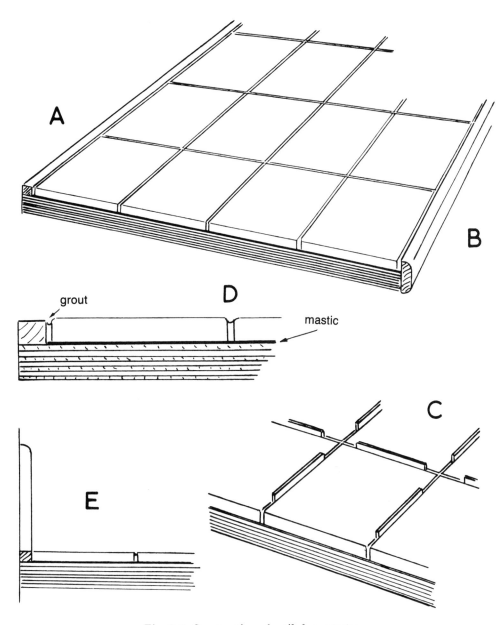

Fig. 9-6. Construction of a tiled countertop.

lines to a concave shape (FIG. 9-6D). A bent piece of ⅛-inch wire makes a suitable tool for doing this.

If there are to be tiles along the wall to act as a splash-back, set them above the rear wood strip over a line of caulking compound (FIG. 9-6E).

INSETTING A SINK

The location of a sink always has to be arranged during early planning, but that is especially true for a sink inset into a countertop for use in a kitchen or bathroom. You must plan the cabinets so that the sink will be located between supports and correctly relate to the plumbing connections.

Sinks come in a great many different styles and sizes. Many of them are almost as wide as a countertop, and if you are fitting a double sink you will have to cut out a large amount. If the edges of the countertop left after cutting are not very wide, you should arrange supports underneath on edge (FIG. 9-7A) instead of flat. You will have to cut back any intermediate lengthwise supports, but it will help if they are allowed to continue as far as possible.

The sink might come with a rubber seal round the edges, or you might have to bed it in a caulking compound. There will be a way of clamping or screwing it in place, and there might also be a paper template showing the size of hole needed. If not, mark and cut a hole in a piece of scrap hardboard first; then try to bowl in that to see what modifications are needed. You must leave a good overlap, so do not cut away any more

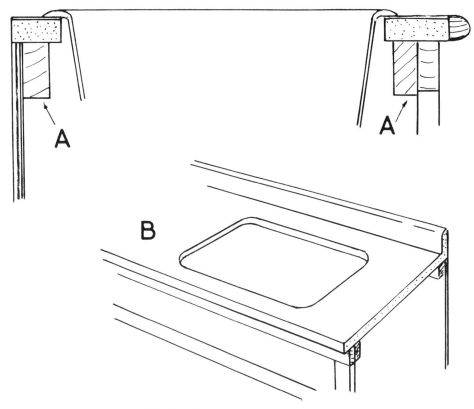

Fig. 9-7. Preparations for insetting a sink.

than is necessary. When satisfied, use the hardboard to mark the shape to be cut. For a single sink, the hole will probably be about 21 inches from front to back and 24 inches long. The length will be nearly twice that for a double sink. Round the corners by as much as the sink will allow (FIG. 9-7B).

You can cut the hole with a portable jigsaw, but because that tool cuts on the up stroke it may splinter a melamine laminated plastic top if you use a coarse blade. Therefore, use a blade with about 12 teeth to the inch, or finer, but check it on some scrap material first, to make sure it can cut the total thickness. You may have to round the edge of the hole to get a close fit. Use ample caulking compound and leave no gaps. Water creeping under the sink edge would cause particleboard to bulge, plywood plies to pucker, or solid wood to swell and eventually rot. Unless the whole top is butcher-block solid wood, keep the butcher-block part away from the sink.

If you decide to set in a countertop range or hot plate, cutting the hole and fitting the unit will be very similar to dealing with the sink. Some ranges allow very little overlap around the edges, however, so when making the hole, be careful to get as large an area of contact as possible.

ACCOMMODATING OTHER APPLIANCES

Some appliances do not require holes cut in the countertop. For example, dishwashers usually go under the counter. The standard refrigerator is higher than a counter and may stand at the end of a counter or come between two sections of it. Slide-in ranges are made to counter height and often a little more than counter width, so they fit between two cabinet ends with tops level. A drop-in range does not require quite as much width and height, so it could probably go above the toe board and have a narrow part of the countertop crossing behind it.

Where countertops have to be cut away or an end section comes against a range or refrigerator, you could just leave the cut ends. With laminated plastic on particleboard or plywood, however, you should cover the ends, especially if a splashboard is involved, in the way described for an open end (FIG. 9-3E).

CHAPTER

Island Units

In a compact kitchen all the work surfaces need to be around the walls, to provide sufficient floor space to move around, open doors, and avoid feeling cramped. More spacious kitchens, however, have enough room to accommodate a work space accessible from all sides. It could be a movable table or a more substantial, permanent unit with storage underneath—comparable to a wall cabinet, but with access on all sides.

In planning an island unit, you must relate it to other furniture in the kitchen. Can it be big enough without restricting floor space? Do you want to sit at it with normal chairs, or should it be high enough for working when standing? Will it be used for meals as well as food preparation? Should it be fixed to the floor or portable? Even a heavy unit can be mounted on casters if you want to be able to move it.

If some of the cook's work will be done on the island unit, you might be able to reduce the number of wall worktops or make one narrower, to provide a more useful floor area around the island unit. This is a situation where a reasonably accurate scale drawing and a card cut to the shape of the proposed unit will help. You can try various positions and check the opening of doors and drawers as well as the movement of the cook and the positioning of stools or chairs.

You must also decide on the probable loads on the island unit. If heavy chopping will be done elsewhere, the unit could be little more than a light table, but if the cook will be chopping on the unit, the top must be stout and the whole structure substantially built, so as not to bounce or move under blows.

If you want to sit at the island using ordinary chairs, the top should be about 30 inches from the floor. You could work at this height while standing, but a 36-inch height would be better for standing work. Sitting at a counter of *that* height, however, requires high chairs or stools. Also, if you want to sit there for a meal, you must allow leg room underneath and the unit might need to be more a table than a storage unit. In any case, if there is space for an island unit, it is worth having. It improves the general appearance of the kitchen while increasing its facilities.

KITCHEN TABLE

In earlier days the kitchen table was the center of activities. For similar reasons, a modern cook might prefer a table to an island counter. This table needs to be more substantial than a dining table and be functional rather than decorative. The table represented by FIGS. 10-1 through 10-3 satisfies these requirements. It could be made with leg space or with a shelf underneath. The shelf framing adds stiffness, but even without a shelf, the table should be rigid enough for normal use. Carried edgewise you should be able to get it through a normal doorway, but check first. It would be frustrating to make a table in your shop and not be able to get it into the kitchen!

Large drawers may weaken rails, but the table in the example has a moderate-size

Fig. 10-1. A kitchen table with drawer, shelf, and laminated plastic top.

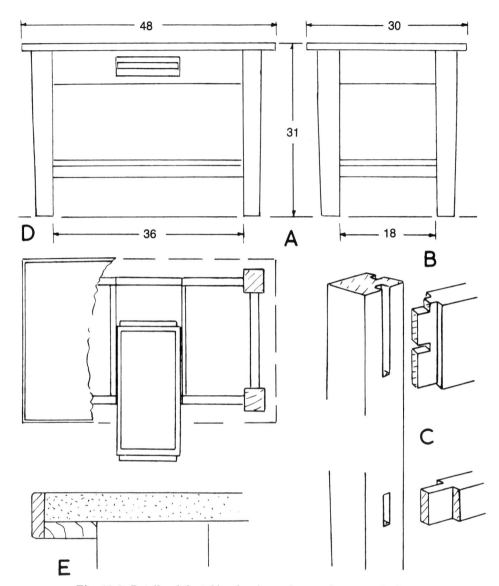

Fig. 10-2. Details of the table, showing a drawer that opens both ways.

drawer going right through, to be pulled out from either side (FIG. 10-1). The sizes suggested in FIG. 10-2A are a guide; adjust them to suit your kitchen. The wood sections specified are for the common furniture hardwoods, but if you want to use softwood, you will have to increase sections slightly.

Rail-to-leg joints are shown with traditional mortises and tenons, but you could use dowels. Drawer guide ends should have dowels. As the drawer is double-ended, you will have to treat both ends as fronts. As shown, the table has a shelf on lower rails, but you could omit this. Following are the basic steps of construction:

• Mark out the four legs (FIG. 10-3A) together to ensure that they match. The top tenons are divided (FIG. 10-2B), but they are plain for the lower rails (FIG. 10-2C). You could leave the legs parallel, but they look better tapered on the outer two surfaces (FIG. 10-2D). That way, the inner surfaces are parallel between opposite legs. Mark the tapers, but do not cut them until after the mortises have been cut.

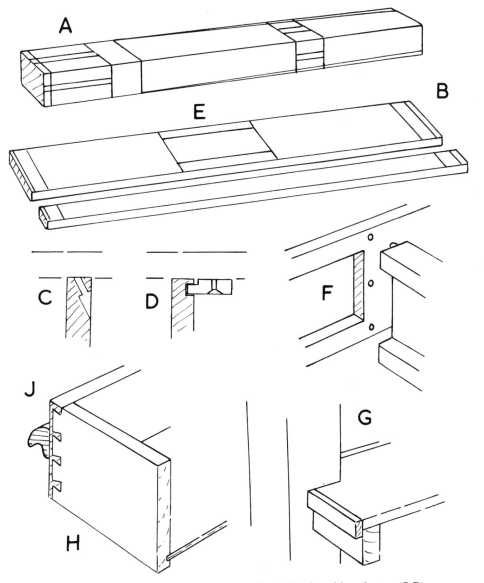

Fig. 10-3. Marking out legs and rails (A,B). Attaching the top (C,D). Shelf corner (G) and drawer (F,J,H) details.

- Mark the top and bottom rails together, so the lengths between the shoulders are the same (FIG. 10-3B). Mark and cut tenons to suit the leg mortises.
- If the top is to be plywood or particleboard, which does not expand or contract in width, drill the top rails diagonally for screws and cut pockets for their heads (FIG. 10-3C). If you are making the top from boards or butcher-block strips, which might expand or contract, plow grooves near the top edges of the top rails, to take buttons (FIG. 10-3D).
- Mark and cut the drawer openings in the long top rails (FIG. 10-3E).
- Make the drawer guides to fit between the rails, with strips top and bottom level with the openings (FIG. 10-3F). Prepare the ends and the rails for dowels.
- Assemble the two long sides. Check squareness by comparing diagonal measurements, and see that the two sides match and do not twist.
- When that glue has set, join the sides with the drawer guides and the other rails. Again, check squareness in all directions.
- If the top is plywood or particleboard (at least ¾ inch thick), with a laminated plastic surface, you should thicken the edges and add a wood edging (FIG. 10-2E). Avoid a molded edge if you expect the table to have to accommodate any clamp-on appliances. Attach the top with glue and screw through the pocketed holes in the rails. If the table is very wide, one or two similar screws in each drawer rail might be advisable.
- If the top is solid wood, use buttons screwed to the top at about 12-inch intervals so they engage with the grooves in the top rail.
- As shown, the bottom shelf is plywood notched around the legs. It could overhang the rails to the edges of the legs, or you could cut it level with the rails and cover the edges (FIG. 10-3G).
- Make the drawer by any of the methods described in Chapter 4. The ends must be flush with the rail surfaces, because you cannot have overlapping fronts on a drawer that has to go both ways. The best construction method, is dovetails, with the bottom fitted into grooves (FIG. 10-3H). Handles should probably extend the width of the drawer, so the cook can find the handle easily by feel (FIG. 10-3J).
- You cannot fit stops to the drawer, so you might have to settle for merely pushing it into a level position. You could, however, let small ball catches into the undersides or edges of the ends—to engage with plates on the rails—to hold the drawer end level when closed but allow for easy pulling either way. This will likely be used for longer cook's tools, but it could have divisions at each end to accommodate small items and cutlery.

Materials List for Kitchen Table

4 legs	4 × 4 × 31
2 rails	1¼ × 6 × 44
2 rails	1¼ × 6 × 26
2 rails	1 × 2 × 44
2 rails	1 × 2 × 26
1 top	30 × 48 × 1 plywood

1 shelf	30 × 48 × ½ plywood
2 thickeners	½ × 1½ × 48
2 thickeners	½ × 1½ × 30
2 edgings	⅜ × 1½ × 50
2 edgings	⅜ × 1½ × 32
2 shelf edgings	⅜ × 1 × 40
2 shelf edgings	⅜ × 1 × 22
2 drawer guides	1 × 6 × 22
4 drawer guides	1 × 1 × 22
2 drawer ends	1 × 4 × 12
2 drawer sides	¾ × 4 × 30
1 drawer bottom	12 × 30 × ¼ plywood
2 drawer handles	1¼ × 1¼ × 12

SQUARE ISLAND CABINETS

This unit is almost a cube and is about the smallest island alternative to the traditional worktop-and-cabinet arrangement. It offers plenty of storage space in cabinets below, about as much as in wall cabinets. The unit shown in FIG. 10-4 is on a plinth, but you could omit that in favor of industrial-type casters. The island unit could then be moved about—perhaps stored in a recess in the room and brought out when needed.

The unit is formed from two identical parts, screwed back to back. Each unit has a framed front and doors mounted on the frame surfaces.

The top can be of any type, but the instructions assumed it will be thick plywood with a laminated plastic surface and wood edging. Nearly all parts are ¾-inch plywood and 1-inch-×-2-inch strips. You can use screws where the screw heads will not show, and dowels elsewhere. If you choose not to paint the exposed surfaces, cover them with suitable veneer.

The sizes shown in FIG. 10-5A allow for the top surface being the same height as wall countertops. The two unit parts are 18 inches × 36 inches. The top can overhang about 2 inches all around. Following are the basic steps of construction:

• Make the two pairs of sides (FIGS. 10-5B and 10-6A). The bottom and back will come inside them, but put a strip across with a recess at the front to take a 1-inch × 2-inch strip (FIGS. 10-5C and 10-6B).
• Make the bottoms (FIG. 10-6C) and back (FIG. 10-6D) to fit between the sides.
• The division (FIG. 10-6E) fits over the bottom and inside the back, with a top recess in line with those at the ends.
• Assemble these parts with glue and screws, but where the bottoms join the ends use dowels into blind holes. That way, nothing will show outside. Make sure the front edges are level and the two cabinets match each other.
• Make the front frames (FIG. 10-6F) level outside and with the central part over the division. The thickness of the bottom should match that of the cabinet bottom.

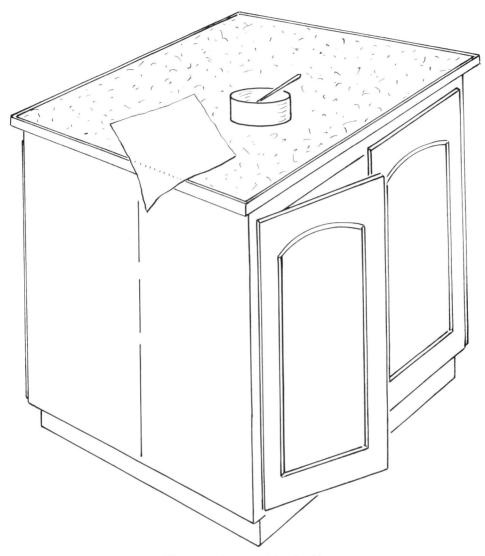

Fig. 10-4. A square island cabinet.

- Join the backs of the cabinets. Fit the front frames. Make sure that the edges and tops are true and match.
- Drill the front strips for screws upward into the top; four in each piece should be enough.
- If there is to be a plinth, make it like an open box with mitered corners and blocks inside (FIG. 10-6G). It should be 2 inches in from the cabinet edges and attached by screwing down through the bottoms.
- If you use industrial casters instead of a plinth, put suitable blocks under each corner.
- Make the doors (FIG. 10-6H) to overlap the openings by ½ inch all around, using any

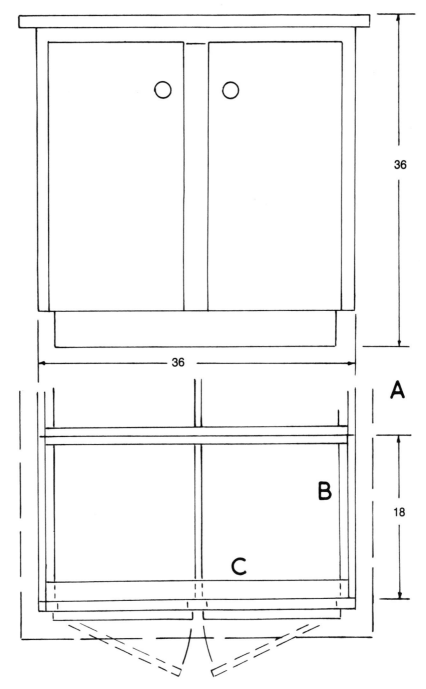

Fig. 10-5. Details of the square island cabinet.

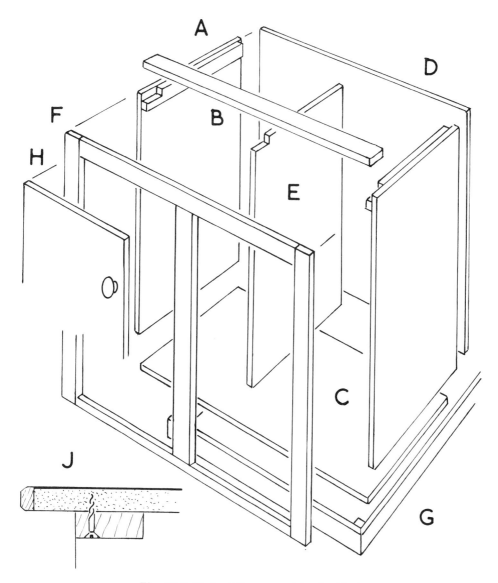

Fig. 10-6. Parts of the square island cabinet.

design to match other doors in the kitchen. Hinge them at the outer edges and fit suitable handles.

• Make the top to overhang the same amount all around, and attach it with screws (FIG. 10-6J).

• Instead of the open cupboards shown in the illustrations, you could fit shelves or trays, with cleats fitted before assembly and all other work done before fitting the top.

Materials List for Square Island Cabinets

4 sides	18 × 32 × ¾ plywood
2 divisions	18 × 32 × ¾ plywood
2 bottoms	18 × 36 × ¾ plywood
2 backs	32 × 38 × ¾ plywood
4 tops	1 × 2 × 18
2 tops	1 × 2 × 36
4 plinths	1 × 4 × 36
6 front frames	1 × 2 × 32
2 front frames	1 × 2 × 36
2 front frames	1 × 1 × 36
1 top	38 × 42 × 1 plywood
4 top edgings	¾ × 1¼ × 43
4 doors to suit	

MULTIPLE ISLAND UNITS

The method used to make a square island unit can be applied to producing similar furniture of other sizes. The square unit contains two double units assembled back to back, but this idea can be modified. Sizes, for example, do not have to be as in that cabinet. Heights should probably be similar, but that unit's basic squares—which are 18 inches—can be reduced or increased to get the piece of furniture you want.

The first increase might be to add another unit at the end of the two forming a square (FIG. 10-7A) or to put another one at the other end (FIG. 10-7B). The overall size, using the original units, would then be about 36 inches wide × 72 inches long. Reducing that to 12-inch squares would give you a size of about 24 inches wide × 48 inches long.

The units do not have to be limited to just cupboards either. You could fit a drawer above each door (FIG. 10-7C) or make a unit with drawers only (FIG. 10-7D).

An end unit need not have a pair of doors. Instead, you could make it into a block of drawers going all the way across (FIG. 10-7E). They could open both ways, as with the table discussed earlier; all could open at one side only; or alternate ones could open at opposite sides (FIG. 10-7F).

Another attractive and useful way of dealing with one or both ends is to fit shelves, perhaps with central posts (FIG. 10-7G) or divisions (FIG. 10-7H). You could curve the shelves at their corners and then reflect this in the top (FIG. 10-7J). Curving a solid or butcher-block top is no problem, but if you have a laminated plastic top with a wood edging, you will have to laminate thin strips of wood around the curves, either taking them all the way or splicing them into solid straight strips.

The island unit might be an ideal place to store chopping and pastry boards on edge. You can arrange that by leaving a gap behind an end unit or block of shelves (FIG. 10-7K). For rigidity, continue the bottom and any top parts over the gap.

When planning a multiple unit, start by checking the available floor space and assess how much of it you devote to island cabinets while still leaving adequate space to move and work. That will give you an idea of the approximate size of the top. Will it be big

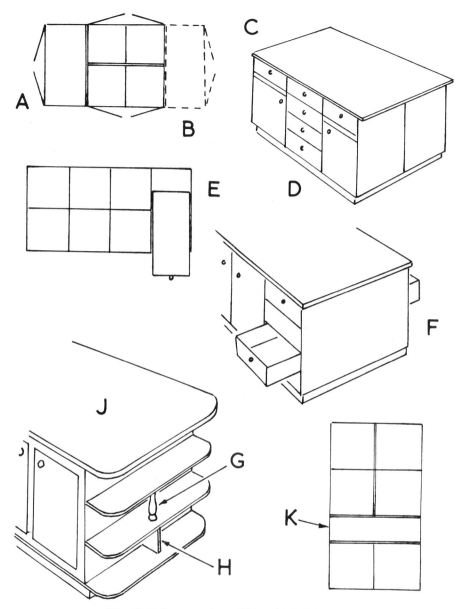

Fig. 10-7. Layouts of possible multiple island units.

enough to be worthwhile? If not, you may have to start thinking again. If you allow for the top overhanging at least 1½ inches all around, the resulting width and length will tell you how much area you have to divide into units.

ISLAND BENCH

Ambitious cooks and professional chefs might prefer an island unit that is more a bench than a table. Because it has to stand up to chopping large quantities of food—including bones—it might look like a table, but it functions more like a workshop bench.

The top should be in butcher-block form, unless you can find well-seasoned solid wood in suitable sizes, and should be made of close-grained hardwood. The lower parts could be softwood, but they would be better also made of hardwood. To add to usefulness and rigidity, you could add racks underneath for pots, pans, and other equipment. For a domestic kitchen the bench need not be too large; FIG. 10-9A suggests possible dimensions. The bench suggested in the illustrations (FIGS. 10-8 through 10-10) has slatted

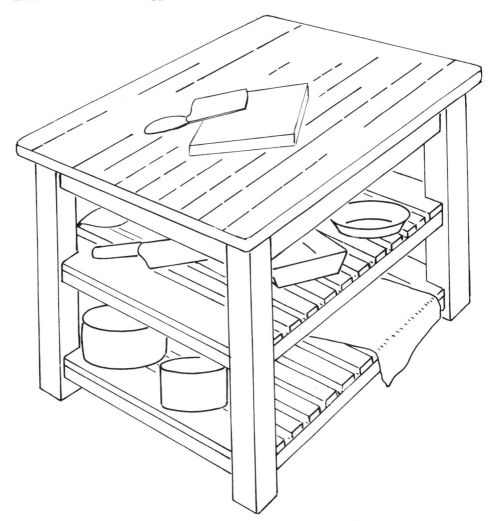

Fig. 10-8. An island bench with slatted shelves.

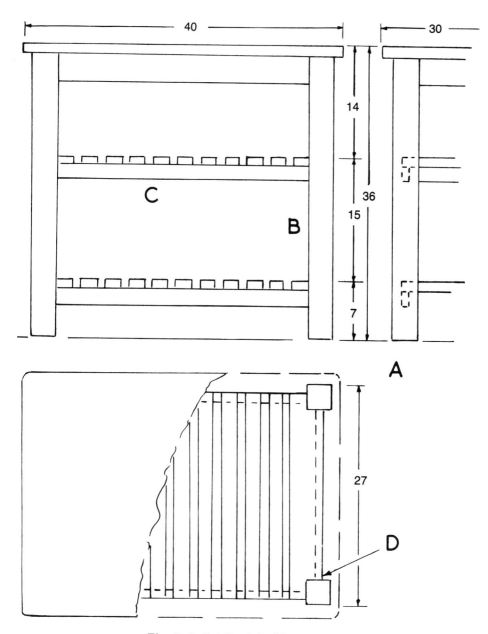

Fig. 10-9. Details of the island bench.

shelves. It is not intended to be used when sitting, so there is no knee room and very little floor clearance. If your cook wants to sit while working on some tasks, you could extend the top at one end by about 12 inches, to accommodate a high stool which might be stored underneath. Following are the basic steps of construction:

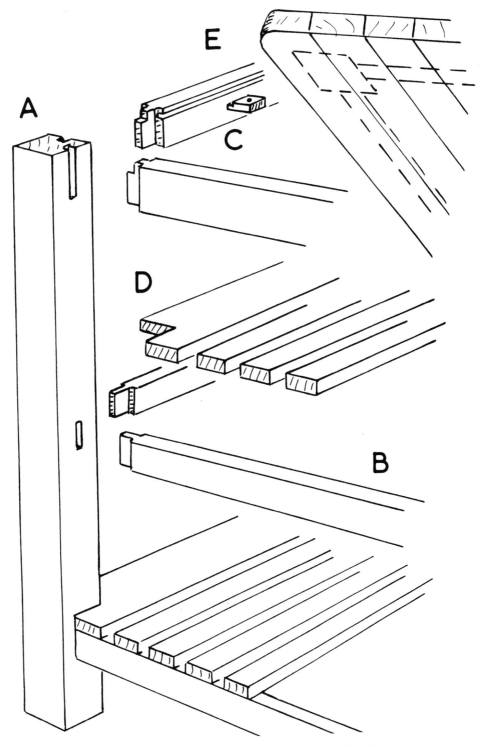

Fig. 10-10. Constructional details of the island bench.

- Start by marking out the four legs together (FIGS. 10-9B and 10-10A). You could dowel the rails, but they are shown with mortise-and-tenon joints.
- Mark out all the rails in each direction together so the lengths between shoulders will be the same (FIGS. 10-9C and 10-10B).
- Plow grooves near the top edges of the top rails to take buttons (FIG. 10-10C) to hold the top.
- Cut the joints or drill for dowels.
- The legs should remain parallel, but before assembly take the sharpness off the leg edges and the edges that will be exposed on rails.
- Assemble opposite pairs of legs and their rails. Check for squareness and lack of twist, and make sure that the two sets match each other.
- Join these assemblies with the rails the other way. Compare diagonals in all directions and see that the legs stand level.
- Make and fit the shelf slats. Cut the end ones to notch around the legs and come level with the outside edges of the rails (FIGS. 10-9D and 10-10D). Space the other slats evenly with gaps of about 1 inch. Glue and either nail or screw the ends, preferably using noncorrosive fastenings. Take the sharpness off exposed ends and edges.
- Make the top by gluing sufficient strips to make up the size (FIG. 10-10E). Allow a 1½-inch overhang, and round the edges and corners.
- Attach the top with buttons in the grooved rails, screwed upward. Place buttons about 1 inch from each leg and others at about 10-inch intervals.

Materials List for Island Bench

4 legs	3 × 3 × 36	
2 rails	1 × 3 × 38	
2 rails	1 × 3 × 28	
4 rails	1 × 2 × 38	
4 rails	1 × 2 × 28	
4 slats	1 × 4 × 30	
18 slats	1 × 2 × 30	
1 top	1½ × 30 × 40	

SIDE SHELF UNIT

Having shelves at the end of an island unit may not be the best arrangement for your kitchen, particularly if the end faces a little-used wall or a narrow or congested part of the floor. Shelves at one or both sides can make the things they store more accessible. And if the shelves are also intended for display, placing them at the side will probably better serve that purpose.

Several variations are possible. The multiple units desired earlier could be made into an assembly with side shelves. The unit shown in FIG. 10-11 has a block of drawers at one end, a double-door cupboard at the other, and back-to-back shelves in the middle. Suggested sizes are only a guide (FIG. 10-12A); you will have to adapt them to suit your

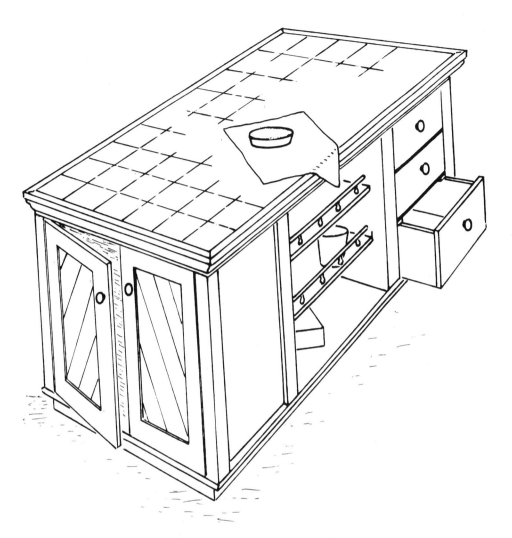

Fig. 10-11. A side shelf unit with a tiled top.

needs and space. If shelves are not needed on both sides, one side could have doors. The suggested unit has a plinth all around and a tiled top, but any other top would suffice.

The unit is made as one assembly—not in sections to be brought together after making. This means that there are no double thicknesses. It also means that you must check access sizes to ensure that a unit made in your workshop can pass through doorways on its way to the kitchen. If necessary, you can save a few inches of width by leaving the top off until the unit is in place.

Most parts are ¾-inch plywood. Some moldings are included, and there are turned pillars under the rails on the shelves. You could simplify the design, however, if a plainer finish would better match other cabinets in the kitchen. If you decide on a tiled top, you can reduce work if you arrange the top to take whole tiles. Start with those measurements

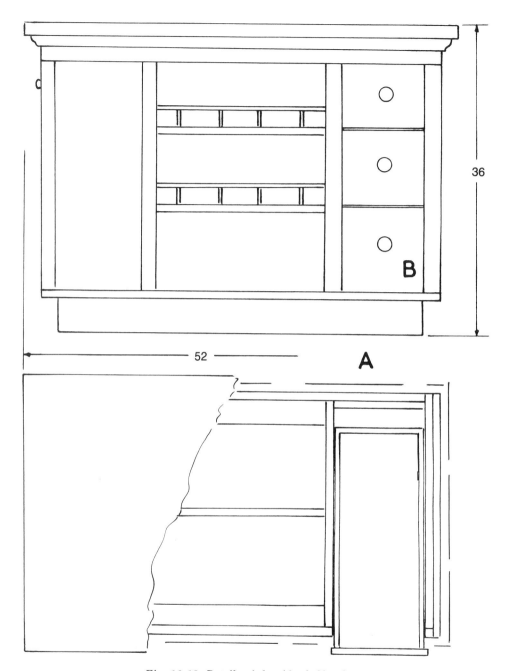

Fig. 10-12. Details of the side shelf unit.

and relate other sizes to them. Doors are shown with diagonal tongue-and-groove board panels, but you could make doors and drawer fronts to match the doors of other cabinets. The height is the same as the wall cabinets, but you could reduce it if your cook prefers a lower work area. Following are the basic steps of construction:

• Mark out the bottom first (FIG. 10-13A). The upright parts are 1 inch in from the edge, which will be covered later with a half-round molding.

• Make the three crosswise uprights (FIG. 10-13B). They are the same overall size. Fit notched strips across the top edges to take the lengthwise strips (FIGS. 10-13C, D). On upright #1 (FIG. 10-13E) cut away the plywood notches and mark for both sides of the cupboard on the side with the top strip. Mark for the central division and the shelves on the other side. Mark upright #2 in the same way, but there will not be a piece

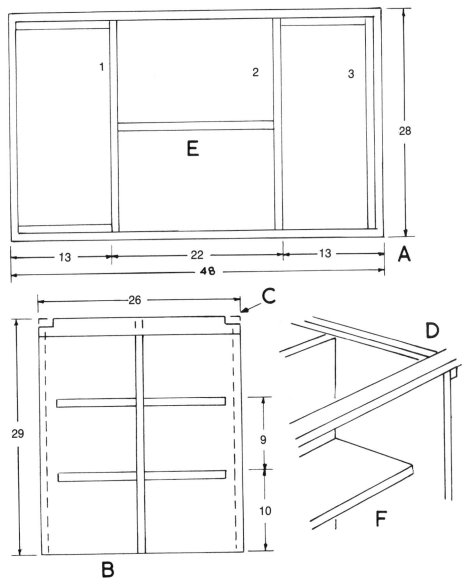

Fig. 10-13. Sizes of parts of the side shelf unit.

connecting at the fronts of the drawers. Mark the inner surface of upright #3 as a pair to #2, but do not cut away the plywood notches.

• Make the division (FIGS. 10-13E and 10-14A) to fit between uprights #1 and #2. Cut plywood for the shelves (FIGS. 10-13F and 10-14B). If you want to have rails and spindles at the front of the shelves, make them now and allow for small tenons on the rail ends into the plywood (FIG. 10-15A). Use bought spindles or turn your own with dowel ends.

• Make the two sides of the cupboard (FIG. 10-14C) and the piece at the back of the drawers (FIG. 10-14D). The tops of these parts come against the underside of the lengthwise strips.

• Prepare all the meeting edges for dowels; ⅜-inch dowels at about 4-inch intervals should be satisfactory.

• Cover the front edges of the shelves and all edges of the bottom with half-round molding (FIG. 10-14E).

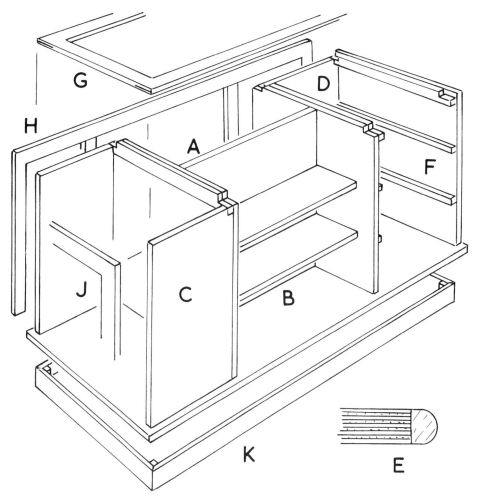

Fig. 10-14. Main parts of the side shelf unit.

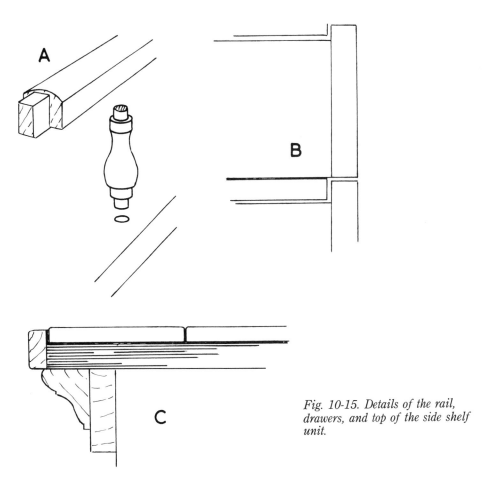

Fig. 10-15. Details of the rail, drawers, and top of the side shelf unit.

- Fit drawer runners to uprights #2 and #3. Three drawers are shown (FIGS. 10-12B and 10-14F), but you could have four or more.
- Assemble the parts made so far.
- Fit lengthwise strips in the top notches, with a piece across the top of the cupboard (FIG. 10-14G).
- Make frames to cover the back and front, with 3-inch-wide strips at the top and 2-inch-wide pieces for the uprights (FIG. 10-14H). There are no pieces across the bottoms of the frames. The intermediate upright pieces should be level with the edge of the shelf openings and cover the edges of the plywood crosswise uprights.
- Make frames for the ends (FIG. 14-10J) in a similar way. The frame on the outside of the end with the drawers is only there for appearance, but the one at the other end will hold the doors, which can be flush or set on the surface. Match the doors to others in the kitchen.
- Make the drawers by any of the methods described in Chapter 4. As there are no drawer rails across the front, you should make the fronts extending upward enough to

hide the ends of the drawer runners (FIG. 10-15B). They could be flush inside the frames or overlap.

• If the top is to be tiled, make its base with a good overhang and edge it to contain the tiles. You could put a molding underneath the edges (FIG. 10-15C).

• Make the plinth like an open box, with blocks inside mitered corners (FIG. 10-14K).

• Fit the plinth with screws downward and the top with screws upward.

Materials List for Side Shelf Unit

1 bottom	28 ×	48 × ¾ plywood
1 top	32 ×	54 × ¾ plywood
3 uprights	26 ×	30 × ¾ plywood
1 division	21 ×	30 × ¾ plywood
3 uprights	13 ×	30 × ¾ plywood
4 shelves	13 ×	22 × ¾ plywood
3 strips	1 ×	2 × 27
2 top strips	1 ×	2 × 48
1 top strip	1 ×	2 × 27
2 side frames	1 ×	3 × 52
8 side frames	1 ×	2 × 30
2 end frames	1 ×	3 × 28
4 end frames	1 ×	2 × 30
2 top moldings	1 ×	2 × 52
2 top moldings	1 ×	2 × 30
2 bottom moldings	¾ ×	52 half-round
2 bottom moldings	¾ ×	30 half-round
4 shelf moldings	¾ ×	22 half-round
2 top edgings	⅝ ×	1½ × 56
2 top edgings	⅝ ×	1½ × 34
4 shelf edge rails	¾ ×	¾ × 22
16 shelf edge spindles	¾ ×	¾ × 4
4 door frames	1 ×	2 × 30
2 door frames	1 ×	2 × 14
2 door frames	1 ×	3 × 14
door panels to suit		
1 drawer front	¾ ×	10 × 12
2 drawer fronts	¾ ×	9 × 12
1 drawer back	⅝ ×	9 × 12
2 drawer backs	⅝ ×	8 × 12
2 drawer sides	⅝ ×	9 × 29
4 drawer sides	⅝ ×	8 × 26
3 drawer bottoms	12 ×	26 × ¼ plywood

ISLAND UNIT WITH TRAYS

Drawers and cupboards can take care of most cooks' needs, but trays might be favored because they can be lifted out—complete with their contents—and put on the countertop. The exposed ends of a block of trays might not be attractive and could admit dirt and insects, but you could hide and protect the trays with a drawer below and a front high enough to fit over the trays.

Another problem that a tray unit can help solve involves space. Due to limited kitchen area, your island unit might have to be fairly narrow. Although the cook might want to work all around the unit, most of the access to storage will be from one side.

The unit shown in FIG. 10-16 is an example of an arrangement with hidden trays and a comparatively narrow top. You should not make a unit of standard height any narrower than this—unless it will be fixed to the floor—as it could easily tip over. Storage arrangements in the unit shown are with blocks of trays hidden by deep drawer fronts, intended to be accessible from one side. Between them there is an open part with shelves

Fig. 10-16. An island unit with hidden trays.

that can be reached from both sides. You could have vertical racks instead of shelves, or you could make one end compartment open from the other side.

The sizes (FIG. 10-17A) divide the length into three equal parts. Each end section has three 4-inch trays, with a deep drawer below. If you alter sizes, do not make the drawer too shallow because depth is needed to provide strength when the front is pulled from the top.

The unit's main parts are made of ¾-inch plywood. It has frames at the back and front, which have to be matched in size with tray bearers. The deep drawer fronts can

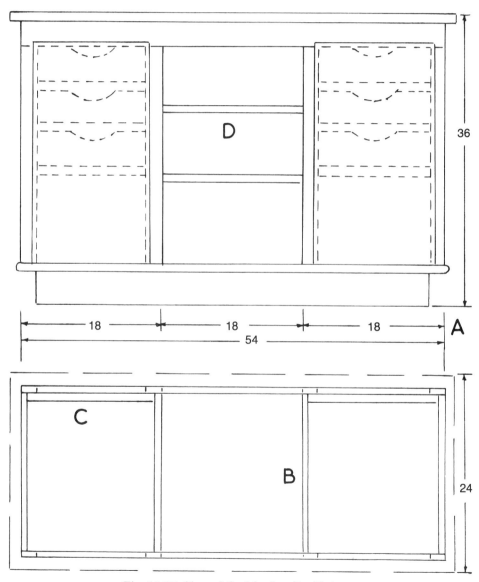

Fig. 10-17. Sizes of the island unit with trays.

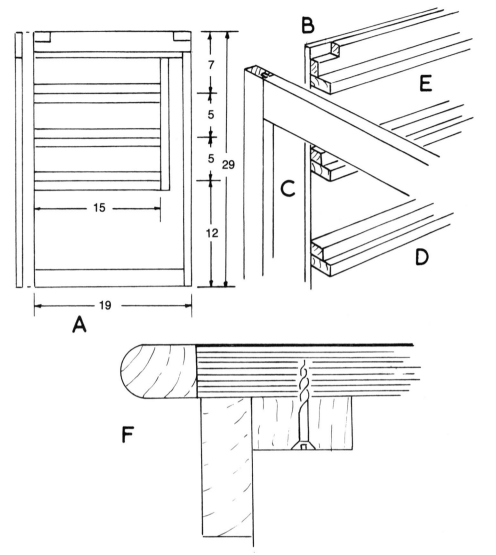

Fig. 10-18. Tray and top details for the island unit with trays.

match doors elsewhere in the kitchen. The top shown is plywood covered with laminated plastic, but any other construction would be suitable. Parts may be screwed where the heads will not show, but use dowels elsewhere. Following are the basic steps of construction:

• Make the four upright plywood pieces (FIGS. 10-17B, 10-18A, and 10-19A). Put a strip across each top, with notches for the lengthwise strips (FIG. 10-18B). Notch the plywood for the inner pieces, too, but only notch the strips at the ends.
• The guides and bearers for the trays have to be related to the widths of the frame uprights, which are nominally 2 inches, but measure their actual width (FIG. 10-18C). Fit

guide pieces that will come level with the edges of the frame uprights, and fit pieces below as tray bearers that extend an additional ¾ inch (FIGS. 10-18D and 10-19B). At the top, put a strip level with the underside of the top frame piece (FIG. 10-18E) to stop the top tray from tilting as it is pulled out. At the bottom put a strip across each part to come level with the edge of the frame side, to act as a drawer guide. Put stop strips behind the tray supports. If you make trays extending to the back, you will have difficulty removing them without pulling the drawer below all the way out.

• Make the bottom (FIG. 10-19C) to the width of the upright plywood pieces plus the thickness of the frame at the back and front. There are no frames at the ends, and the bottom can finish level with the end upright pieces. Before assembly, cover the edges of the bottom with half-round molding (FIG. 10-14E). If the drawer fronts are to overhang the bottom, however, stop the molding on each side of the openings.

• Make upright plywood pieces as backs for the tray sections (FIGS. 10-17C and 10-19D).

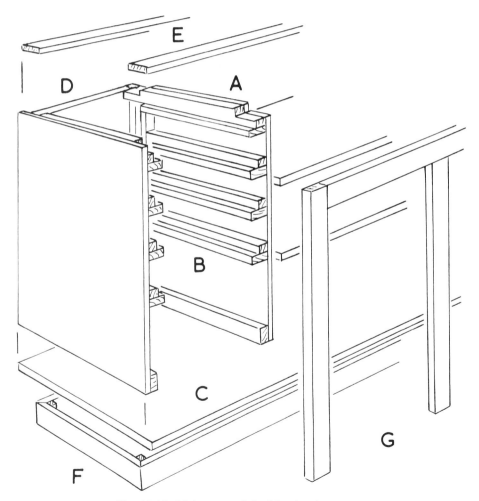

Fig. 10-19. Main parts of the island unit with trays.

They fit between the crosswise parts and below the lengthwise strips. Frame parts will cover their joints.

• The shelves (FIG. 10-17D) could rest on cleats, or you could dowel them to the upright plywood pieces. Prepare the shelves and their attachments.

• Have the lengthwise strips (FIG. 10-19E) ready. Drill the parts for screws and dowels, then assemble (with glue) all the parts made so far. The parts should hold each other square, but you might wish to check by comparing diagonals.

• Make the plinth to stand in from the bottom edges 2 inches all around. Miter the corners and strengthen the joints with blocks inside (FIG. 10-19F). Screw it to the bottom.

• Make frames for the back and front (FIG. 10-19G). Make the outer edges level with the edges of the carcass and the intermediate uprights level with the edges of the uprights next to the shelves. The frames have no bottom rails. Check the relation of tray and drawer bearers and guides to the frames, and make any adjustments necessary to get edges level.

• Fit the frames in place.

• Make the two drawers (FIG. 10-20A). Start with the sides and make sure that they will slide between their guides. Use any of the joints described in Chapter 4, but make sure that the front joints are strong because of the load they will bear when the tall front is pulled from near the top; dovetails would be the best (FIG. 10-20B) approach. Let a plywood bottom into grooves. The drawers can run close to the guides, or you can make them narrower to leave space for metal runners, which might require deeper wood guides to allow for their width.

• The tall false fronts look like doors, so make them to match the doors of nearby cabinets. In the example the fronts are plain plywood with solid wood lips on the edges, but you could use any other type of door in a similar way.

• Make the front to overlap the frame like a door. Let the front finish on the bottom or overhang it.

• Fit a handle centrally near the top. If, however, it can be located farther down without requiring the cook to stoop, the leverage on the joint with the box part of the drawer will be reduced (FIG. 10-20C). A long handle is easier to reach than a knob.

• Join the tall false front to the inner front with glue and screws driven from inside. Check each for squareness in fit over the front frame before finally tightening screws.

• The trays are simple boxes with hollowed fronts to serve as handles. Arrange the fronts to be about ½ inch back from the frame surface. As there are 24 identical corners, you can save effort by using any facilities for series production you might have. Finger or comb joints are suitable (FIG. 10-20D).

• Let the plywood bottoms into grooves (FIG. 10-20E), let them into rabbets, or simply nail them on. Carefully round the front hollows. Make the trays an easy fit, so the cook has no trouble withdrawing them.

• If you make the top with a fairly wide edging (FIG. 10-18F), there will be enough wood to allow corners to be well rounded. An island unit is more likely to be knocked than the corners of a wall counter, so avoid anything approaching sharpness. Allow up to 2 inches overhang all around. Fix with screws driven upward through the lengthwise strips.

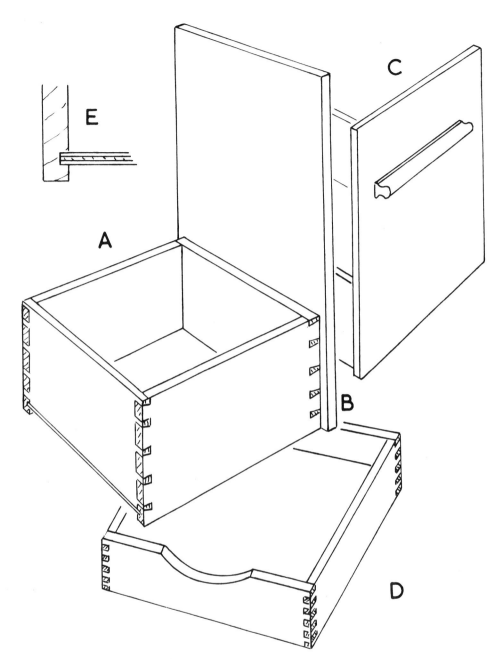

Fig. 10-20. Details of drawer and tray.

Materials List for Island Unit with Trays

4 uprights	19	×	30 × ¾ plywood
1 bottom	21	×	56 × ¾ plywood
1 top	24	×	60 × ¾ plywood
2 backs	17	×	30 × ¾ plywood
2 shelves	19	×	19 × ¾ plywood
2 drawer fronts	21	×	30 × ¾ plywood
4 top strips	1	×	2 × 20
2 top strips	1	×	2 × 56
4 top guides	1	×	30 × 20
12 drawer guides	1¼	×	1¼ × 20
12 drawer runners	¾	×	2 × 20
4 bottom guides	1¼	×	2 × 20
4 drawer stops	1	×	3 × 15
2 frame tops	1	×	3 × 56
8 frame uprights	1	×	2 × 30
2 bottom edges	56	×	1 half-round
2 bottom edges	24	×	1 half-round
2 top edges	⅞	×	2 × 60
2 top edges	⅞	×	2 × 26
4 drawer sides	⅝	×	12 × 20
2 drawer backs	⅝	×	12 × 20
2 drawer fronts	¾	×	12 × 20
2 drawer bottoms	20	×	20 × ¼ plywood
12 tray sides	½	×	5 × 16
12 tray ends	½	×	5 × 18
6 tray bottoms	16	×	18 × ¼ plywood
2 plinth sides	¾	×	4 × 54
2 plinth ends	¾	×	4 × 24

CHAPTER

Built-in Tables

Most kitchens require a surface of suitable height for use when sitting, relaxing, or eating a meal. The standard counter height of 36 inches is too high to use with a normal chair, but it could be used with a high chair or stool. That may be the answer, particularly in a very compact kitchen, but if you want to use ordinary chairs the surface height should be between 29 and 31 inches.

If there is ample floor space the best arrangement is a normal table standing independent of any counter or cabinet. In many places, however, such a table would be in the way at least part of the time. A good compromise is a surface at table height attached in some way to a cabinet. It might have to be simply a small ledge, if space is minimal, or it could project far enough for four people to sit and eat in comfort.

The extension could be just a table or it could include some storage below, provided there is leg room when users are sitting. The general design could be very similar to the cabinets and their top, or it could be more like a plain table. The surface could be suitable for working on—possibly for rougher work than you want to do on the countertop—or it could be finished to dining table quality.

Whatever approach you choose, the table will project into the room, so check with drawings or a temporary mock-up to ensure that there is sufficient space and that the table will not be in the way at any time. If there is not enough space for a permanent table, you may have to make one that folds.

SLIDING SHELF

A ledge that can be pulled out from under a counter at table height can serve as extra working surface or as a table for a single person to sit at with a normal chair.

The sliding shelf shown in FIG. 11-1 can be made to the width of a cabinet unit and will pull out to about 18 inches, assuming the cabinet depth is about 23 inches. Therefore, it will provide a useful area of about 18 inches square.

The shelf is a piece of 1-inch plywood, and the guides should also be 1 inch thick. Sizes will depend on the cabinet, but you should locate the shelf 6 inches below the top counter surface (FIG. 11-2A). You can deepen the top piece on each cabinet side to make a guide (FIG. 11-2B) and add another strip below to form a bottom guide (FIG. 11-2C). Space the guides so that the plywood shelf slides fairly tightly at first; otherwise it may develop a sag.

You may have to adapt the front frame if it continues over other units, but there should be a piece across to cover above the shelf (FIG. 11-2D). The piece below could link with uprights around a door (FIG. 11-2E). Arrange the space between the frame parts to make a slot that continues the lines of the guides.

Make the shelf to project up to 1 inch when it is pushed fully in. To enable you to pull it out, there has to be a hollow under the shelf front (FIG. 11-2F) and a matching hollow in the front frame rail below it (FIG. 11-2G). If you make the solid wood lip on the front of the shelf to suit this, you can cut the hollows to match with a router or by other means.

Put stops on the lower guides (FIG. 11-2H). After sliding in the shelf, screw a strip across it (FIG. 11-2J) to come against the stops. If you arrange the stops so that 5 inches of the shelf remains between the guides, the unit should be stiff enough for normal use. If you ever need to remove the shelf, you can withdraw the screws by reaching from the cupboard below.

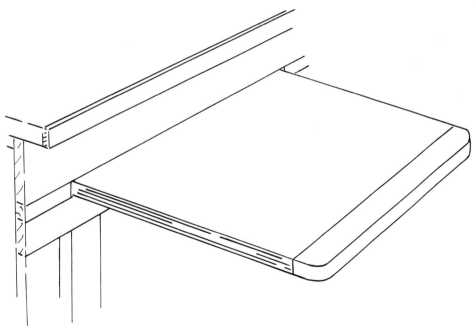

Fig. 11-1. A sliding shelf provides extra work area.

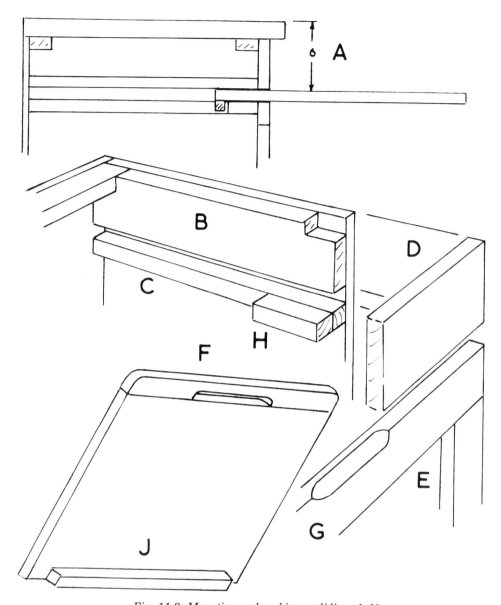

Fig. 11-2. Mounting and making a sliding shelf.

Round the projecting part of the shelf. The top of the shelf in the example is untreated, but you could surface it with laminated plastic or wood veneer. If so, remember to allow for the extra depth when locating the guide strips.

FOLDING TABLES

Tables that fold under counters are handy, but they involve certain limitations of size. If the table is to be 30 inches from the floor, the space it folds into must be that height, so the length the table extends has to be 30 inches or slightly less. There also has to be one or more legs, and if they are hinged anywhere except at the extreme end of the tabletop there must be space for their lower ends to project inside the cabinet when folded.

The folding table shown in FIG. 11-3 is a light table that conforms to these limitations. To accommodate such a table, arrange an opening at a suitable place under a countertop, probably between two ordinary units. If a toe board and cabinet bottom continue across, they must leave clearance for the folded table to reach the floor vertically under the rail on which it hangs. The toe board will probably be far enough back, but you will have to notch the cabinet bottom. The space inside can be used for storage, but access to it will be by lifting the table.

The table can be any width you wish, but 20 inches is suggested (FIG. 11-4A). The main parts are ¾-inch or 1-inch plywood. Simple pieces of plywood are shown, but you could use a veneer or laminated plastic top with solid-wood edging. You might then finish

Fig. 11-3. This table folds into a cabinet.

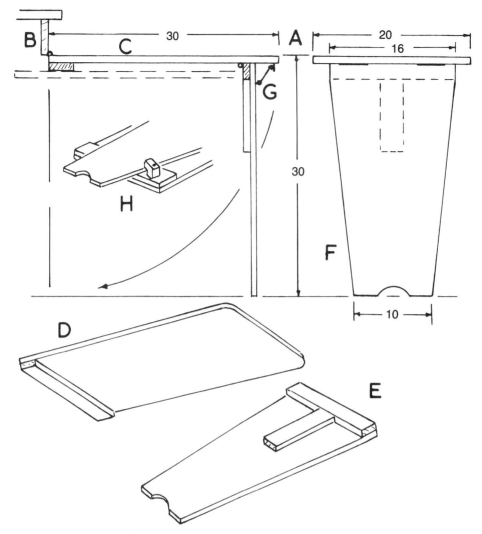

Fig. 11-4. Sizes and details of the folding table.

the leg to match. Solid parts are 1-inch-×-3-inch strips. Following are the basic steps of construction:

• Arrange a rail above the opening to set the correct height (FIG. 11-4B). There must be clearance behind it to enable the folded leg to swing up behind it almost 5 inches. With normal cabinet height and construction this should be possible.

• Make the tabletop (FIGS. 11-4C, D), with a strip across the inner end and rounded outer corners. Make its width to fit easily in the opening and its length to hang with a little clearance above the floor.

• The leg (FIGS. 11-4E, F) has a strip across the top and tapers to the foot. If you cut a hollow in the foot end, it will be better able to stand on a slightly uneven floor.

- Use two 4-inch hinges at each pivot point. Let them into the wood so that the knuckles are clear but so that the wood surfaces close almost together. Where screws go into plywood only, use the longest screws you can without breaking through. The hinge between leg and top should allow the leg to open only just to square.
- There are several ways of holding the leg upright. A simple one is to use a long hook and eye (FIG. 11-4G).
- To keep the leg in the folded position, make a small turnbutton to fit over the narrower part (FIG. 11-4H).
- Hinge the table to the edge of the top rail and test the action. It should hang vertically without fastening, but if necessary you could fit spring or magnetic fasteners.

Materials List for Folding Table

1 top	20 × 30 × ¾ or 1 plywood
1 leg	16 × 30 × ¾ or 1 plywood
1 top strip	1 × 3 × 21
1 leg strip	1 × 3 × 17
1 leg stiffener	1 × 3 × 12

END TABLE

In many kitchens the most convenient place to put a permanent extending table is at the end of a row of cabinets. It could serve as a dining area away from the immediate cooking area and as a divider if another part of the room is used for other purposes. The table could be stepped down from the counter level for use with ordinary chairs, or it could continue at counter level for use with high stools. The table shown in FIG. 11-5 is at the lower level and has ample leg room because there are no drawers, shelves, or cabinets built-in below. Chairs can fit at the end as well as at the sides, so four people should be able to eat here in comfort.

The cabinet next to this table should have a level end, although the worktop may overhang in the usual way. You can let the cabinet back extend behind the table or use separate plywood there, but extending the back would contribute to strength. You could also add a table to an existing cabinet end, but it is better to treat the assembly as a whole in new work. Following are the basic steps of construction:

- The size of the top determines many other sizes, so make it first (FIG. 11-6A). It is shown as plywood covered with laminated plastic, with the corners angled and with a wood edging (FIG. 11-7A), but you could use any other type of tabletop to match the countertop.
- Stiffen the underside of the top with strips parallel with the edges (FIGS. 11-6B and 11-7B). If you can fit these strips before adding the laminated plastic, you can drive screws downward. Otherwise, screw upward with counterbored holes in the strips.
- Where the table comes against the cabinet end, cut away the top to notch around (FIGS. 11-6C and 11-7C). The simplest approach is to cut back to the supporting strip, but if the

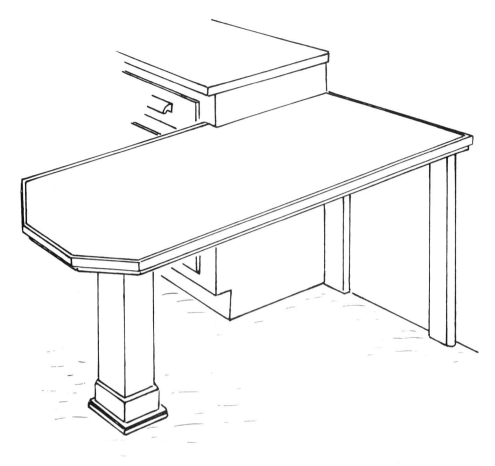

Fig. 11-5. This end table is stepped down from the countertop and has a pedestal support.

overhang would then interfere with a door or drawer on the cabinet, cut back less and include a packing when you screw to the cabinet.

• At the wall end make two legs and a crosspiece to screw to the top (FIGS. 11-6D and 11-7D), with either its own plywood backing or the extension from the cabinet back. Arrange the width across the legs to fit inside the top stiffeners.

• The pillar (FIG. 11-6E) is square and attached to the tabletop. It could be screwed to the floor, but you might find that unnecessary. Join pieces to make a 5-inch-square section (FIG. 11-7E). At the top add square strips (FIG. 11-7F), which can be drilled for screwing upward into the tabletop. Be careful to finish the top square in both directions, as this affects the final attitude of the pillar. If it is out of vertical, it will be visually obvious.

• At the bottom, miter four pieces around the pillar and then add a square below to extend an additional 1 inch (FIG. 11-6F). Bevel the top edges of the upright strips (FIG. 11-7G) and the edges of the base (FIG. 11-7H).

• Mark the position of the table on the cabinet end, then make a trial assembly to make sure that the top will be level and the parts fit squarely. For finishing, the best approach is to stain and polish or paint the parts before final assembly with glue and screws.

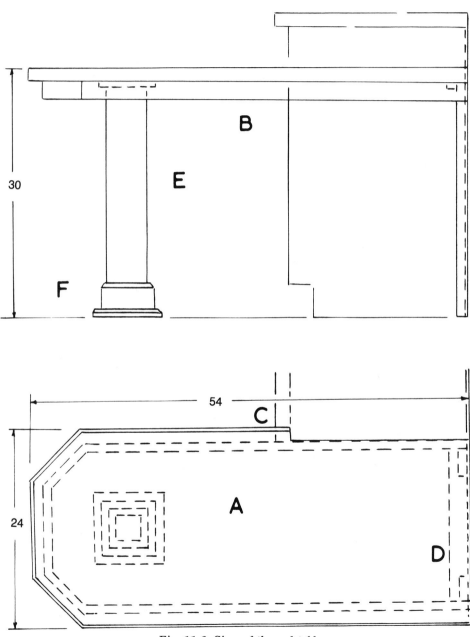

Fig. 11-6. Sizes of the end table.

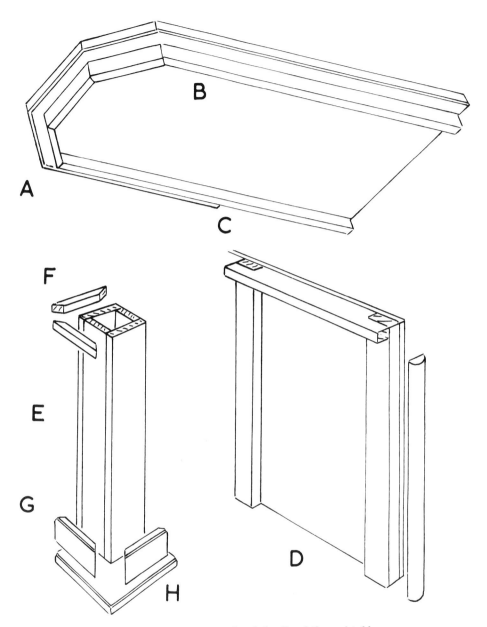

Fig. 11-7. Constructional details of the end table.

Materials List for End Table

1 top	24 × 54 × 1 plywood
1 top edging	3/8 × 1 1/4 × 50
1 top edging	3/8 × 1 1/4 × 30
3 top edgings	3/8 × 1 1/4 × 12

2 top stiffeners	1 ×	2 × 50
3 top stiffeners	1 ×	2 × 12
2 legs	1 ×	3 × 30
1 top piece	1 ×	3 × 24
1 leg edge	30 × 1½ half round	
2 pillars	¾ ×	5 × 30
2 pillars	¾ ×	3½ × 30
4 pillar tops	1 ×	1 × 10
4 pillar bottoms	1 ×	3 × 10
1 pillar base	1 ×	10 × 10

COUNTER-HEIGHT TABLE

If you want a counter-height table, you could simply make the end table described in the preceding section the same height as your countertop. However, the counter-height table to be discussed in this section offers a variation (FIG. 11-8). In effect, the cabinet

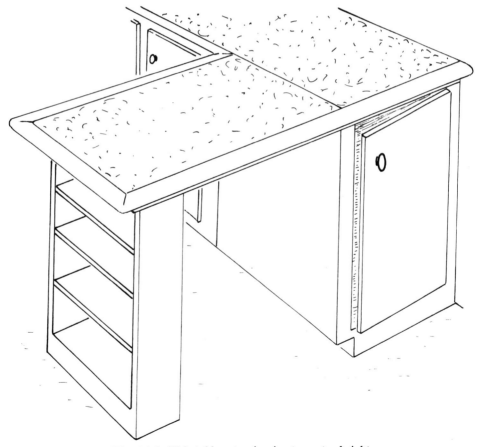

Fig. 11-8. This table extension is at counter height.

extends under the table and has an end door. The projecting table is supported by a block of shelves, which could serve as a bookcase or as extra storage for small items. The table could be used with tall stools, which might be stored underneath. Sizes (FIG. 11-9A) can be varied without affecting the general design.

The tabletop will have to match the countertop because the pattern must continue

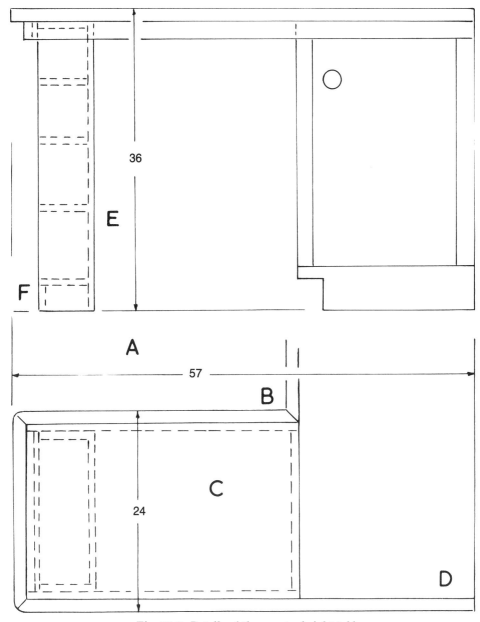

Fig. 11-9. Details of the counter-height table.

around the angle. The top in the example is laminated plastic on thick plywood with a wood edging. The following instructions below apply to the table, but they assume that the main part of the counter was made as described elsewhere in this book—with the end unit having a door in its side and the front (which will come under the table) closed.

• Cut the plywood and laminated plastic level with the end of the cabinet. Cut back the edging at the front to miter to the table edging (FIG. 11-9B). The example has a 2-inch wood edging which is well rounded (FIG. 11-10A), but you could treat other edgings in the same way.

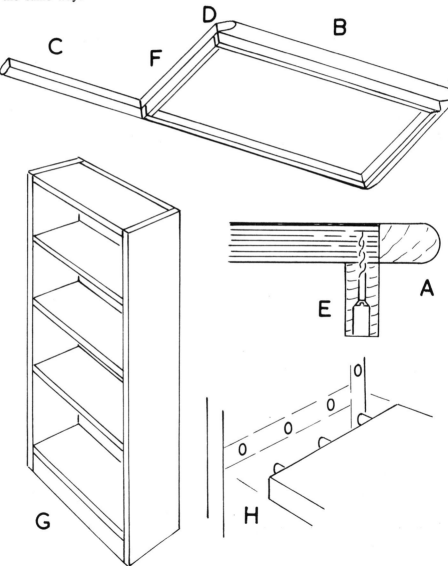

Fig. 11-10. Construction of parts of the counter-height table.

- Make the tabletop (FIGS. 11-9C and 11-10B). It will butt against the main countertop, so make sure the edge there is straight and the meeting edge of the tabletop is both straight and square.
- Fix the edging with mitered joints at the front. Let the outer piece extend to cover the counter end (FIGS. 11-9D and 11-10C). On the other side miter the table edging against the counter edging (FIG. 11-10D).
- Frame the top underneath. If you cannot screw downward before fitting the laminated plastic, use counterbored screws from below (FIG. 11-10E). The end strip (FIG. 11-10F) will be used to screw the tabletop to the front of the countertop.
- The support with shelves is made as a unit (FIG. 11-9E). Its width should fit between the framing strips under the top and its height must bring the tabletop horizontal when screwed to the countertop. You can make its depth to suit your needs, but as drawn 7 inches deep. You could use solid wood or ¾-inch plywood with solid wood on exposed edges. Space shelves to suit your needs.
- Allow for a solid front to bring the bottom shelf to a height to match the cabinet toe board (FIGS. 11-9F and 11-10G). The back fits between the sides. The top is used to screw into the tabletop.
- For joints at the top the best approach is dovetails, but you could use dowels.
- You could fit the shelves into dado slots in the sides, but with plywood it would be simpler to use dowels (FIG. 11-10H). Use dowels for the back as well.
- Try the parts in position, then stain and polish or paint them before final assembly.
- Join the support to the tabletop. Bring the table to the counter edge and pull it close with screws before joining the outer edging to the countertop end.

Materials List for Counter-height Table

1 top	22 × 36 × 1 plywood
1 top edging	1 × 2 × 58
1 top edging	1 × 2 × 36
1 top edging	1 × 2 × 26
2 top stiffeners	1 × 2 × 36
2 top stiffeners	1 × 2 × 26
2 support sides	1 × 7 × 36
6 shelves	1 × 7 × 24
1 front	1 × 4 × 24

BREAKFAST BAR

Another approach to a kitchen eating area is the counter or breakfast bar, usually distinguishable from the working area. If the breakfast bar projects squarely to the wall countertop, it keeps the eaters away from the cooking area and allows the cook to serve from that side.

Such a bar could be at table height for use with chairs, but tall stools are most often used. If desired, the bar can include storage space, to allow cutlery and eating utensils to be easily within reach. The breakfast bar shown in FIG. 11-11 has sufficient length and

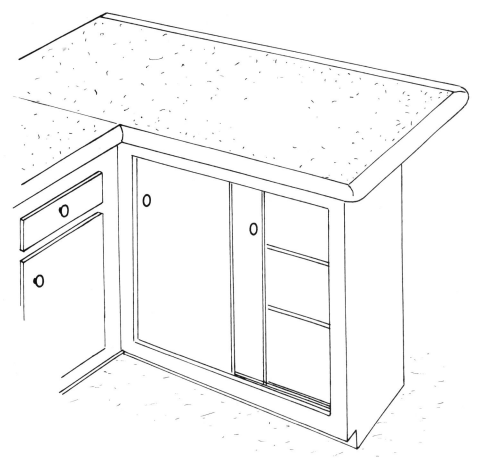

Fig. 11-11. A breakfast bar as seen from the cook's side.

knee room to accommodate several people on stools, which can be stored underneath.

The breakfast bar is made as a unit and then attached to the end of the counter cabinet. The cabinet end and countertop should be level with the breakfast bar top. The top edging will be mitered when the bar is added, but there are no other alterations except screwing or bolting through. The bar top can match that of the adjoining countertop.

Decide well ahead of time on sizes. In the example (FIG. 11-12) the top area is 57 inches long. The 27-inch width is divided underneath to provide 12 inches of clear space. The other side has a cabinet with sliding doors opening to the kitchen side and another cabinet against the wall cabinet which opens toward the sitting side. The cabinets underneath, which provide support, are made separately and brought together under the top (FIG. 11-13A). The cabinet facing outward should be the same width as the end of the wall cabinet. The other cabinet makes up the length to within 3 inches of the end of the bar top. Make sure the cabinets match when they are brought together, so there is a straight line facing the outer side. The door on the cabinet next to the wall will be outside this line, unless you fit a flush door. Following are the basic steps of construction:

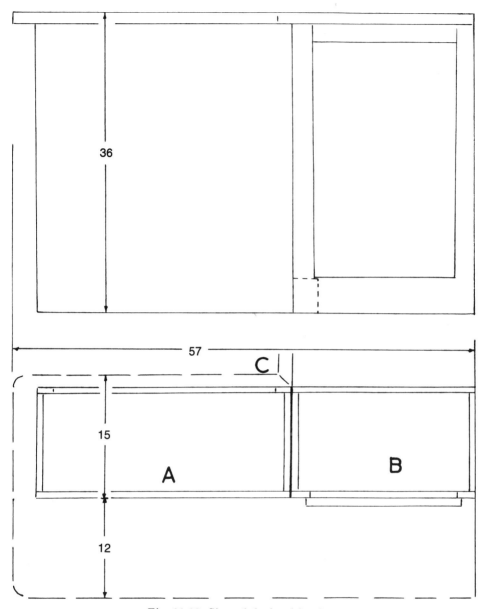

Fig. 11-12. Sizes of the breakfast bar.

• The cabinet with the sliding doors is made like a open box, with ¾-inch plywood. The back (FIGS. 11-12A and 11-13B) sets the size. It fits over the other parts and reaches from the floor to the underside of the countertop.
• Make the pair of sides to fit against the back, with corners cut out at the front for a toe board to match that of the wall cabinets (FIG. 11-13C). Include an upright strip at

the front in the total width (FIG. 11-13D). This strip and the top rail are supported by a notched piece on each side.

• Make the bottom to fit inside, notched around the upright strips. If you leave the toe board until after you fit the cabinet in place, you can ensure a close fit against the next toe board.

• The sliding doors are pieces of ¼-inch plywood, made as described in Chapter 4. Make the top guide strip and fit it under the top rail (FIG. 11-13E). Put the other piece on the front edge of the bottom.

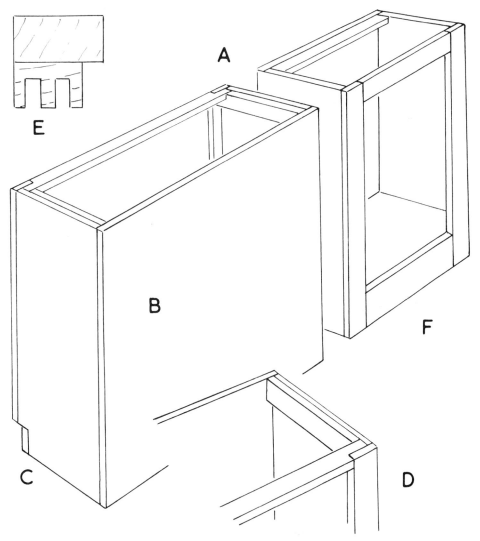

Fig. 11-13. Units that make up the breakfast bar.

- Make the two sliding doors and fit them with handles—or cut holes or slots—for gripping.
- The other cabinet is also made like an open box (FIGS. 11-12B and 11-13F). The front frame should raise the cabinet bottom to the same level as the other cabinet, but you do not need to set back a toe board.
- Make a door for this cabinet to match other doors, and hinge it at the wall side.
- You will probably want to fit shelves in both cabinets. They can rest on cleats and be arranged to suit your needs.
- The top can be any type to match the adjacent countertop, but for this example the top is plywood covered with laminated plastic and with a wide wood edge (FIG. 11-10A).
- Make the bar top so it will have the plywood edge level with the cabinets below and will butt closely against the wall countertop. You can then miter its edging to the other edging (FIG. 11-12C). Fit edging all around, except for the gap against the countertop.
- Join the cabinets together with screws or bolts.
- Check levels and adjust if necessary, then screw the cabinets securely under the bar top. The open 12-inch side cantilevers from the cabinets. It will be stiff enough, but the screws at the farther side will have to take the load if anyone leans on or hits heavily near the open edge. Therefore, use plenty of screws through the strip over the sliding door and a strip inside the other cabinet.
- Join the breakfast bar to the end wall cabinet. A strip of 1-inch-×-2-inch wood on the wall under the end of the open side will increase stiffness.

Materials List for Breakfast Bar

1 top	27 × 57 × 1 plywood
1 back	36 × 36 × ¾ plywood
1 back	24 × 36 × ¾ plywood
4 sides	14 × 36 × ¾ plywood
1 bottom	14 × 36 × ¾ plywood
1 bottom	14 × 24 × ¾ plywood
1 top edge	1¼ × 2 × 60
1 top edge	1¼ × 2 × 40
1 top edge	1¼ × 2 × 30
2 top strips	1 × 2 × 14
1 top strip	1 × 2 × 36
1 top strip	1 × 2 × 24
2 uprights	1 × 2 × 36
2 front frames	1 × 2 × 36
1 front frame	1 × 2 × 24
1 front frame	1 × 4 × 24
1 toe board	1 × 4 × 36
2 door guides	1 × 2 × 36
2 sliding doors	20 × 34 × ¼ plywood
1 wall cleat	1 × 2 × 12

CABINET EXTENSION

In some kitchen layouts it is helpful to have the worktop extended squarely to the wall, to provide more area or to divide the food preparation area from another part of the room. The extension can serve as a table, but the cook can also use it as a working area. The extension could also contain a sink or range—if available space elsewhere is very restricted—but sinks and ranges are usually better backed by a wall.

The extension might form part of a room divider, with more storage or cabinets above, as described later. If it is to be primarily a work area, leg room will not be needed and the space below the countertop can be filled with cabinets, racks, or shelves, to increase general storage capacity and match the cabinets along the wall.

The simplest way to make the unit's carcass is to make cabinet units and join them together. You can make them in sizes to suit your needs, but the example shown in

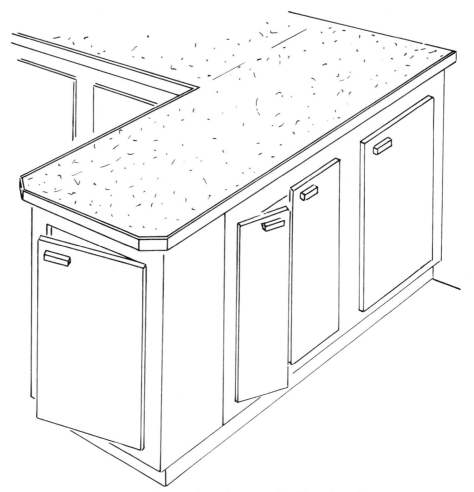

Fig. 11-14. This extension takes top and cabinets into the room.

FIG. 11-14 uses four identical units of a width based on the width of a wall cabinet: about 24 inches. One cabinet fits across the end of the wall cabinets, two fit back-to-back, and another fits across the end (FIG. 11-15A). This makes the cabinet extension 36 inches long and 26 inches wide, going 12 inches farther along the wall than the wall cabinets. The top will overhang about 2 inches all around. You could make the back-to-back units wider or narrower, if that would provide the extension you need. The end wall cabinet should be made with a closed front as wide as half its depth (12 inches) and a door alongside (FIG. 11-15B) so the extension cabinet can butt against it.

If you decide on four identical cabinets, be careful to get sizes exact, so they can fit together correctly. The first measurement is the width, which must match the end of the wall cabinet (FIG. 11-15C). The depth back to front must be exactly half this (FIG.

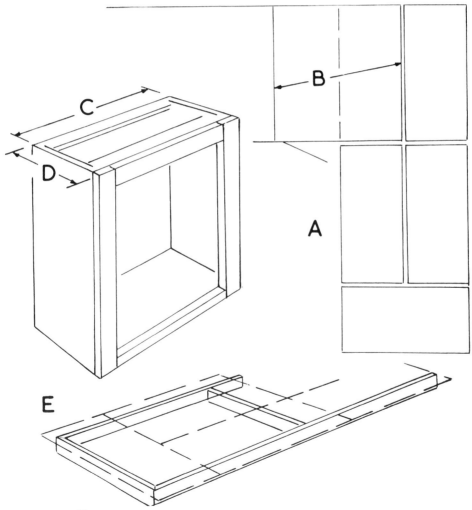

Fig. 11-15. Using similar units to make the cabinet extension.

11-15D), and the total height must bring the countertops level. Allow for the cabinets resting on a plinth, which provides the toe boards all around (FIG. 11-15E), at a height to match those under the wall cabinets.

Although the cabinet carcasses are the same, you can vary the doors, which may

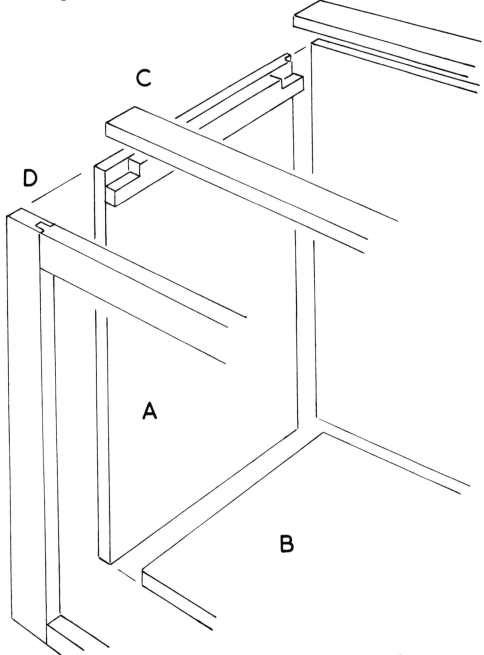

Fig. 11-16. Constructional details of a unit for the cabinet extension.

be single, double, or sliding. The doors inside the angle have to swing in order to minimize interference with each other, and you might prefer sliding doors on the extension. You could also put a sliding door on the end wall cabinet, arranged so it slides behind the closed front.

You can make the cabinets in a manner basically similar to those described in Chapter 5. Main parts can be ¾-inch plywood. None of the backs show, so they can be thinner plywood let into rabbets. Because the top edges of the backs will not show, they can overlap the lengthwise strips. You can use screws and glue to assemble parts where heads will not show, but elsewhere use dowels in blind holes. The front frame is part of each cabinet and should be included in the total depth. Following are the basic steps of construction:

• For each cabinet, make a pair of ends with notched strips at the top (FIG. 11-16A). Rabbet the rear edges to suit the plywood back.
• Make a bottom to fit between the sides (FIG. 11-16B) and two strips of the same length for the top (FIG. 11-16C).
• Cut a back to fit. Assemble all parts so far.
• The sections of wood for the front frames should match similar parts on the wall

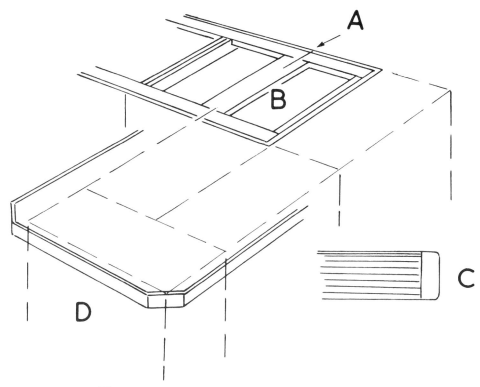

Fig. 11-17. Joining the extension top and the main top.

cabinets, but they will probably be 1 inch × 2 inches at the top and sides and the same as the plywood at the bottom (FIG. 11-16D). Tenon or dowel the corners and attach the frame to the front of the cabinet.

• Make all the units to this point. Check them against each other and adjust if necessary.

• Join two of them back to back and one to the end of this pair. Add the one that will fit against the wall cabinet.

• Make the plinth (FIG. 11-15E) about 2 inches in from the edges. Its short side will come against the toe board of the wall cabinet. The main purpose of the crosspiece is to keep the sides at the right distance until you have screwed the plinth in place.

• Make a trial assembly. To get a tight fit, final cutting of the short plinth end should be delayed until this stage.

• While cabinets are temporarily in place, you can measure and cut the parts for the top. It will probably be best if the top on the wall cabinet finishes in line with the edge of the extension top (FIG. 11-17A), so that the extension goes across in a single parallel piece. Put a wide strip across the wall cabinet to support the joint (FIG. 11-17B), allowing for the amount the extension top will overhang its cabinets.

• Cut the top of the wall cabinets to length. Make the top on the extension with an edging similar to that of the main counter top. The example uses a narrow strip of wood (FIG. 11-17C) with the outer corners beveled (FIG. 11-17D). Miter the edging where they meet at the inner angle.

• You could join the top to the extension cabinets before assembly to the wall cabinets, but it is easier to tightly fit the cabinets and then pull the joint in the top as close as possible while you screw upward from below through the flat strips.

Materials List for Cabinet Extension

8 sides	12 × 32 × ¾ plywood
4 bottoms	12 × 25 × ¾ plywood
4 backs	24 × 25 × ½ plywood
8 top strips	1 × 2 × 13
8 top strips	1 × 2 × 25
8 front frames	1 × 2 × 25
4 front frames	1 × 2 × 24
4 front frames	1 × 1 × 24
1 plinth	¾ × 4 × 60
2 plinths	¾ × 4 × 24
1 plinth	¾ × 4 × 40
1 top joint cover	1 × 4 × 24
1 top	28 × 66 × 1 plywood
1 top edging	½ × 1¼ × 60
1 top edging	½ × 1¼ × 40
1 top edging	½ × 1¼ × 36
Doors to match	

12
CHAPTER

Shelves

The simplest way to provide storage on the wall above a countertop is with shelving. Open shelves can provide a considerable amount of storage space, and all of it is visible so you can easily find what you need.

Large numbers of open shelves loaded with a variety of goods can look untidy, so you have to weigh easy access against appearance when you plan shelves. As a compromise, you could have wall cabinets, some with solid and some with glass doors, and shelves between, below or above. Another solution is to dress-up the shelves, with low rails with spindles across their fronts. This arrangement is particularly good if you have plates or glassware you want to display without a glass front.

In planning shelves, you must consider the way you are furnishing the kitchen. In a modern arrangement open wall shelves are few. A strictly traditional kitchen, however, could have more shelves than wall cabinets. If the kitchen is to be functional rather than decorative, you will probably provide a larger proportion of shelves.

As mentioned earlier, very basic shelves are more functional, than attractive. However, you can shape their edges, put shaped pieces under the edges, or use decorative supports at the ends. And if the shelves come between wall cabinets, there will probably be enough decoration in the cabinet doors or shaped sides to offset the plainness of the shelves.

Material for shelves needs to be stiff in its length more than its width, so for long shelves use solid wood instead of plywood or particleboard. These materials have the same strength in all directions, so they are better for short shelves or shelves with close supports. Heavy weights obviously require a stiff shelf, but even a moderate load can cause sagging over time.

SIMPLE SHELF

A simple shelf may be supported on metal brackets (FIG. 12-1A), but these are usually not very attractive. You *can* get good-looking brackets, but as part of the furnishings of a kitchen you might decide to use wooden brackets instead.

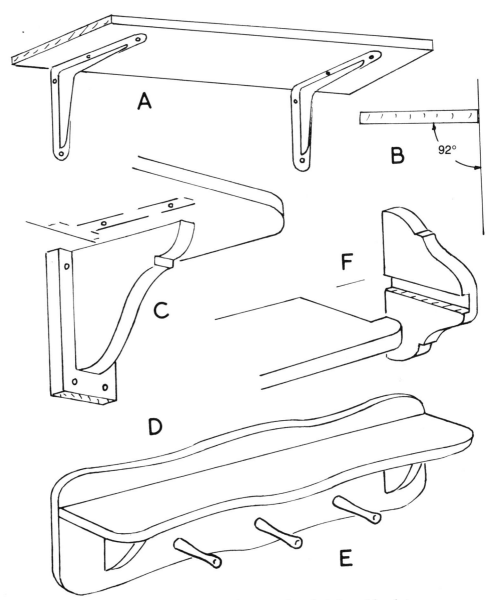

Fig. 12-1. *A simple shelf can have metal or shaped wood brackets, with or without a back.*

If you test the squareness of bought metal brackets, you will find that most are a degree or so wider than 90 degrees. This is to prevent the shelf from tilting forward. Shelves should always be very slightly higher at the front than at the back (FIG. 12-1B). If you are uncertain about the verticality of the wall, try a spirit level front to back on a shelf and set it by that.

For an independent shelf with wooden brackets, you can screw the shelf down into the brackets, but you have to allow for screws from the brackets into the wall. You could use a vertical piece behind each bracket to take the screws (FIG. 12-1C). You could also have a piece of wood as long as the shelf, and shape its edge to match the shelf edge (FIG. 12-1D). The long backing piece lends itself to fitted hooks or pegs below for hanging cloths and other things. Pegs could be turned or bought as Shaker pegs (FIG. 12-1E).

Simple single shelves are likely to come into your planning after you have arranged wall cabinets—possibly with shelves built between and around them—but keep an eye open for other gaps that might be filled by shelves. For example, you might put one over a doorway or on a blank piece of wall. You might also put shelves in places too high for other use. Such shelves could store items rarely needed or those intended to be more ornamental than functional.

Instead of using brackets underneath, you might want end supporting brackets above as well as below, with the shelf in dadoes. If the shelf is notched around its supports, dadoes can go right through and be hidden (FIG. 12-1F).

BLOCKS OF SHELVES

If you want two or more shelves between end supports, the construction is similar to that of a bookcase. Several joints are possible. A simple dado has its end exposed, unless the shelf is wider and notched around (FIG. 12-2A). If the shelf and support are the same width, you must stop the dado to hide it. You can do so by rounding the shelf to match a router-cut groove (FIG. 12-2B) or by trimming the dado square with a chisel (FIG. 12-2C).

If the joint needs strengthening and screws through the supports are not acceptable (FIG. 12-2D), you can drive screws diagonally upward from below (FIG. 12-2E). If there is a back to strengthen the joint, a screw near the front of top and bottom shelves should be enough. In some blocks of shelves you can use vertical pieces at the ends to add strength as well as hide open ends of dadoes (FIG. 12-2F) and improve appearance.

Shelves can rest on cleats (FIG. 12-2G), as they usually do inside cabinets, but cleats are unattractive. Where they would show, use dowels instead (FIG. 12-2H). If the outside surfaces are hidden in cabinets or elsewhere, the dowels could go through; otherwise they should be in blind holes.

You can buy a variety of metal fittings to support shelves between sides. Most of these have a row of holes, so positions can be altered. A basic type has a peg to go in the hole and a hook to support the shelf (FIG. 12-2J). You can make similar things by cutting flats on bits of dowel rod (FIG. 12-2K). In both cases, when the shelf is in position the pegs cannot come out, but by removing the shelf you can move the pegs to a different position. If the arrangement is open-fronted, there is nothing to stop a shelf on these

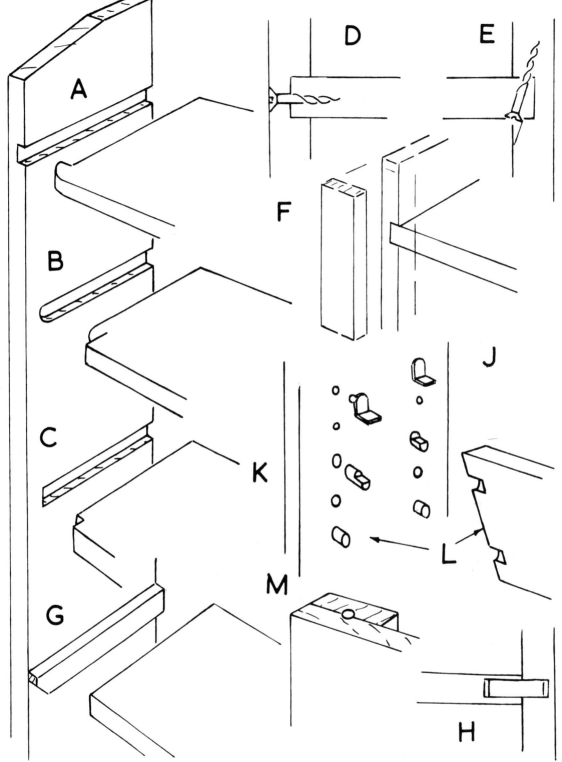

Fig.12-2. Shelves can have dado joints in various forms or be made to adjust or lift out.

supports from being pulled forward. However, if you use full dowels in half holes (FIG. 12-2L), shelves remain positioned. You can drill a half hole by clamping a piece of scrap wood against the shelf when drilling (FIG. 12-2M), or try drilling a pair of shelves at a time.

BASIC SHELF UNIT

A block of shelves should have an outside structure of sides, top, and bottom securely joined together, so that whatever the number of shelves, they will be secured in their dadoes or supports by sides that cannot move outward. The unit should have a back, unless you want it to be open to the wall. It could also have some decoration, but you should make the carcass in the basic way. The unit will probably link with cabinets or other assemblies, so the shelf unit can be functional while the adjoining parts provide decoration in their outline or doors.

The unit shown in FIG. 12-3 (left) is a straightforward block of shelves. If it is to stand alone, you could shape the ends for decoration. The main parts are hardwood finished

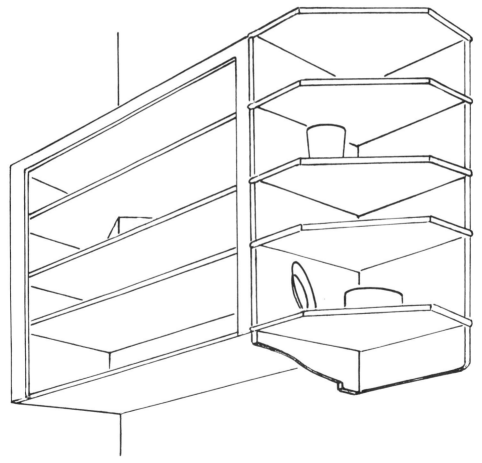

Fig. 12-3. This basic shelf unit has a block of corner shelves fitted against it.

⅝ inch thick, and the back is ¼-inch plywood, preferably with a face veneer to match the solid wood parts. FIGURE 12-4A suggests sizes, but you will probably have to adjust them to match adjoining cabinets or to suit available wall space. Following are the basic steps of construction:

• Mark out the pair of ends (FIG. 12-4B). Rabbet the rear edges to take the back plywood (FIG. 12-4C). The dadoes go through the front edges and into the rabbets.
• Mark out the top and bottom the same size (FIG. 12-4D).
• The suggested corner joints are through dovetails (FIG. 12-5A), but other corner joints are suitable. Cut the joints.

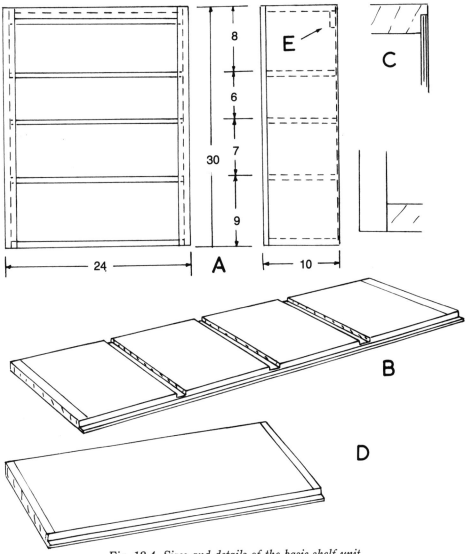

Fig. 12-4. Sizes and details of the basic shelf unit.

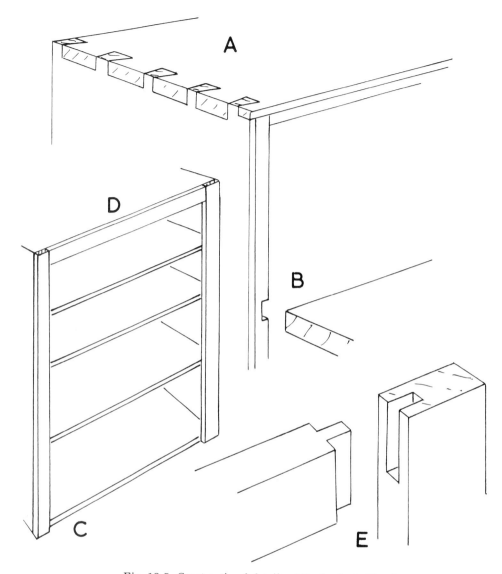

Fig. 12-5. Constructional details of the basic shelf unit.

• Cut the dadoes (FIG. 12-5B) and make the shelves, using the top and bottom lengths between joints and the dado depths as a guide to shelf length.

• Assemble all the parts made so far. Pull the corner joints tight and plane off any excess tails and pins after the glue has set. Slide in the shelves with glue and fit the back to hold the assembly in place.

• Make the front uprights (FIG. 12-5C) and the front top piece (FIG. 12-5D) to match the carcass sizes. Stub tenons (FIG. 12-5E) will keep these parts level; fit them to the front of the block. You can use glue, with pins set and stopped.

- Put a strip across under the top to take screws into the wall (FIG. 12-4E). This will take the main load, but you could add screws lower down.

Materials List for Basic Shelf Unit

2 sides	$\frac{5}{8} \times 9\frac{5}{8} \times 31$
1 top	$\frac{5}{8} \times 9\frac{5}{8} \times 25$
1 bottom	$\frac{5}{8} \times 9\frac{5}{8} \times 25$
3 shelves	$\frac{5}{8} \times 9\frac{3}{8} \times 25$
1 top front	$\frac{5}{8} \times 1\frac{1}{2} \times 25$
2 side fronts	$\frac{5}{8} \times 1\frac{1}{2} \times 31$
1 back	$24 \times 30 \times \frac{1}{4}$ plywood
1 screw strip	$\frac{5}{8} \times 1\frac{1}{2} \times 25$

CORNER SHELVES

A block of shelves set into an angle is an obvious choice for a kitchen corner, but this arrangement can be used in several other places. For example, if you do not fit a basic shelf unit against wall cabinets, you could improve its appearance and usefulness with corner shelves at one or both ends (FIG. 12-3, right).

The sizes of the block of corner shelves shown in FIG. 12-6A are arranged to match the basic unit described earlier, but you can adapt the sizes to suit your needs. Because as the top of the unit is above the sight line, it is left plain. The bottom could be the same, but shaping it improves its appearance. If the corner shelf is placed alongside a basic shelf unit, this shaping is only necessary on the side projecting forward; the other side can remain plain. But if the shelves are in the corner of a room or they are to join units on an external angle, shape both sides.

The corner unit is best made of solid wood $\frac{5}{8}$ inch thick. Thinner wood might look neater but would not allow much thickness for cutting dadoes. The grain of the shelves should be parallel with that of their diagonal fronts. Following are the basic steps of construction:

- The two backs are joined by a rabbet in one of them (FIG. 12-6B), so cut one that much narrower than the other.
- The top also fits into a rabbet, the same depth as the dadoes (FIG. 12-6C). The shelves, bottom, and top will then all be the same.
- Cut the dadoes and shape the bottom(s) of the backs (FIG. 12-6D).
- Make the shelves. Each projects $\frac{1}{2}$ inch and is notched over the thickness of the back (FIG. 12-6E). You can round the exposed edges. If you are fitting the unit into the corner of a room, check its actual angle, which may not be exactly square. Cut the shelves to this angle.
- Join the shelves to the back with the rabbet, then add the other back. At the top, screw downward into the backs. At the bottom, use screws diagonally upward (FIG. 12-2E) if necessary. One or more screws each way below the top will take the weight. Other screws lower down will pull the backs tight to the wall.

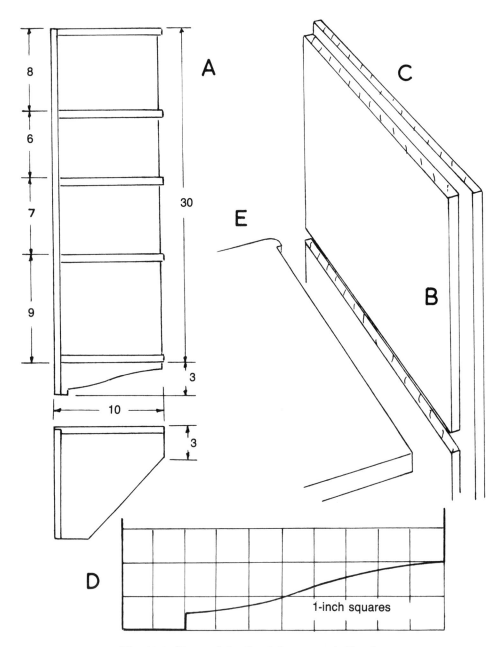

Fig. 12-6. Sizes and details of the corner shelf unit.

Materials List for Corner Shelves

1 back	$\frac{5}{8} \times 10 \times 36$
1 back	$\frac{5}{8} \times 9\frac{3}{4} \times 36$
5 shelves	$\frac{5}{8} \times 11 \times 16$

DISPLAY SHELVES

If you want to display valuable plates or other tableware on a shelf, it must have a positive stop at the front. In some cases a notch in the shelf or a shallow rail might keep items in place, but a higher rail on spindles is safer and more decorative as well. If the shelves are part of a row of wall cabinets, you can leave the ends plain, but if the display shelves hang independently, you might want to shape extending parts. The display shelf shown in FIG. 12-7 will hang without touching other furniture.

For the sizes suggested in FIG. 12-8A the main parts could be ⅝-inch hardwood. If you use softwood, increase thicknesses to ¾ inch. The back between the shelves is ¼-inch plywood, but there is a solid wood back above the top shelf, to provide stiffness and take the hanging screws. The plywood back may finish at the bottom shelf or continue to the ends of the sides. Following are the basic steps of construction:

- The key parts are two sides, so mark them out first (FIG. 12-8B). Continue the rabbet for the plywood to the end, if that is what you want, or stop it at the bottom shelf. At the top of each side, cut away to take the top solid back (FIG. 12-8C).

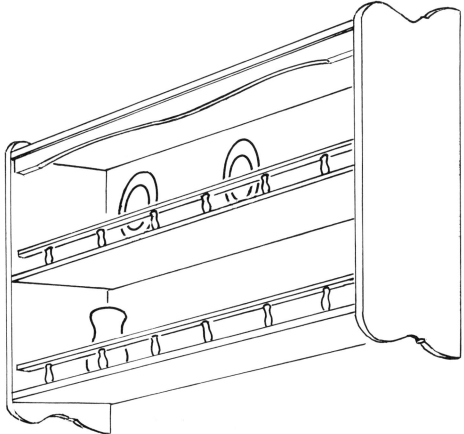

Fig. 12-7. These display shelves have shaped ends and rails to keep items in place.

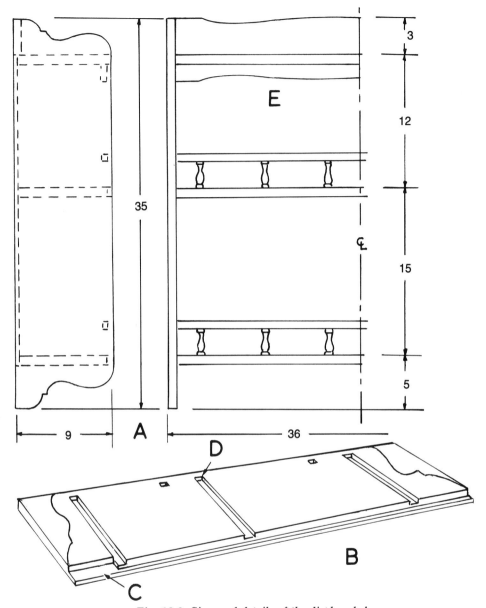

Fig. 12-8. Sizes and details of the display shelves.

- Prepare the wood for the shelves and cut the dadoes in the sides. Stop them ¼ inch back from the front (FIG. 12-8D) and cut the ends of the shelves to suit.
- The shaped ends of the sides are the same (FIG. 12-9A), so to ensure uniformity cut a card template of the shape. Mark and cut the shapes. Remove saw marks and sand the ends. The top curves may be too high for surface details to be seen, but the bottom

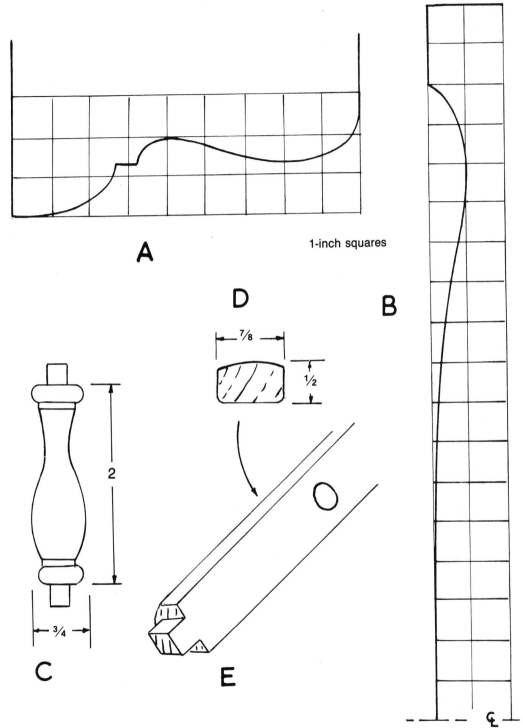

1-inch squares

A

D

B

7/8

1/2

2

3/4

C

E

Fig. 12-9. Outlines of the curved shapes and details of the rails and spindles.

shaping should be smooth. If the top of the unit will be high, you might not have to worry about the edge of the solid wood back above the top shelf, but if it is visible you might wish to shape it (FIG. 12-9B).

• You could add a strip under the front of the top shelf (FIG. 12-8E) to improve appearance. It need not be tenoned to the sides; you could use dowels or depend only on glue. The strip should repeat the curve of the solid wood back.

• You might have to relate the rail sizes to the spindles, depending on the dowel ends. If you turn them yourself (FIG. 12-9C), ¼-inch dowel ends can go into rails about ½ inch × ⅞ inch (FIG. 12-9D). Shape the rail sections and cut small tenons to fit into the sides (FIG. 12-9E). Spindles at 6-inch centers should be satisfactory, but if the shelf will display small things, make the spindles closer together.

• When you assemble the unit, screw the ends of the top solid wood back into the sides and put two or three screws upward through the shelf into the back before fitting the plywood, which goes over the top shelf and against the solid wood back.

• You will probably need to drive one or two screws diagonally upward through the ends of the bottom shelf to strengthen the dado joints.

• Drill the solid wood top for the main hanging screws. You might need one or two more screws lower in the plywood to keep the unit close to the wall.

Materials List for Display Shelves

2 sides	⅝ × 9 × 36
3 shelves	⅝ × 8¾ × 37
1 back	⅝ × 3 × 37
1 back	36 × 37 × ¼ plywood
2 rails	½ × ⅞ × 37
12 spindles	¾ × ¾ × 4

COUNTERTOP SHELVES

A row of low shelving at the back of a countertop can take the place of a splash-back for at least part of the length of a working area. This shelving could be conveniently located below a window, where the top provides a ledge. These shelves could also fill part of the space under a wall cabinet, or you might carry them around a corner at the end of a counter.

You can vary the size to suit your needs, but the block should not be too wide, or it will use up precious work space. If you want the shelf to accommodate books, their size might determine the minimum width. Height limitations might be important in some parts and not others, so you might make a long block of shelves with its top stepped to two levels. On a long countertop, you could make a block of shelves up to 8 feet long, but there is probably a break in the counter for a sink or range and you could not carry the shelves past that.

How you go about making these shelves depends on what you want them to hold as well as on their design. If you have vertical divisions no more than 15 inches apart, the top would be stiff enough if ½ inch thick. If, however, you space supports farther apart or you use softwood, the top would have to be thicker. Hardwood, with its front edges rounded or molded, looks neat if not too thick. The back could be plywood, but its thickness uses up depth, which may be limited. You could also use laminated plastic, with its decorative surface forward. This would make a good combination if the plastic has the same pattern as the countertop. Otherwise, a light color might be desirable, to more clearly display what the shelves contain.

You might have to base shelf sizes on particular items, such as books. As cookbooks tend to require a taller space than other things do, you might want to have two levels alongside them for spice jars or sets of bottles or containers. Scales might get their own compartment. For much of the length, the height should be no more than 12 inches. The cook will soon find plenty of things to push into the space. You could also include one or more small drawers, to break up the plain appearance of a long stretch of shelves.

The specimen shelving shown in FIG. 12-10 includes several features you might wish to incorporate in the shelving you make to suit your countertop. If the shelving comes across the end of the countertop against a wall, the corner could have a post or, to give maximum access, there could be a division one way or even diagonally.

The example is drawn (FIG. 12-11A) with a section at the left to hold large books against a corner wall. That height is then divided into two for spice jars or other containers. Beyond that the assembly steps down both in width and height (FIG. 12-11B). The length of this reduced-size which can continue as far as desired, is divided into 15 inch bays, with one bay arranged to take two drawers. If the end is exposed, the top and bottom can continue a few inches past the last upright.

You could join the parts in any way, from nailing or screwing to dowels or dado joints. The diagram suggests dado joints; the wood should finish ½ inch thick or slightly more, then you can cut the dadoes ³⁄₁₆ inch deep. If you prefer dowel joints, three ³⁄₁₆-inch dowels in each joint should be satisfactory. At the bottom they could go through, but at the top they should be in blind holes taken as deep as possible. Following are the basic steps for constructing a countertop shelf:

- The top and bottom make a pair except for the step-down of the top. The bottom could be a wide board reduced in width for the narrow part, but it is better to glue on a strip to make up the wider part (FIG. 12-12A).
- Mark and cut the dado grooves. The uprights are set back ½ inch from the front edges, so stop the dadoes there (FIG. 12-11C).
- At the end against the wall, cut rabbets of the same size as the dadoes. At the other end allow 3 inches past the last upright, unless that end will also be against a wall or cabinet.
- Make the three taller uprights. All are the same size, but the one against the wall (FIG. 12-11D) is plain, one has a stopped dado for the shelf (FIG. 12-11E), and the other has a matching groove for the shelf and another groove at the opposite side for the lower top (FIG. 12-11F).

- Make the shelf (FIGS. 12-11G and 12-12B), and notch it so the fronts come level.
- Make the top (FIG. 12-12C) level at the wall end, but with about ¾ inch overhang at the other end, where the outer corner should be rounded.
- The long top fits into a dado groove on the tall upright and then should be marked and grooved to match the bottom. Stop the grooves in both parts ½ inch from the front edge.
- If you wish to fit drawers or just a shelf, make a division (FIG. 12-11H) as you did in the higher part. This need not be central; the upper drawer could be shallower than the lower one.
- Mount the bottom on 1-inch-square strips (FIG. 12-12D), carried around the difference in width and across the open end.
- In front of this, fit strips to make a base (FIG. 12-12E). They look best if the tops are about ⅟₁₆ inch below the surface level and the front edge is beveled (FIG. 12-13A). Attach with glue and a few pins, punched below the surface and stopped. Miter at the change of bottom width.
- Laminated plastic is less than ⅟₁₆ inch thick, so you do not have to let it in at the back, but if you keep its edge below the top surface of the shelves, it will not show. You could use contact cement, but you will have to use some fine nails as well. Drill for each nail, or the plastic might splinter.
- You can make the drawers by any of the methods described earlier, but dovetails are best. Let plywood bottoms into grooves. If the false fronts are ½ inch thick (FIG. 12-13B), they will finish level with the shelf top and bottom and can overlap the uprights. Fit knobs or handles as desired.
- If you want to carry the countertop shelves around a corner, you could dowel the top and bottom. Ordinary uprights placed not too far from the corner might be sufficient to support the top (FIG. 12-13C), but you can add corner supports.
- At the corner, you could add a square or turned post (FIG. 12-13D). You could also treat the corner with a normal (FIG. 12-13E) or diagonal (FIG. 12-13F) division.

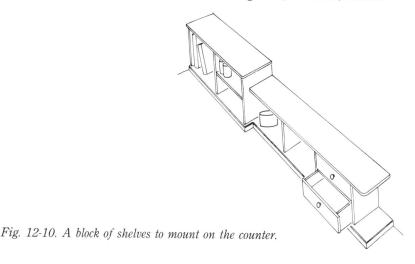

Fig. 12-10. A block of shelves to mount on the counter.

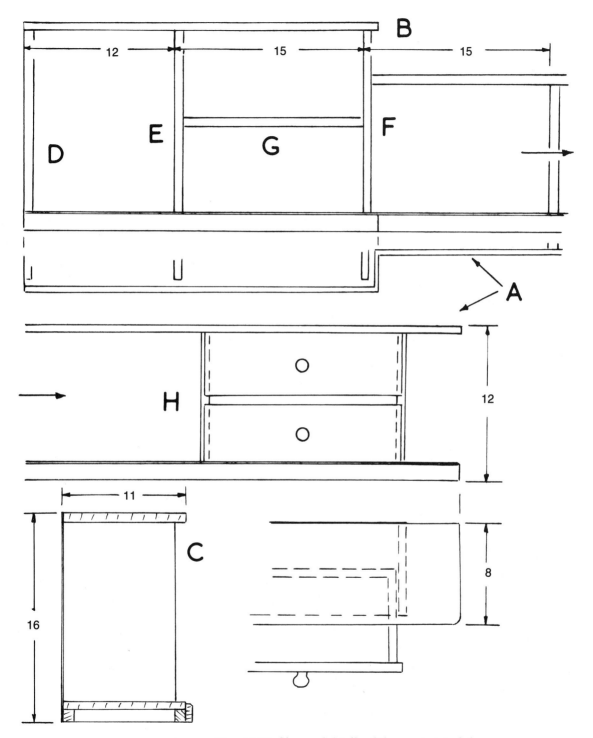

Fig. 12-11. Sizes and details of the countertop shelves.

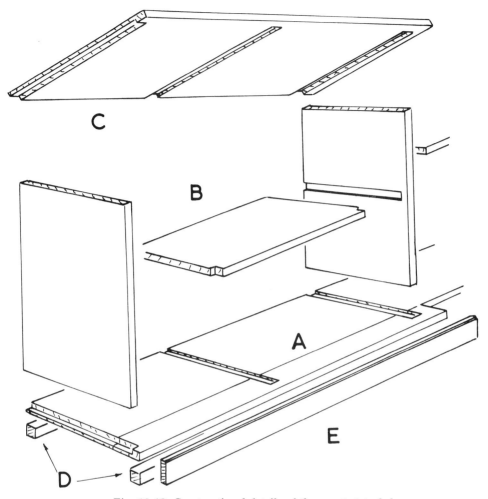

Fig. 12-12. Constructional details of the countertop shelves.

• Stain and polish or paint the shelving before mounting it on the countertop. A few screws downward into the countertop might suffice, but you could drive screws through the back into the wall to keep it close. Put washers under screw heads there.

Materials List for Countertop Shelves

1 bottom	$\frac{1}{2} \times$	8×80
2 bottom supports	$1 \times$	1×80
1 bottom	$\frac{1}{2} \times$	3×30
1 bottom edge	$\frac{1}{2} \times 1\frac{1}{2} \times 30$	
1 bottom edge	$\frac{1}{2} \times 1\frac{1}{2} \times 60$	
1 top	$\frac{1}{2} \times$	11×30
1 top	$\frac{1}{2} \times$	8×54
3 uprights	$\frac{1}{2} \times 10\frac{1}{2} \times 16$	

1 shelf	½ × 10½ × 16
3 uprights	½ × 7½ × 12
1 shelf	½ × 7½ × 16
4 drawer fronts	½ × 5 × 16
2 drawer backs	½ × 4½ × 16
4 drawer sides	½ × 5 × 8
2 drawer bottoms	8 × 16 × ¼ plywood
1 back	16 × 28 laminated plastic
1 back	12 × 50 laminated plastic

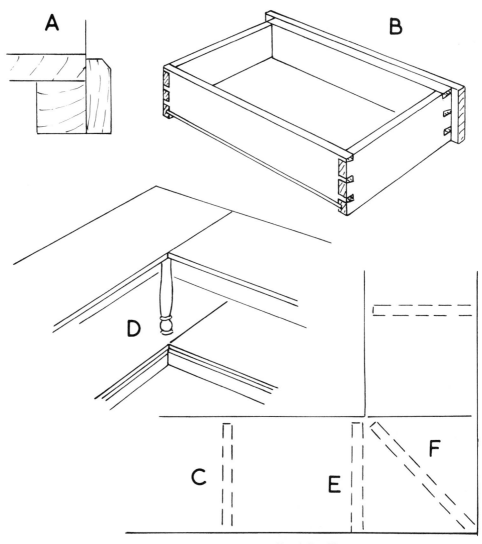

*Fig. 12-13. Base and drawer details (A,B). How to carry
the shelves around a corner (G-F).*

TALL SHELVES

If the base of a block of shelves is on the countertop, you must keep it reasonably narrow so as not to take up too much of the working area. However, if the block is tall, you can make the upper part extend farther out from the wall without interfering with normal food preparation. This is often done with wall cabinets, but you can arrange shelves in the same way.

The block of tall shelves shown in FIG. 12-14 is a self-contained unit, but you could arrange it between cabinets or alongside one cabinet. With its shaping, it would make a good end to a series of cabinets.

The whole unit could be solid-wood, mostly ¾ inch thick, but some parts could be plywood with solid-wood edging. You could make the two sides of solid wood and other parts of lipped plywood. If the sides are plywood, the brackets between the narrow and wide parts would have to be matching solid wood. The top extends over the sides and front and will look best with molding underneath. The vertical divisions are intended to support magazines as well as cookbooks. FIGURE 12-14 shows one drawer, but you could omit this in favor of extra shelving, or you could put a shelf at the bottom of the narrow part.

Check the suggested sizes (FIG. 12-15A) against your available space and to see if the cook will be able to reach everything that will be stored on these shelves. Following are the basic steps of construction:

- Make a pair of sides (FIGS. 12-15B and 12-16A). A piece 7 inches wide goes right through. Glue on a 5-inch piece to make up width, but before adding it, shape the bracket end (FIGS. 12-15C and 12-16B). Rabbet the rear edges to take the plywood back.
- You could fit the horizontal part with dowels, but the drawing shows dado joints (FIG. 12-16C), stopped at the front edges.
- At the top there is a piece across at the front (FIG. 12-15D) and one at the back inside the plywood (FIG. 12-15E). The back piece provides strength for screwing what could be a heavy weight to the wall. You can dowel or tenon these pieces (FIG. 12-16D). Cut the mortises (FIG. 12-16E).
- The shelf at the bottom is notched around the sides and could have a rounded front (FIG. 12-15F). Secure the strip across below with glue, or use dowels.
- The two wide shelves should be the same length as the bottom shelf, but notch them to finish flush with the front edges of the sides (FIG. 12-17A).
- One shelf is plain, but the other has to take the divisions, which could be doweled. They stop ¾ inch from the front edges of the shelf and can be fitted into dado grooves (FIG. 12-17B).
- Make the two strips (FIG. 12-15D, E), with tenons to fit the side mortises.
- Prepare the top. You can use plywood, even if other parts are solid wood, but you will have to cover its edge with half-round molding. How much extension you allow depends on the molding you will fit under it. The diagram assumes that the molding will

Fig. 12-14. A block of tall shelves can rest on the countertop, with the upper part extending farther out from the wall.

be about 1½ inches on the vertical face and 1 inch wide. The top can then overlap 1½ inches at the sides and front.

• The two divisions could have straight front edges, but as shown they are cut away to give easier access to books and magazines (FIG. 12-17C). Make them to fit into the

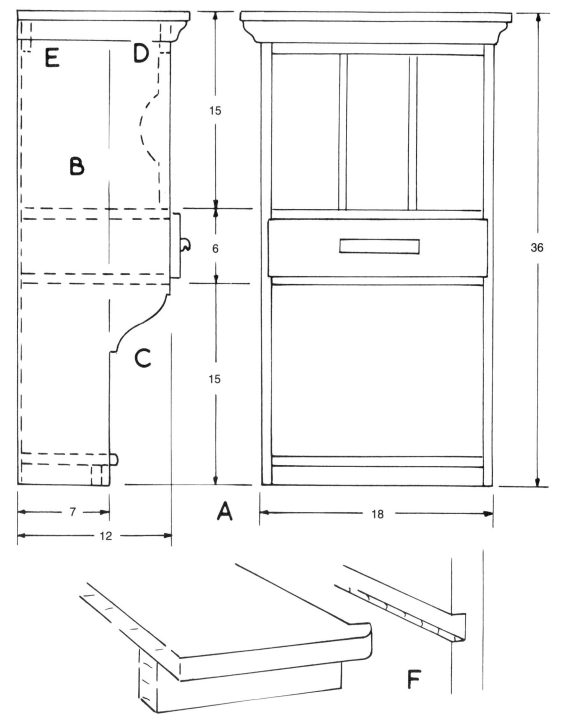

Fig. 12-15. Sizes and details of the tall shelves.

grooves at the bottom. They *could* go into grooves at the top, but it is easier to just screw downward into them.

• Assemble all the crosswise pieces to the sides, except the top. Fit the divisions and glue and nail or screw the back into the rabbets.

• Screw the top onto the framework and the divisions. Add the molding, mitered at the front corners.

• Make the drawer described earlier for the countertop shelves (FIG. 12-13B), but allow the false front to overlap all around to about half the width of the surrounding front edges.

• Try the block of shelves in position. Drill for screws to the wall, then stain and polish or paint the wood before finally fixing the unit in place.

Materials List for Tall Shelves

2 sides	$\frac{3}{4} \times 7 \times 38$
2 sides	$\frac{3}{4} \times 5 \times 28$
1 shelf	$\frac{3}{4} \times 8 \times 20$
1 strip	$\frac{3}{4} \times 1\frac{1}{2} \times 20$
2 shelves	$\frac{3}{4} \times 12 \times 20$
2 top rails	$\frac{3}{4} \times 3 \times 20$
2 divisions	$\frac{5}{8} \times 11 \times 16$
1 back	$18 \times 36 \times \frac{1}{4}$ plywood

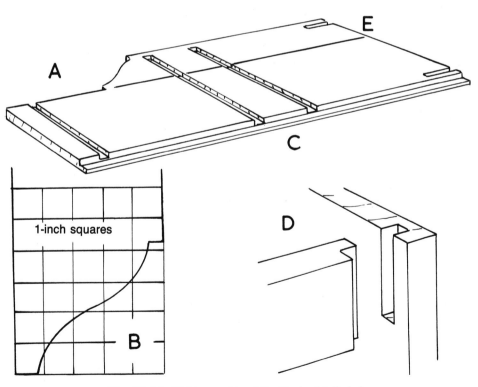

Fig. 12-16. Making a side of the block of tall shelves.

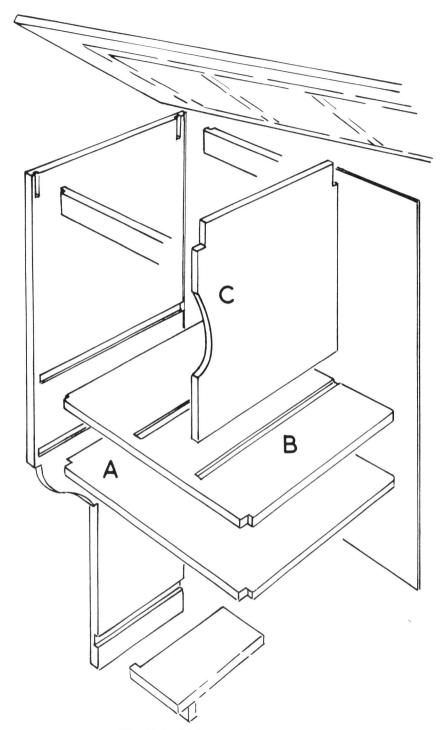

Fig. 12-17. Main parts of the block of tall shelves.

1 top	14 × 22 × ¾
1 molding	1 × 1½ × 22
2 moldings	1 × 1½ × 14
1 drawer front	⅝ × 4½ × 18
1 drawer front	⅝ × 5½ × 18
2 drawer sides	⅝ × 4½ × 13
1 drawer back	⅝ × 4 × 18
1 drawer bottom	13 × 18 × ¼ plywood

WIDE SHELVES

A block of narrow shelves might be satisfactory if left comparatively plain, particularly if there are decorative cabinets or other wall furniture nearby. But if you increase shelves' width, they become a major feature in the decoration of the kitchen. Breaking up the plainness with drawers improves the visual effect and provides storage space as well. Otherwise, the shelves' main decoration might be at the top. For example, a block of

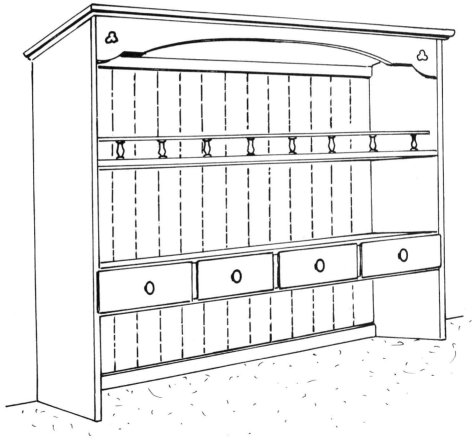

Fig. 12-18. A block of wide shelves with rails, a decorated top, and drawers.

shelves that reached the ceiling could have a molding there. A shaped and pierced piece at the front of the top could also draw attention away from the plainness of the shelves. And a rail on spindles can improve appearance as well as keeping items from falling off the shelf.

This block of wide shelves shown in FIG. 12-18 is a combination of country and modern styles. The sides rest on the countertop, but otherwise it does not interfere with the work space. The shelves could have two or four drawers. Narrow drawers slide better than wide ones, however. As shown, one shelf has a rail supported on spindles. A shaped and pierced board comes under an overhanging top. The back could be plywood, but it is shown as tongue-and-grooved boards. In general the effect is very similar to the upper part of a Welsh dresser.

Solid wood throughout is recommended, but you could use plywood with solid wood lips matching the surface veneers. For straight parts you could use particleboard with wood veneer surfaces and edges, but you could not edge it for the decorative shaped front shown in the illustration. The tongue-and-grooved wood for the back does not have to be of the same wood as the other parts, but you could stain it to match. If you buy the material already prepared, get the thinnest and narrowest boards available; ½-inch-×-4-inch pieces would be fine. Thicker pieces would work, but they would entail deeper rabbets in the sides and slightly narrower shelves. You also might be able to get plywood patterned to look like narrow boards. Following are the basic steps of construction:

- Prepare the wood for the pair of sides. Cut rabbets to suit the tongue-and-grooved or plywood back (FIG. 12-20A).
- The shelves are let into stopped dado grooves (FIG. 12-20B).
- At the top there is a mortise for a rail that supports the back (FIG. 12-20C) and a similar one at the bottom. You could tenon the front board, but it is easier and just as satisfactory to use dowels (FIG. 12-20D).
- Mark the position of the end of the shelf rail (FIG. 12-19A), but do not cut a mortise there until you have prepared the rails and tenons.
- Mark and cut the three shelves (FIG. 12-19B) to the same size to fit the grooves. You will have to prepare the two lower ones to take the drawer dividers. For two drawers there can be just one divider at the center, but you will need three dividers for four drawers (FIG. 12-20E). The grain of the dividers should be upright. You could dowel them, but they are shown with dado joints.
- Make the top and bottom strips (FIGS. 12-19C, D) the same length between shoulders as the shelves. Bevel the exposed edges.
- Shape the front piece at the top, as you please; FIG. 12-19E shows a suggested outline. The piercing is made with three overlapping holes. If possible, use a Forstner bit to get clean holes. Clean the shaped edge of the board of saw marks and round off the angular section. Prepare it and the sides for dowels.

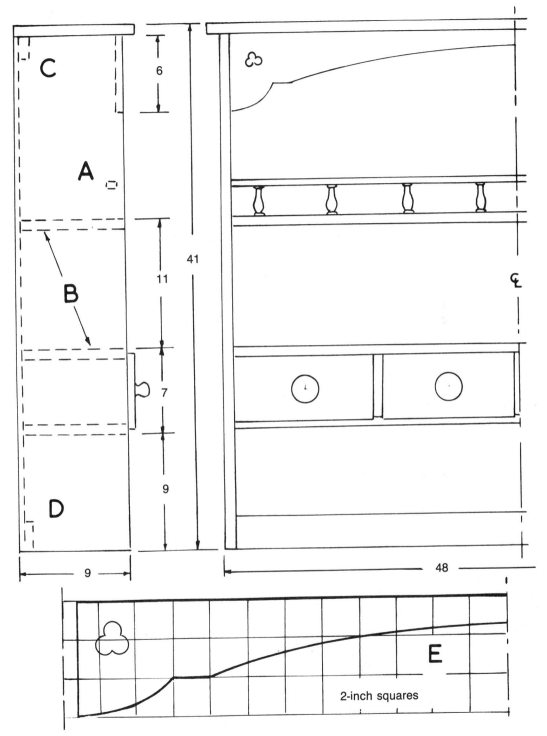

Fig. 12-19. Sizes of the block of wide shelves.

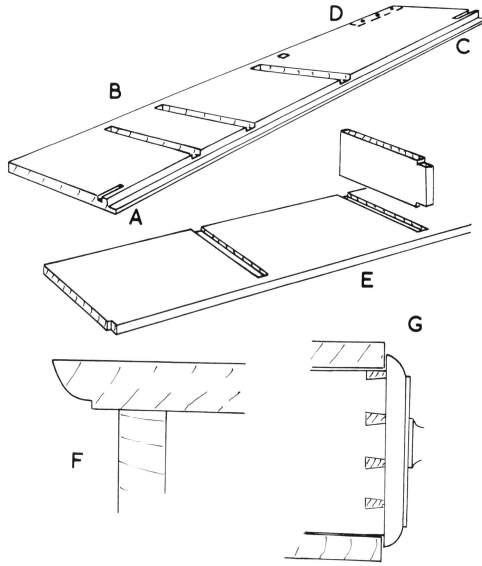

Fig. 12-20. Construction of the block of wide shelves.

• If you wish to add a rail and spindles to the top shelf, prepare the wood for the rail and turn sufficient spindles (FIGS. 12-9C-E). Cut mortises in the sides to match the tenons. If you use straight-grained hardwood and space spindles not more than 6 inches apart, the rail should be stiff enough, but make it a little larger if you think it necessary. Rounding the larger section well reduces its clumsy appearance.

• Assemble the drawer dividers to their shelves. Join all the crosswise pieces to the sides. Put the assembly front down on a flat surface. Compare diagonals to check squareness, and sight across the sides to see that there is no twisting.

• Attach the tongue-and-grooved boards at the back, with nails or screws. Do not force them too tightly together as a little slackness will allow for expansion and contraction. With narrow boards, one nail or screw central in the board at each crossing should be enough and will allow for changes in width without risk of splitting.

• The top overlaps about 1 inch at the sides and front. It could be plain, but a molded edge is more attractive (FIG. 12-20F).

• Make the drawers as described earlier for the countertop shelves (FIG. 12-13B), but allow the false fronts to overlap the surrounding wood to about half the thickness of the edges. You could make drawer fronts to match others in the kitchen or give them molded edges, preferably matching the molding on the block top (FIG. 12-20G). Fit suitable knobs or handles.

• Drill the top and bottom back rails for screws to the wall. There should be no need for any attachment to the countertop.

Materials List for Wide Shelves

2 sides	¾ × 9 × 42
3 shelves	¾ × 9 × 48
2 rails	¾ × 3 × 48
1 top rail	¾ × 6 × 48
3 drawer dividers	¾ × 9 × 7
1 top	¾ × 10 × 52
1 rail	⅝ × 1 × 48
8 spindles	¾ × ¾ × 4
1 back	41 × 48 tongue-and-grooved boards
4 drawer fronts	⅝ × 6 × 13
4 drawer fronts	⅝ × 7 × 13
8 drawer sides	⅝ × 6 × 10
4 drawer backs	⅝ × 6 × 13
4 drawer bottoms	9 × 13 × ¼ plywood

SPINDLE-SUPPORTED SHELVES

Turned wood parts always add a decorative feature to an otherwise plain design. They tend to look lighter than plain square parts and give an open feeling to an assembly. Used between shelves, they provide an open effect on units that would otherwise need solid ends or brackets. Such shelves can suit bathroom or kitchen. In a compact bathroom, shelves with spindles give a more spacious feeling than shelves that are more boxed in.

The shelves shown in FIG. 12-21 have brackets under the bottom shelf and turned spindles to support the other. As shown, the brackets could also carry a rail for towels.

The back could be plywood with a suitable face veneer, but you might want to paint edges black to hide the plies, or frame around the back with solid wood. If you cannot turn your own spindles, you can buy suitable ones with square ends; they are intended to be used for making stools. The square ends allow you to cut the parts to length within quite a wide range. Following are the basic steps of construction:

• Make the three shelves (FIG. 12-22A) with rounded front corners and edges. Mark the positions of the brackets and posts.
• Cut back the plywood carefully to avoid splintering. Round the corners and sand the edges. Mark the positions of the shelves. The lower gap is 1 inch larger than the top gap, to provide a balanced appearance.
• Mark out the two brackets (FIG. 12-23A) with the grain diagonal. Mark the hole position if you wish to fit a rail.

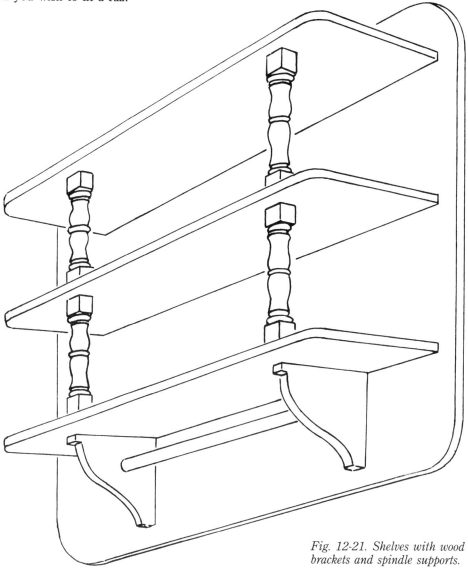

Fig. 12-21. Shelves with wood brackets and spindle supports.

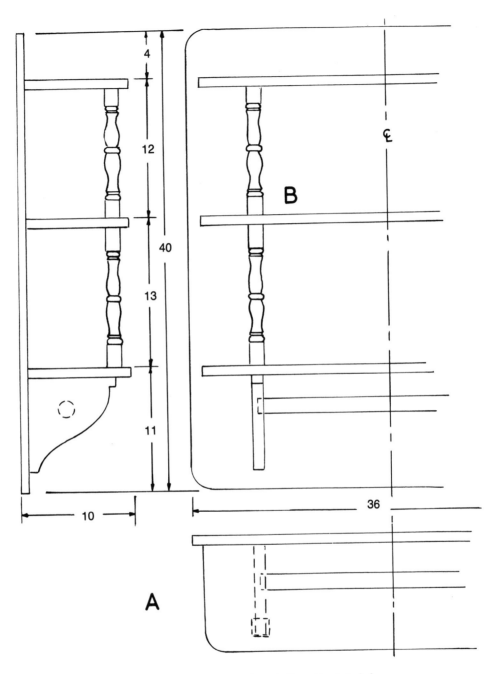

Fig. 12-22. Sizes of the spindle-supported shelves.

• Make sure that the wood edges of the bracket are square. Remove saw marks from the front edges.

• The spindles all have turned parts the same size (FIG. 12-23B), but those in the lower space are 1 inch longer overall. Turn the set of four spindles with some excess left at the ends.

• Mark out the mortises on the shelves and the tenons on the spindles (FIG. 12-23C). At the middle shelf (FIG. 12-22B) the mortise goes through and the tenons enter from opposite sides, so their length should be less than half the thickness. At the top and bottom shelves, the mortises do not go through, so cut the tenons to suit.

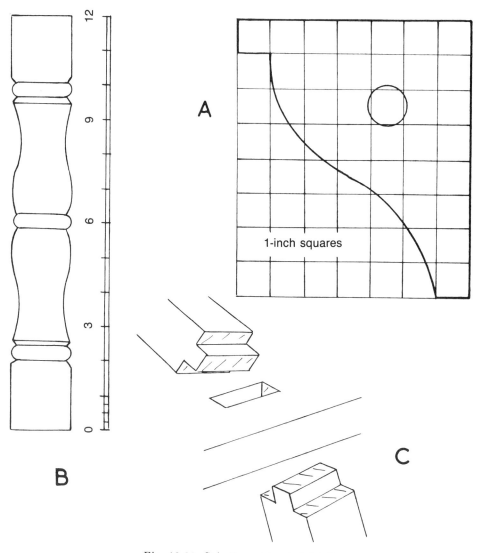

Fig. 12-23. Spindle and bracket details.

- To ensure squareness, start assembly at the bottom. Join the bottom shelf to the back with glue and screws. Position the brackets and fit them with glue and screws through the back. One screw driven downward through the shelf into each bracket, just behind the spindle position should suffice. You could counterbore and plug the hole if you do not want the screw head to show. Include the towel rail, which could be a piece of 1-inch dowel rod or plated metal tube, in holes drilled about halfway through each bracket.
- Add the next shelf with screws through the back, and position the two spindles as you assemble. Do the same with the top shelf.
- Two screws through the back above the top shelf will hang the assembly, but another screw lower down will keep the back close to the wall.

Materials List for Spindle-supported Shelves

3 shelves	¾ × 9½ × 36
2 brackets	1 × 7 × 12
4 spindles	1¾ × 1¾ × 14
1 back	36 × 40 × ¾ plywood
1 rail	30 × 1 round

PLATE RACK

At one time, kitchens of large houses had extensive plate racks, where plates stood on edge and were separated by vertical rods. Few modern kitchens have space for so extensive a rack, but you might like to include a small plate rack in your wall shelves and cabinets.

The rack shown in FIG. 12-24 has two levels and is an independent unit, but you could adapt the design to fit between cabinets or other blocks of shelves, particularly in a country-style kitchen. The sizes shown in FIG. 12-25A will suit the largest dining plates, but you could fit smaller plates in as well, perhaps two or more to a compartment.

You could use softwood for the rack, but a light-colored hardwood would be better. The rods are common dowel rods. Traditional plate racks were bare wood, but you could finish your rack with clear varnish or lacquer. Suggested construction is with dowels, although you could use mortise-and-tenon or dado joints for some parts. Following are the basic steps of construction:

- Make the pair of sides (FIG. 12-25A). The top will be doweled or screwed on, but you could dowel the two pairs of rails that support the plates with ½-inch dowels (FIG. 12-25B). There is a wider piece toward the back for clearance, arranged to provide a 7-inch gap (FIG. 12-25C). This suits plates from 9 to 12 inches in diameter. Gaps between the rows of vertical rods are about 8½ inches. Adjust this if you want to fit plates of very different sizes.
- You can leave the back of the rack left open to the wall or rabbet the sides to take ¼-inch plywood.
- Drill all lengthwise pieces together and mark their direction so they will not be turned

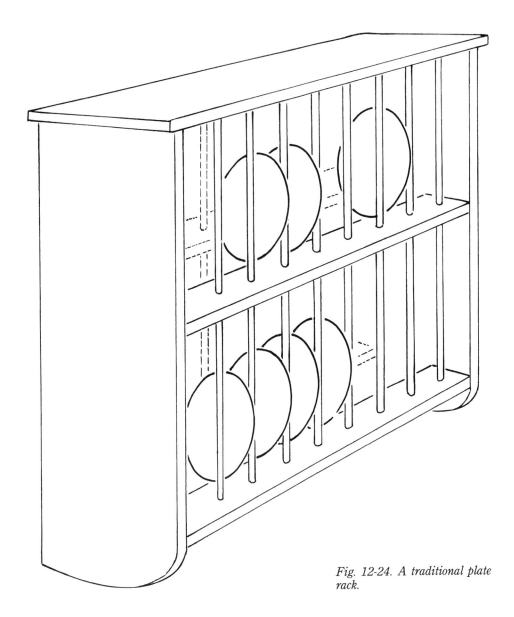

Fig. 12-24. *A traditional plate rack.*

around during assembly. Mark one and clamp all four together, then drill on a press or by some other means that will ensure squareness.

• Holes are needed in the top to take the ends of the vertical rods. Cut the top to overhang 1 inch at the sides and front. Rabbet the rear edge if you are fitting a plywood back. Use one of the strips to mark and act as a drilling guide for the top holes, which should only go halfway through the wood.

• Make a strip under the upper rear rail (FIGS. 12-25D, E) for screwing to the wall. Put another under the top if you think it necessary.

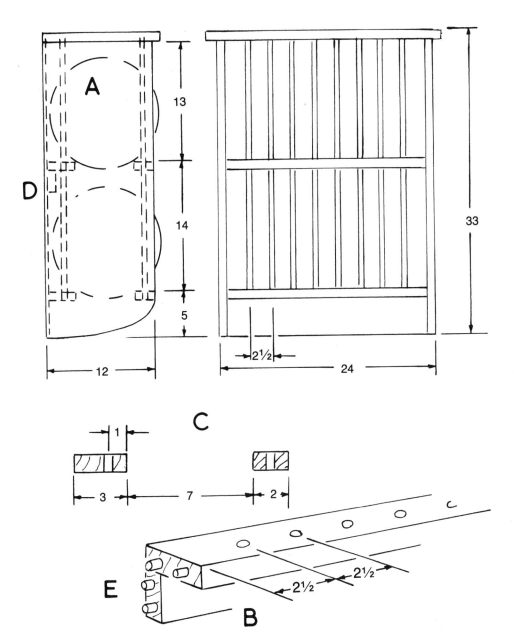

Fig. 12-25. Suggested sizes and details for the plate rack.

- Assemble the strips with their dowels to the sides. Add the top and the back.
- Stand the unit upside-down, so you can insert the rods via the bottom rails. Insert the rear ones in first. To avoid getting glue where it is not wanted, pass a rod through until it is ready to go into the top. Put a little glue in the top hole and smear a little on the part of the rod that is about to go into the hole in the bottom rail. You should

not need any glue where the rod goes through the upper rail. Wipe off excess glue as you fit each rod.

• Do a complete row in this way, then cut off any surplus rods extending below the bottom rail. Repeat the procedure with the front row of vertical rods.

Materials List for Plate Rack

2 sides	¾ ×	12 × 34
1 top	¾ ×	13 × 28
1 back	28 ×	34 × ¼ plywood
2 rails	1 ×	2 × 26
3 rails	1 ×	3 × 24
16 rods	30 × ½ diameter	

13

Basic Hanging Wall Cabinets

To be most easily noticed, items should be displayed at or near eye level. That applies to goods on store shelves as well as to food and equipment in a kitchen. These things are more visible and accessible at eye level than in cupboards under the counter or in drawers. This idea applies even more to bathrooms because space limitations cause most items to be stored low and out of reach.

Cabinets on the wall must have their bottoms high enough above any working surface to provide ample clearance. They can then go as high as the ceiling, but that will put the upper parts out of reach or require a step stool. The amount such cabinets project from the wall is determined in part by the need to avoid interfering with the counter surface below. Carefully weigh these needs when you plan the capacity of your wall cabinets.

In a bathroom a projection of only a few inches may serve for a medicine cabinet. In a kitchen you can provide a projection of 7 to 12 inches, or a little more if the bottom of the cabinet is higher. As you plan, consider clearances. When bending forward, will the cook bump into cabinet? Will swinging doors have enough clearance or will they be a nuisance when open?

If you have a series of cabinets under a countertop, it makes sense to match them with a series of hanging cabinets or cupboards on the wall. The appearance of the hanging cabinets should complement the lower cabinets. As the former more prominent, regard them as the leaders in the overall planning of your kitchen. Chapter 14 deals with the arrangement of multiple wall cabinets, but here we consider simpler individual hanging cabinets, which might form the basis of more complex cupboard assemblies.

When planning and making these cabinets, remember their location and visual impact. You will be looking mostly level or upward, so you will see their undersides, which would be hidden in floor cabinets. So avoid such things as putting the shelves on cleats, which are acceptable lower down but are unattractive when in full view. Instead use dado joints or dowels. On the other hand, the tops of these cabinets will usually be out of view, so they do not need a special finish. If you use a plywood back, you do not need to let it into a rabbet in the top. It can lap over the rear edge of the top, as its edge will not show. If you plan pierced or shaped decoration, consider the angle of view. Saw marks that would not matter when you look down would appear ugly as you look up.

As for doors, consider ones that slide and stay out of the way. Glass sliding doors look attractive if positioned between solid doors. If you use wide swinging doors, arrange for them to go all the way back rather than stay square to the front when open, to reduce the hazard and nuisance of a door at 90 degrees. Double doors might be a better choice, as the amount of projection is halved.

SINGLE CUPBOARD

A small single hanging cabinet presents a basic method of construction that applies to other assemblies. The cupboard shown in FIG. 13-1 would suit either a bathroom or a

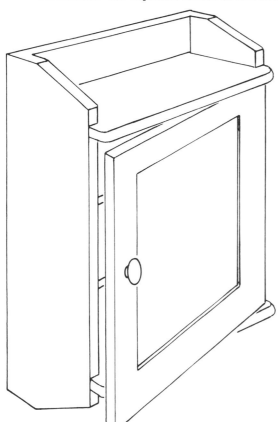

Fig. 13-1. A single hanging cupboard suitable as a medicine cabinet.

kitchen. As shown, it is plain, but you could shape the ends and make the door in a different design. The door is shown with a plywood panel, but you might prefer a mirror.

The diagrams (FIGS. 13-2 and 13-3) allow for using softwood and finishing the unit with paint. The back has solid parts for strength and for screwing to the wall. The unit has two shelves, but you can adapt internal arrangements to your needs. Following are the basic steps of construction:

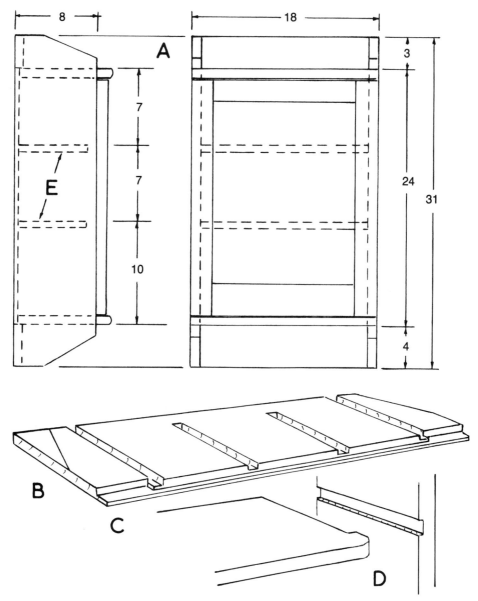

Fig. 13-2. Sizes and construction of the single hanging cupboard.

- Start with the pair of sides (FIGS. 13-2B and 13-3A). Cut a rabbet the full length to suit the plywood back. Cut grooves all the way across for the top and bottom. Cut stopped grooves for the shelves. At the top and bottom, increase the width of the rabbet to take the solid wood backs above and below the end grooves (FIG. 13-2C).
- The top and bottom (FIG. 13-3B) project at the front enough to overhang the door and

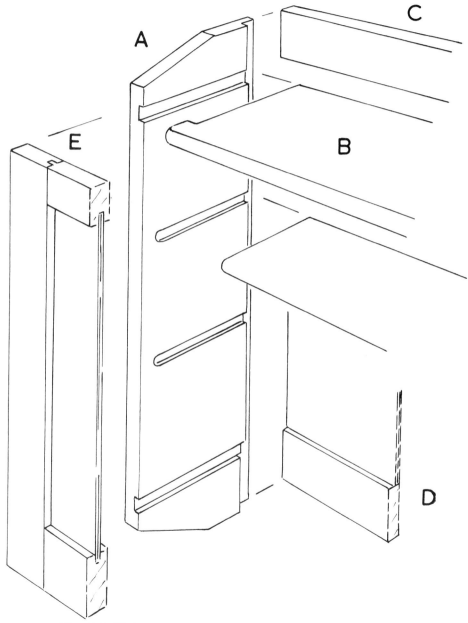

Fig. 13-3. Fitting together the parts of the single hanging cupboard.

an additional ¼ inch for a rounded edge. Cut the corner to fit over the end of the groove (FIG. 13-2D).

• Make the shelves to fit their grooves (FIG. 13-2E). You can round the front edges if desired.

• Make the top and bottom solid backs (FIGS. 13-3C, D). They are shown straight, but the exposed edges could be shaped.

• Have the plywood back ready. Assemble the top, bottom, and shelves to the sides. Check squareness and fit the top and bottom back strips with screws into the sides. You can use one or more screws through the top and bottom into the back pieces. Fit the plywood back with glue and screws or nails.

• Make a framed door (FIG. 13-3E) to fit easily between the top and bottom and with a width to match the overall width of the cabinet. Let in hinges, preferably brass, at one side. Provide a spring or magnetic catch at the other side, and fit a knob.

• It should be sufficient to drill for two widely spaced screws at the top and one centrally at the bottom. Paint the cabinet before hanging it.

Materials List for Single Cupboard

2 sides	¾ × 8 × 33
1 top	¾ × 9 × 18
1 bottom	¾ × 9 × 18
2 shelves	½ × 7 × 18
1 back	¾ × 3 × 18
1 back	¾ × 4 × 18
1 back	18 × 25 × ¼ plywood

SMALL MIRROR CABINET

You cannot have too many mirrors in a bathroom, and at least one would be welcome in a kitchen. An obvious place to add one is on the front of a cabinet. The cabinet shown in FIG. 13-4 is small, with a mirror over the whole door, held there with metal clips. You could hinge the door as in the preceding section, but pivoting it on screws is preferable.

It might be advisable to start with the mirror. You could get a standard size mirror and arrange the other sizes to fit around it. (FIG. 13-5 serves as a general guide to sizes). Get the metal clips from the mirror supplier. They are plated and bent to fit over the edge of the mirror and be screwed to the wood door (FIG. 13-5A). You could make them from strip brass, but the purchased, plated ones look better. Following are the basic steps of construction the small mirror cabinet:

• The door is best made of ⅝-inch or ¾-inch hardwood plywood. Most of this material is made with thinner plies than fir plywood and is therefore stronger where it has to be drilled for screw pivots. Make the door to the size of the mirror. At the opening edge, cut a finger grip about 3 inches long (FIG. 13-6A).

• Rabbet the rear edges of the pieces to make the case. The back can be thin plywood or tempered hardboard. The top and bottom are wide enough to extend over the door.

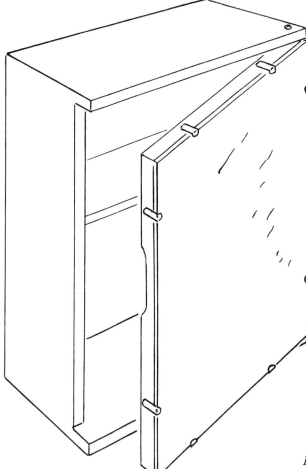

Fig. 13-4. A small cabinet with a mirror-fronted door.

• If you are using screw pivots, bevel the pivoting to give clearance as the door swings open (FIG. 13-5B). The other side has a square edge.

• Dovetails are best for the corner joints (FIG. 13-6B), but if you will be using a painted finish, rabbeted and nailed joints are simple and inconspicuous (FIG. 13-6C).

• Make the shelf and cut grooves in the sides for it.

• Assemble the case, with its plywood back to hold it square.

• The door should have a little clearance at top and bottom and be the same width as the overall width of the case.

• Mark and drill the top and bottom for the pivot screws (FIG. 13-5C). The screws need not be thicker than #6 gauge. Put the door in position and use these holes as guides to mark the position of the holes in the door. Drill undersize holes in the door. Put washers under the screw heads. Fit a catch at the other side of the door.

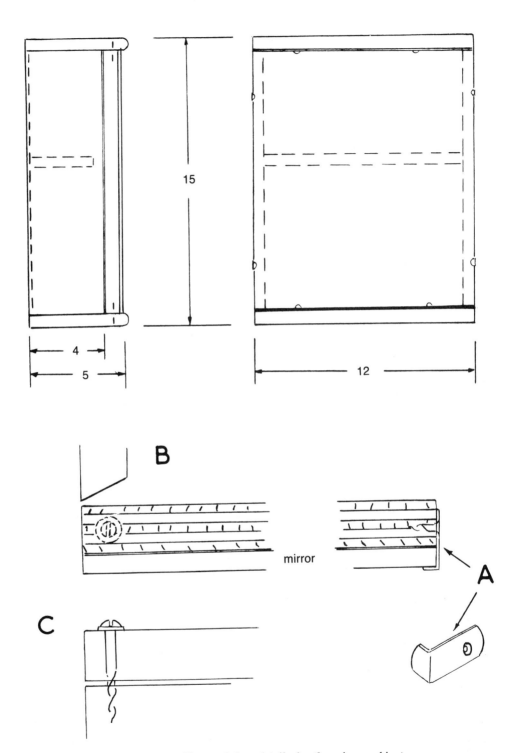

Fig. 13-5. Sizes and door details for the mirror cabinet.

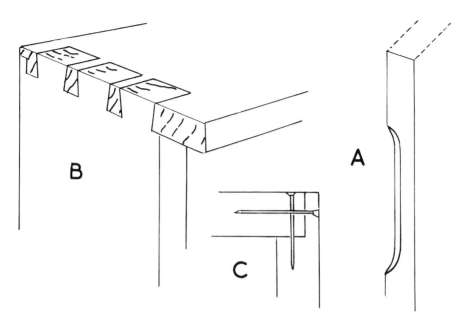

Fig. 13-6. Corner joints and door-pull details for the mirror cabinet.

• After a trial assembly, separate the parts and finish the wood with paint or stain and polish. Then mount the mirror on the door, pivot the door, and screw the cabinet to the wall.

Materials List for Small Mirror Cabinet

1 door	12 × 14 × ¾ plywood
2 sides	⅝ × 4 × 15
1 top	⅝ × 5 × 13
1 bottom	⅝ × 5 × 13
1 shelf	½ × 3½ × 13
1 back	12 × 14 × ¼ plywood

MATCHING CABINET

If the room has a pattern of cabinets with matching fronts under the counter, some of the cabinets attached to the wall above should match. You could have a series of cabinets along the wall—as described in Chapter 14—to carry the overall pattern, but if there is no reason to do otherwise, you could simply make an individual cupboard or cabinet to match.

The cabinet shown in FIG. 13-7 is made similar to the lower cabinets and can have doors of the same pattern. As shown, it has extending shelves, which can be at one or both ends. Internal shelves are shown, but you could arrange the inside to suit your needs. You could even include some of the cook's tool fittings described later in this chapter.

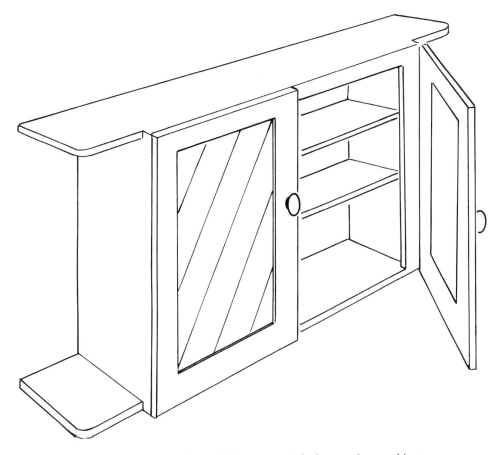

Fig. 13-7. A wall cabinet with doors to match those on lower cabinets.

Sizes can match existing cabinets or your available wall space, but the cabinet shown in FIG. 13-8A is a useful size and has double doors. A narrower version could have a single door, but if you plan to put a single door on a wide cabinet, make sure that there is space for it to open without becoming an obstruction.

Construction of this cabinet is straightforward. The sides have dado joints to the top. You could reinforce them with screws driven downward, as their heads will not be visible from a normal position. The joints at the bottom could be the same, but it would be better to use wedged tenons to resist any downward loads on the bottom. Following are the basic steps of construction:

• Mark out and cut the pair of sides (FIGS. 13-8B and 13-9A). Allow a little extra length on the tenons at this stage.

• Mark out the top and bottom together, to get the key sizes the same, but the top must have dado grooves (FIGS. 13-8C and 13-9B) whereas the bottom has mortises (FIGS. 13-8D and 13-9C). Cut the joints before rounding the corners.

- The simplest way to fit the back is to nail it on. It could then extend to the ends of the shelves (FIG. 13-9D). If you prefer not to have the back extending behind the outside shelves, rabbet the sides for it and cut back the top and bottom rear edges for the plywood to overlap (FIGS. 13-8E and 13-9E).
- The inside shelves (FIG. 13-9F) fit into stopped grooves.
- Have the plywood back ready. Assemble the parts and use the back to keep the assembly square. At the top, drive at least two screws downward into each joint. At

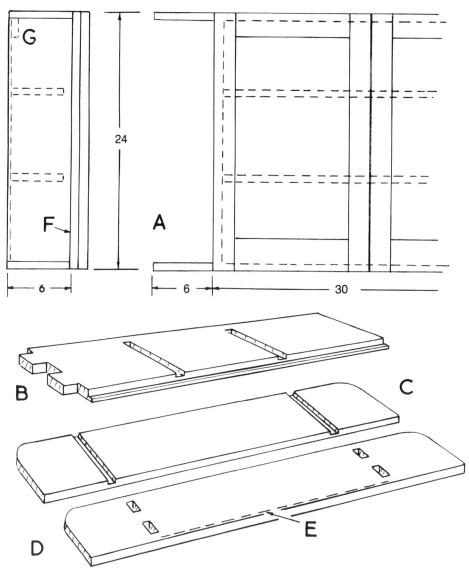

Fig. 13-8. Sizes and details of parts of the matching cabinet.

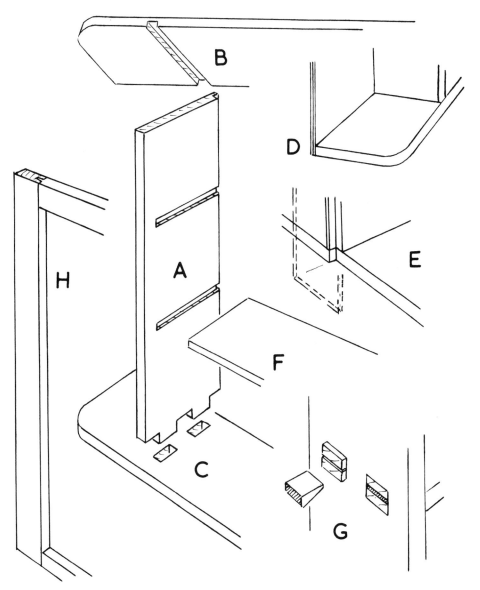

Fig. 13-9. Main parts of the matching cabinet.

the bottom, put saw cuts in the tenons. After gluing, drive wedges into the saw cuts (FIG. 13-9G) and cut the ends off level.

• Make a front frame (FIGS. 13-8F and 13-9H) as for the lower cabinets, but you could make this one thinner. Stub tenons will keep the parts level. Fit the frame in place.

• Make the doors in the same way as you did those below the counter. If you want to use ordinary hinges and the doors are to swing all the way back, the front frame should be as thick as the doors, to provide clearance in front of the extending shelves. Hinges of the throw-clear type will automatically provide enough clearance, even if the frame is thinner.

• Fit handles or knobs to the doors and arrange catches at the inside of the top and bottom.

• If the plywood used for the back does not seem strong enough to take the weight of screwing to the wall, put a strip across under the top (FIG. 13-8G) and screw through that to take the weight. Drive one or two more screws lower down to hold the cabinet close to the wall.

Materials List for Matching Cabinet

2 sides	$\frac{3}{4} \times 6 \times 26$
1 top	$\frac{3}{4} \times 6 \times 44$
1 bottom	$\frac{3}{4} \times 6 \times 44$
2 shelves	$\frac{5}{8} \times 5 \times 31$
1 back	$24 \times 30 \times \frac{1}{4}$ plywood
1 back strip	$\frac{3}{4} \times 3 \times 31$
4 front frames	$\frac{5}{8} \times 2 \times 26$
2 front frames	$\frac{5}{8} \times 2 \times 16$
2 front frames	$\frac{5}{8} \times 1 \times 16$
Doors to suit	

COOK'S TOOL CABINET

Cooks who take their work seriously accumulate a large number of tools. Some may be stored quite satisfactorily in a drawer, but others need more careful storage as they could be damaged by close contact with other tools. This is particularly true of knives, which need to be sharp to do their job. Tossing them all together in a drawer or tray will soon blunt them. Moreover, this storage method increases the risk that someone will cut himself looking for a certain knife.

Knives should be stored individually. You can get knife blocks that stand on the countertop, but these blocks can get in the way. A better solution is a rack, with individual slots, located away from the worktop. Better still, you could build a cabinet for the rack and include storage space for other tools.

The tool cabinet shown in FIG. 13-10 has a knife rack that can be tilted forward for easy storage and removal. The blades are protected, but you can see them through a transparent plastic front. Whatever else goes in the cabinet is up to the cook, but there is space for many hanging tools inside the door. You can use spring clips (preferably plated or covered with plastic) for some tools, while others can hang outside the cabinet.

FIGURE 13-11A shows suggested sizes, which you can adapt when you have sorted and measured the tools to be stored. The cabinet could be much bigger than shown, with double doors. Increasing its depth would allow you to fit drawers or trays. A rail below the bottom could take several hanging tools, or you could it for a towel (FIG. 13-11B). If your main concern is the safe storage of knives, count and measure them first. Allow for one or two spare slots. Based on information you can settle the sizes of the unit. Following are the basic steps of construction:

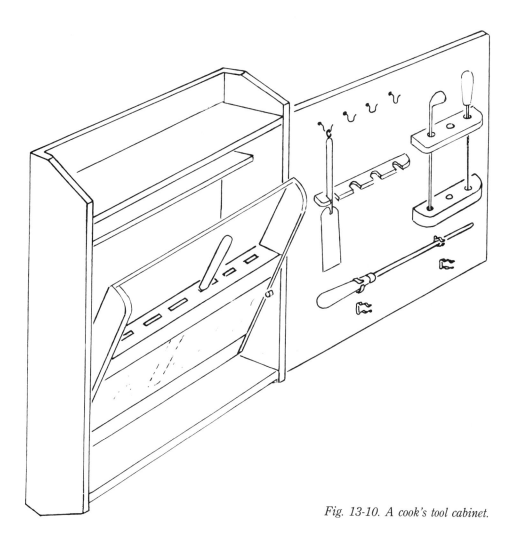

Fig. 13-10. A cook's tool cabinet.

• Start with the knife rack. Use close-grained hardwood for the thick pieces. The back could be plywood. There is no need to make slots to fit knife blades closely; you might be able to decide on one or perhaps two, slot sizes that will serve all knives. In FIG. 13-12A all slots are ¼ inch wide. Slot length should be slightly more than the width of the largest blade. The rack shown takes blades up to 9 inches long with handles up to 6 inches long (FIG. 13-12B).

• You could cut slots through a solid block, but it is easier to get accurate results by using two parts. The diagram shows a flat back piece (FIG. 13-12C) glued to a front piece in which the slots are cut (FIG. 13-12D).

• The bottom block (FIG. 13-12E) is solid. Cut rabbets in both pieces to take ⅛-inch plexiglass or similar transparent plastic.

• Put uprights across the ends, and close the back with plywood.

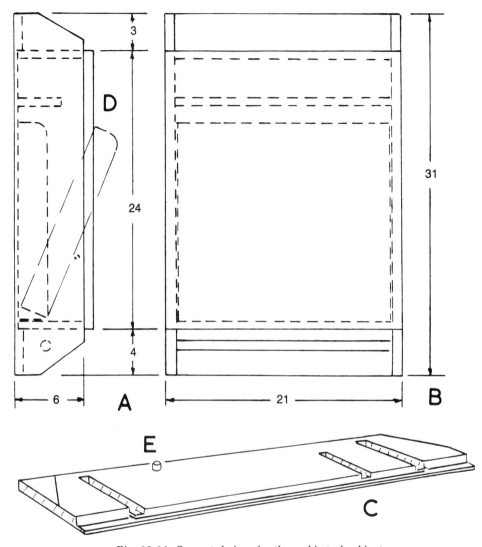

Fig. 13-11. Suggested sizes for the cook's tool cabinet.

• The cabinet is made very much like the single cupboard discussed earlier in this chapter (FIG. 13-2). Refer to those instructions for details. Use the knife rack as a guide to internal sizes.

• Mark out a pair of sides (FIG. 13-11C), with rabbets at the rear edge for plywood and widening parts for solid pieces at the top and bottom. Cut stopped grooves for the cabinet top and bottom and for a shelf, if you wish to fit one.

• Make the cabinet top and bottom with notches to fit the stopped grooves. Make the shelf the same length. Cut the solid back strips.

• Try the knife rack against one side before assembly, and decide how much you want

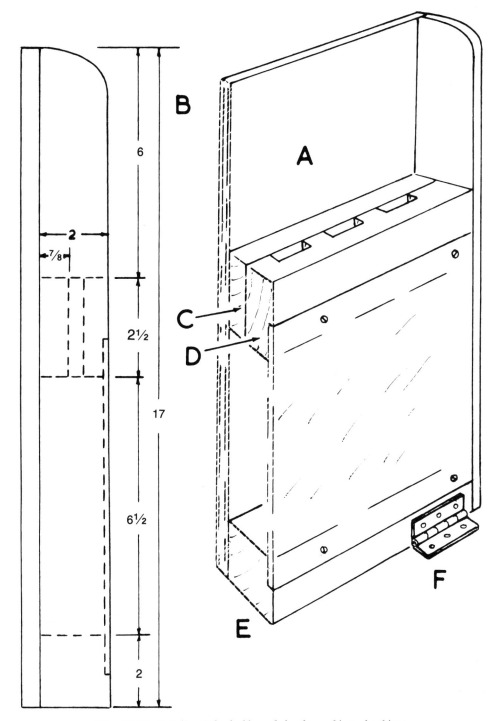

Fig. 13-12. *Details of the knife rack in the cook's tool cabinet.*

it to tilt forward (FIG. 13-11D). Based on this test, position a short ½-inch dowel on each side to act as stops (FIG. 13-11E).

- Have the plywood back ready, then assemble all the parts of the cabinet made so far.
- Make the door from thick plywood, with solid wood lips all around (FIG. 13-13A).
- FIGURE 13-13 suggests ways of hanging cooks' tools. Several will hang on hooks, but you could add a notched strip lower down to limit their swaying when the door is moved (FIG. 13-13B).
- Some tools can pass through holes and their ends rest in other holes drilled only partly through another block (FIG. 13-13C). Some tools are better held with spring clips (FIG. 13-13D). Try laying the tools on the door (lain flat) to get the best arrangement.
- Fit the knife rack with hinges on its front edge (FIG. 13-12F). The rack's own weight will keep it upright, and you can pull it forward by gripping its edge or a knife. Hinge the door at one side, fit a catch at the other side, and add a handle.

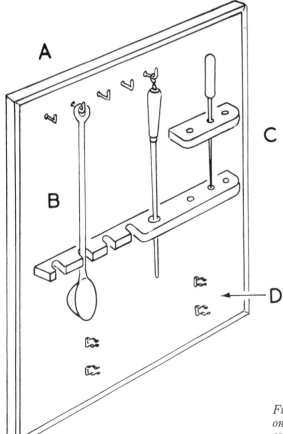

Fig. 13-13. A sample arrangement of tools on the inside of the door of the cook's tool cabinet.

Materials List for Cook's Tool Cabinet

1 knife rack	$\frac{7}{8} \times 2\frac{1}{2} \times 21$
1 knife rack	$1\frac{1}{8} \times 2\frac{1}{2} \times 21$
1 knife rack bottom	$2 \times 2 \times 21$
2 knife rack ends	$\frac{1}{2} \times 2 \times 19$
1 knife rack back	$17 \times 21 \times \frac{1}{2}$ plywood
2 cabinet sides	$\frac{3}{4} \times \quad \times 23$
1 cabinet top	$\frac{3}{4} \times 6 \times 23$
1 cabinet bottom	$\frac{3}{4} \times 6 \times 23$
1 shelf	$\frac{5}{8} \times 5 \times 23$
1 back	$21 \times 24 \times \frac{1}{4}$ plywood
1 back	$\frac{3}{4} \times 3 \times 3$
1 back	$\frac{3}{4} \times 4 \times 23$
1 door	$21 \times 25 \times \frac{3}{4}$ or 1 plywood
4 door edgings	$\frac{1}{2} \times 1 \times 26$

CORNER CUPBOARD

A cupboard with a door fit diagonally across a corner fills a gap attractively and provides storage space in either a kitchen or bathroom, but the actual storage space inside is not as great as might be expected. Making it simply a triangular shape provides minimal capacity. It should have sides square to the wall. The more they project, the more the capacity—but the smaller the door width. You have to compromise.

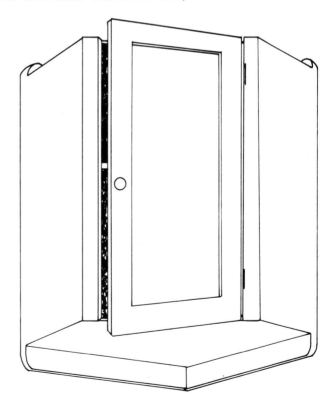

Fig. 13-14. A small corner cupboard.

The cupboard shown in FIG. 13-14 has reasonable proportions. As shown in FIG. 13-15A, it has narrow projections and a fairly wide door (about 12 inches). If you increase the projections, the area inside increases but the door gets narrower.

Before starting construction, measure the angle of the corner of the room in which the cupboard will hang. If you make the cupboard 90 degrees and the corner is a few degrees more than that, you will not be able to fit the cupboard closely to both walls and there will be at least one unsightly gap. And if the corner angle is a few degrees *less* than 90 degrees, you can get a better-looking fit at the front, but there will be gaps to the rear. To deal with an error in the corner, set an adjustable bevel to the actual angle and use that instead of a square when marking out shelves and other parts that should match the angle of the corner.

The parts against the wall extend above and below the cupboard. This allows the top and bottom to fit into grooves in the same way as shelves, and thus simplifies construction. The door fits flush between the sides. In some corner cupboards or cabinets, the door hinges directly to the pieces projecting from the wall, but the acute angle beside the door provides a weak fastening for the hinge screws. It is better to miter narrow strips, so the hinges are square on both surfaces (FIG. 13-15B).

You can use any wood, but a good hardwood looks best. Most parts could be plywood or veneered particleboard, with exposed edges lipped. It is difficult to cut good dado joints in plywood and almost impossible in particleboard, so for those materials join-in the top, bottom, and shelf with dowels. If you use solid wood, have the grain of the top, bottom, and shelf diagonal to the corner. Following are the basic steps of construction:

• This job is easier with a full-size section drawing. Draw it on scrap plywood (FIG. 13-16A), using the actual angle of the room corner. At the point, you can lap one piece on the other and screw them, but a rabbet is shown (FIG. 13-16B).
• Mark out the two broad sides (FIG. 13-15C). Allow for the difference in width due to the overlap at the point, so the cupboard extends the same amount along each wall. What you do at the top and bottom depends on anything the cupboard needs to match. You could shape (FIG. 13-15D) them or simply cut them straight across 2 inches from the grooves (FIG. 13-15E).
• Grooves for the top and bottom go all the way through. As shown, the shelf (FIG. 13-15F) is straight across, but it could be narrower or the same shape as the top and bottom. It will then reach the inside of the door. Decide what will best suit your needs.
• Make the top and bottom the same. Check that when they are closely in the grooves both ways, their fronts come level with the sides.
• Make the shelf, either cut straight across or the same shape as the top and bottom.
• Join the two broad sides with glue and screws. Join in the top, bottom, and shelf, with glue and screws from outside. Sink all screw heads below the surface so the sides fit close to the walls. You will probably have to plane off the sharpness at the point to fit into the corner.
• Use your full-size drawing to get the sections and angles for the facing pieces. Prepare strips. The sides (FIG. 13-16C) will be level with the wall and mitered to the door posts

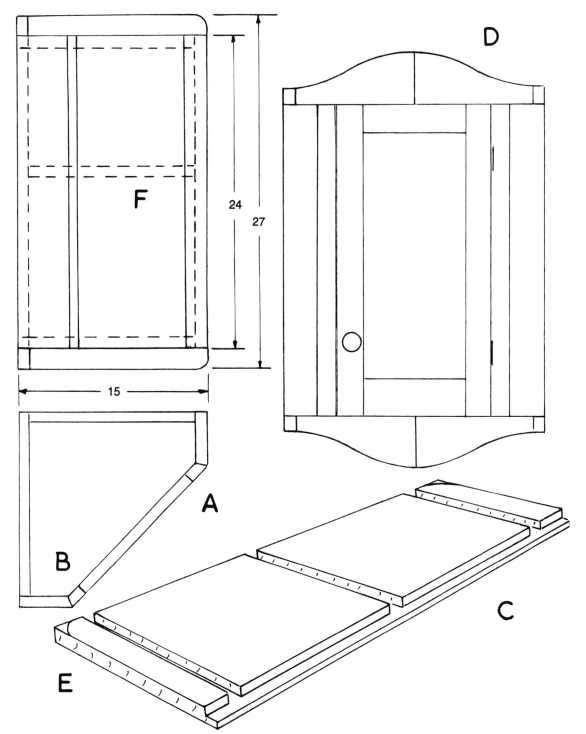

Fig. 13-15. Sizes and side details of the corner cupboard.

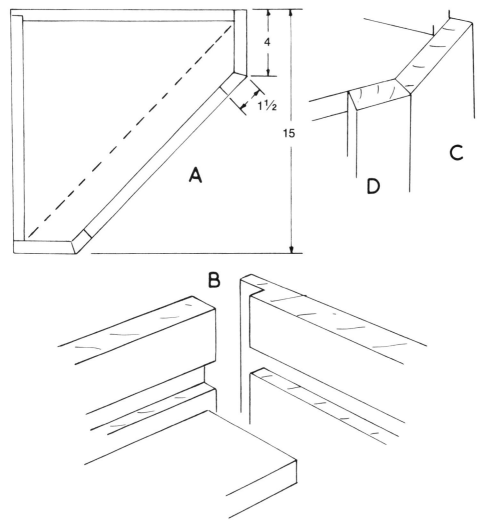

Fig. 13-16. Section and details of the corner cupboard.

(FIG. 13-16D). Cut the strips longer than needed at this stage, but they have to finish level with the cupboard top and bottom. When assembling the cupboard, make sure the door posts are parallel; otherwise the door would have to be made out of square, and that would be visually obvious.

• Glue the mitered pieces to each other and then to the broad sides and the top and bottom. Reinforce the joints with fine nails, set below the surface and stopped.

• When the glue has set, try the cupboard in the corner. You can make slight adjustments by planing the edges.

• The door can be similar to others in the kitchen, but a paneled door is suggested. Make it to fit between the door posts and overlap the cabinet top and bottom. Let hinges in at one side. The best place for a catch is under the top or the shelf (if it is full width). Put a knob or handle on the opening side. If the user will have to reach high or over a countertop, the handle should be fairly low.

• To hang the unit, you can drive screws into the wall inconspicuously from inside the cupboard.

Materials List for Corner Cupboard

2 sides	¾ × 15 × 29
2 sides	¾ × 4 × 26
2 door posts	¾ × 1½ × 26
1 top	¾ × 14 × 22
1 bottom	¾ × 14 × 22
1 shelf	¾ × 12 × 22
2 door frames	¾ × 2 × 26
1 door frame	¾ × 2 × 14
1 door frame	¾ × 3 × 14
1 door panel	11 × 23 × ¼ plywood

WRITING-FLAP CABINET

A cook might be glad to have a special rack for personal notebooks, recipe cards, and other such things. If the same unit has a pull-down flap for writing on, the cook can make notes away from the mess of the worktop.

The cabinet shown in FIG. 13-17 has a divided top section for notebooks and papers. The compartment below includes a flap front that provides a writing area over 12 inches square. There is space behind for pads, pens, and many other small things. FIGURE 13-18A suggests sizes, which you can modify to suit your needs. When planning this unit, allow enough of the flap to go under its shelf when lowered, to support the surface in normal use. A quarter of the amount projecting should be about right. In the drawing there is about 3 inches under the shelf for a flap projection of 12 inches.

You could make most of the parts with plywood or veneered particleboard, with suitable edging, but the instructions are for solid wood. Even if you make nearly all the parts of solid wood, you might want to use plywood for the flap because it does not warp or shrink. As shown, the unit has solid wood pieces across at top and bottom of the back, with thin plywood between. Following are the basic steps of construction:

• Mark out the pair of sides (FIGS. 13-18B and 13-19A). Rabbet the rear edges for plywood and increase the width of the rabbets for the top and bottom solid strip backs, as described for other projects in this chapter. The two top stopped grooves across are for shelves that will come flush with the front edges of the sides. The groove for the lower shelf allows for it being set back to clear the flap when raised (FIG. 13-18C). Shape the top and bottom ends of the sides as shown or to match other cabinets.

• Make the top two shelves (FIGS. 13-18D and 13-19B), notched to fit the grooves in the

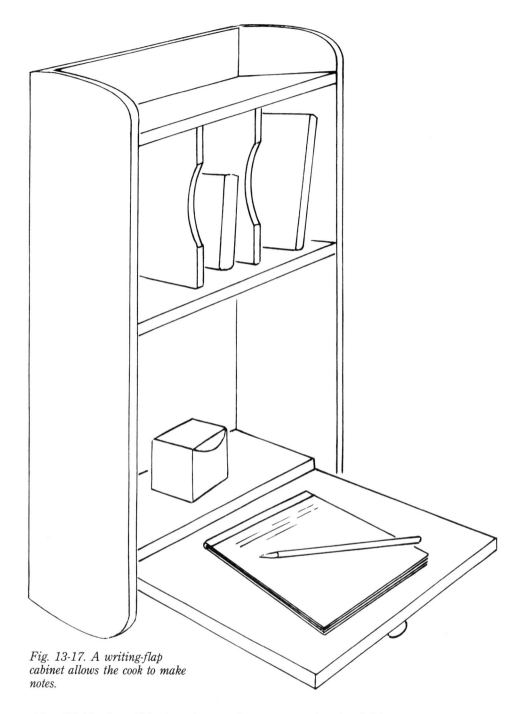

Fig. 13-17. A writing-flap
cabinet allows the cook to make
notes.

sides. Divide the widths into three and cut grooves for the divisions, which can stop
1 inch from the front edge (FIG. 13-19C).

• The divisions can have hollowed front edges (FIG. 13-19D) and should be well rounded.

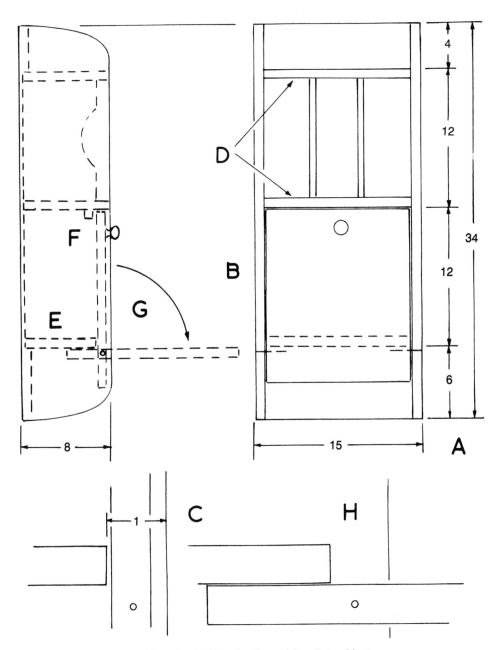

Fig. 13-18. Sizes for the writing-flap cabinet.

- Make the bottom shelf (FIGS. 13-18E and 13-19E) to match the grooves in the sides.
- Put a strip across under the middle shelf at the same distance from the back as the width of the bottom shelf, to act as a stop for the flap when raised (FIGS. 13-18F and 13-19F).
- Prepare the solid and plywood back parts.

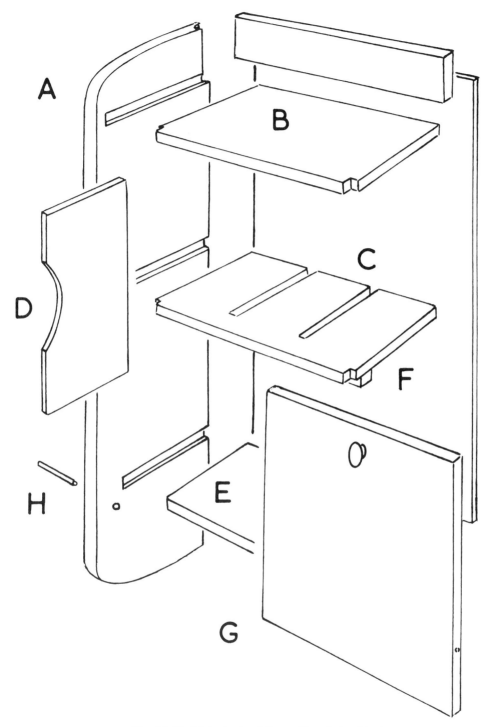

Fig. 13-19. Main parts of the writing-flap cabinet.

- Join the divisions to their shelves, then the shelves to the sides. Add the back parts. Check squareness and make sure that the sides are parallel for a good fit on the flap.
- Make the flap (FIGS. 13-18G and 13-19G) to fit easily between the sides. Round the top and bottom edges if you wish. Fit a knob or handle near the top edge.
- The pivot point on each side has to be located so that the flap will be upright when closed and it fits under the shelf when open (FIG. 13-18H). The pivots could be stout screws (2 inches long by at least #12 gauge), but it is better to use pieces of noncorrosive metal rod $\frac{3}{16}$ inch diameter (FIG. 13-19H). Mark and drill the sides. Put the flaps in position and mark and drill through. Drill a short distance into the flap and insert the rods, so you can try the action. If necessary, you can relocate the holes slightly as you drill the full depth.
- Drive in the rods until the ends are level with the surface. If you want to be able to remove the rods, however, let project a little, preferably with rounded ends for the sake of appearance.
- A small ball catch at one side will hold the flap in its up position.

Materials List for Writing-flap Cabinet

2 sides	$\frac{3}{4} \times 8 \times 36$
2 shelves	$\frac{3}{4} \times 8 \times 16$
1 shelf	$\frac{3}{4} \times 7 \times 16$
2 divisions	$\frac{1}{2} \times 7 \times 13$
1 back	$\frac{3}{4} \times 4 \times 16$
1 back	$\frac{3}{4} \times 6 \times 16$
1 back	$15 \times 26 \times \frac{1}{4}$ plywood
1 flap	$\frac{3}{4} \times 14 \times 17$

CABINET WITH LIFTING DOOR

If you need maximum access to the inside of a hanging cabinet, and you want to be able to open it without interfering with any adjoining cabinet, you can arrange the door to lift rather than swing from one side. Hinging a door at the top is easy, but you need a way to hold it up. You could use a rope over a pulley at the ceiling, but in most situations that rope will hang rather unattractively when not in use. A better solution is to use a strut to hold the door horizontal or just above that.

The cabinet shown in FIG. 13-20 is plain, but you can use this lifting door arrangement with cupboards or cabinets of any pattern, provided that the door can be made to overlap the front edges.

The sizes suggested in FIG. 13-21A are for a cabinet with a 24-inch-square door, but you can use any other size. The door could match those elsewhere in the kitchen, but it is best with the back left plain or with a flat frame about 3 inches wide at the side with the strut.

The cabinet is a square box with thin plywood let into the back. Dovetails would make the best corner joints, but any corner joints would suffice. As shown, the shelves

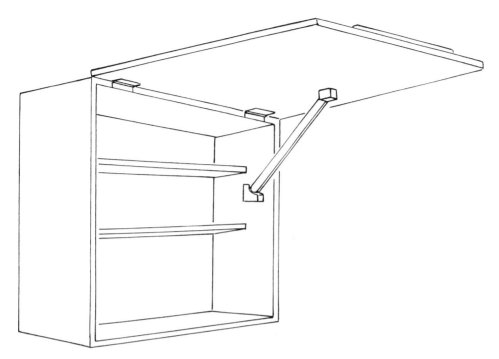

Fig. 13-20. A lifting door on a cabinet provides maximum access to the interior.

are fitted with dado joints. General construction is as described for several other cabinets in this chapter. The following instructions only refer to the fitting of the door.

- Make the door to cover the front of the cabinet. At the top, fit hinges so the door can swing clear. Two 3-inch brass hinges would be suitable.
- Fit a handle at the lower edge, or recess the rear of the bottom edge, so you can pull it forward. There should be no need for a fastener, as the weight of the door should keep it closed.
- The strut must be arranged to hang vertically inside the door when it is closed (FIG. 13-21B). When the door is up, it should rest against a block on the side of the cabinet (FIG. 13-21C). You might have to experiment if your cabinet and door are other sizes, but the layout shown allows the strut to hold the door horizontal. It hangs clear of the block when the door is closed.
- Make the strut parts of close-grained hardwood, even if the rest of the cabinet is softwood. Round the ends and edges of the strut (FIG. 13-21D). Using pivot screws, attach it to a block which will allow it to swing closed just clear of the door (FIG. 13-21E). The strut should move easily on the screw.
- The block to fit inside the cabinet may be thicker than the strut. Hollow it to match the curve of the strut (FIG. 13-21F).
- Attach the pivot block to the inside of the door so that the strut hangs just clear of the inner surface of the cabinet side (FIG. 13-21G).

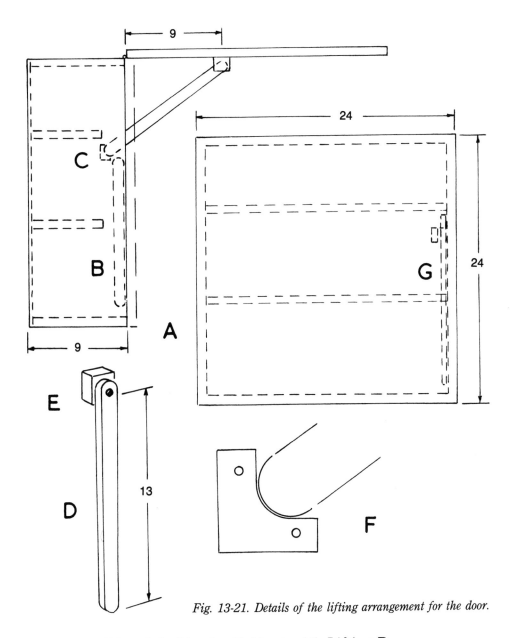

Fig. 13-21. Details of the lifting arrangement for the door.

Materials List for Cabinet with Lifting Door

4 sides	¾ × 9 × 26
1 back	24 × 24 × ¼ plywood
2 shelves	¾ × 7 × 26
1 door to match	
1 strut	½ × 1 × 15
1 pivot block	¾ × 2 × 2
1 stop block	¾ × 2 × 2

14
CHAPTER

Multiple Hanging Wall Cabinets

If a kitchen has a long countertop with cabinets underneath it, it almost certainly has a comparable length of wall above it where hanging cabinets could be positioned. In other parts of the room there might be wall space over equipment other than a counter, which could accommodate a single cabinet (as described in Chapter 13) or a longer line of cabinets.

A bathroom might not have as much space available, but it could still have a line of shallower cabinets along a wall, some of them possibly with mirror fronts. In a compact bathroom a higher position on a wall might be the only place where such storage could be provided without interfering with the normal use of the room.

A long line of identical doors might not be the most attractive arrangement, however, even if the individual doors are nicely molded or decorated in some other way. When planning these cabinets therefore, consider breaking the line somewhere. Perhaps there is a window, which provides a natural and sufficient break. Or there might be a hood over a range, which projects from the wall between cabinets. A section of open shelves might also provide a break somewhere along the line of cabinets—not necessarily at the center. Or perhaps one or more cabinets could be glass-fronted. The glass could have a leaded pattern and the cabinet used to display your best china. A light inside the cabinet would make this arrangement even more attractive.

Early on, you must decide how you will make the multiple cabinets. If the line is not too long you can make one unit of the full length and divide it into compartments. The size of such a unit, however, might make it difficult to get it from your shop to the kitchen or bathroom and to lift and hold it in position while screwing it in place. The alternative is to make units of one or two compartments and then assemble them in position. If there is to be a front frame, it could go the whole length or over a group of units. Molding along the top front edge could also be in one piece, to give the front a unified appearance even when the compartments behind are made up of several parts.

If the arrangement is to be more than just a straight line, deal with any changes of direction by using a linking unit. At an internal or external corner, a unit need not be bigger than necessary to take care of the change of direction, but it should have panels to fit against the ends of the straight parts. If a part of the corner projects from the wall section as a working area or table, and you want to build a unit above it for more storage space or as a room divider, you will have to blend it in with the hanging wall cabinets, even though it is made separately.

Pictures of older kitchens show collections of a great many things brought together without consideration of the whole room. The various appliances and equipment may be functional, but little thought was given to the overall effect or the relationship of one piece to another.

The modern kitchen is planned as a whole. A large part of this general effect comes from the hanging wall units, which not only provide a considerable amount of storage but are the kitchen's most prominent feature.

Progress in bathroom planning has not kept up with that of kitchens. Many bathrooms are still just individual units, which to a certain extent is unavoidable. However, cabinets can provide a linkage between some items and give the whole room a coordinated effect.

You must carefully consider taller items, as you plan hanging wall cabinets. A refrigerator will stand above the counter level, yet it might not reach the height plan for the wall cabinets. You could therefore put a shelf over the refrigerator, to provide continuity with the cabinets on either side. If you make a higher floor-standing cabinet, probably at the end of a counter, treat that as part of the whole assembly and blend it into the cabinets under the counter and those on the wall. Such a cabinet helps combat the plainness of a long line of cabinet doors.

In a bathroom, you might have to exercise more ingenuity if you want a worthwhile arrangement of hanging cabinets fitted around plumbing and other projections vertically on a wall. Either be careful not to obstruct anything that might require maintenance or arrange what you fit to be easily removable.

PLANNING

Hanging wall cabinets are usually arranged in a way similar to those below the countertop, to provide a symmetrical appearance. They do not *have* to be so arranged however. The general pattern of doors should be similar to those below, but you might find you can use different ones that are of the same family. The widths and spacings also do not have to be the same as those of the lower doors, but you have no reason to do otherwise the matching of doors is a good starting point in planning a long series of cabinets.

In the most basic form (FIG. 14-1) the matching doors give an appearance of uniformity. You can avoid the stark, clinical appearance with attractive veneers or colored plastic facings. The picture cabinets are not necessarily an unattractive arrangement,

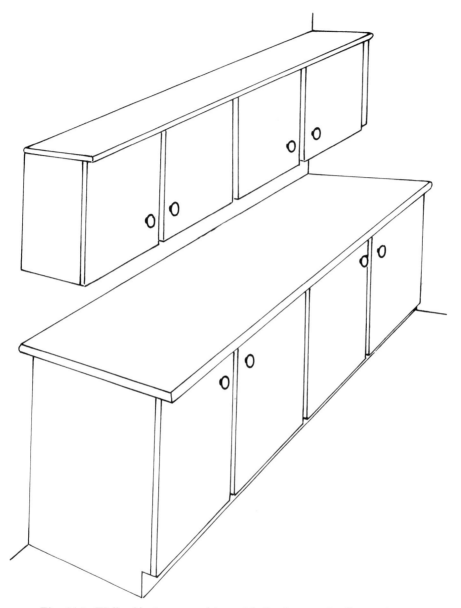

Fig. 14-1. Wall cabinets arranged to match the doors under the countertop.

however. It certainly looks functional, and an efficient look might be what you want in a kitchen.

As shown, there are two pairs of doors at each level, but the same planning could be carried through with other arrangements. Note that the knobs are high on the lower doors and low on the upper doors, for ease of operation.

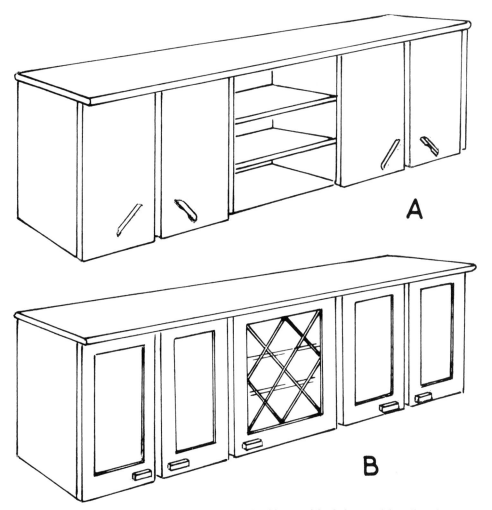

Fig. 14-2. You can break the pattern of cabinets with shelves and handles (A) or with a glazed door (B).

If desired, you could break the pattern of these cabinets with shelves between narrower pairs of doors (FIG. 14-2A). The shelves could be narrow or wide, to suit both the desired visual effect and the items the shelves will contain. You might have to consider the overall length, however, as you should not make the doors too narrow. The doors need not all be the same width, and you may find that a single door is better than two very narrow ones. You can further alter the appearance of these cabinets by using handles instead of knobs. Handles set diagonally might be all that is needed to make otherwise plain doors attractive.

A glass panel in a door will always improve the appearance of a row of solid doors. For a bathroom, you could clip a mirror on the front of a plain door, but for a kitchen you should put the glass in a frame. Glass could be patterned or obscure, but clear glass is better for displaying items on shelves.

Leaded glass is attractive, either with a square or diamond arrangement (FIG. 14-2B). You can get lead strip with an adhesive to put on sheet glass. There are also plastic substitutes that look like lead or others with a bronze effect. Lay out the pattern on paper and put the glass over it while you attach the strips, so you get a balanced result. Do not make the pattern too small if you want to be able to see what is inside. If you use such glass, you must fit it into a rabbeted frame, so it looks like a paneled door. Doors at the side of the cabinets can be plain, but doors framed with plywood panels look better (FIG. 14-2B). The drawing shows straight wood handles at the lower edges of the doors.

Further decoration could come from a molding around the top of the cabinet. The doors could overlap the carcass at the top as well as at the sides or bottom. Or you could have an overhanging top, as shown in FIG. 14-2. This type of top stops dust from getting inside if a door does not close tightly. You could alter this simple overhanging top by putting a molding along its edge, probably a strip deeper than the wood used for the top.

A good way to improve hanging wall cabinets is to include shelves outside the cabinet line. Other matching shelves could come between cabinets. Shelves provide visible storage of items and give the cook a chance to brighten the kitchen with plants or vases of flowers. Adding rails on spindles to the shelves helps guard against things being knocked over and improve the shelves' appearance, too.

FIGURE 14-3A shows shelves with rails on cabinets with shaped, paneled doors, but you can use rails with simpler cabinets as well. If the end shelves are very large they will need support at the back and a corner post. As shown, the rails are light and are supported with slim spindles. Shelves farther along in the line of doors need not be spaced the same as at the ends, but they look better if they are.

With its shaped doors and turned spindles, the cabinet in FIG. 14-3A looks best capped by a fairly large overhanging molding. There could be knobs or handles on the doors, but finger grooves under the bottom edges are effective and do not break the design line of the door fronts.

When leaning forward, the cook's head must be able clear the edges of the hanging wall cabinets. The problem area is along the bottom edge; it would not matter if higher parts projected more. You might decide, therefore, to design your cabinets in two steps (FIG. 14-3B). The arrangement shown has doors on the surface, with a plywood paneled door at the end, and a glass door with the glass set in molded rails. This type of door lets you show your woodworking skill if you have suitable equipment. The part set back under the doors is shelf, and next to it is a rail for hanging cloths or tools. You could also have drawers at this level. Avoid putting drawers in wall cabinets that are at or above eye level, however because their contents cannot be seen without an effort.

If a window interrupts the line of hanging cabinets, do not be tempted to take the cabinets right to the edge of the window. They would lessen the natural light entering the room. Finish the cabinets a little way back from the window edge (FIG. 14-3C). To

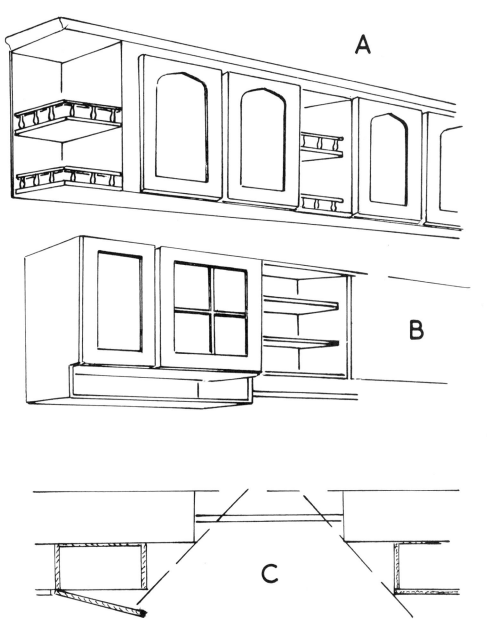

Fig. 14-3. Shaped door frames and shelf rails (A) can decorate cabinets.
Shelves and a glazed door (B) can break up the pattern.
At a window, keep cabinets back so as not to obstruct light (C).

judge how far back the cabinets should go, try holding a piece of plywood of the size of the end of the cabinet in place and see what effect it has on light. You will probably find that you need to allow the light to enter at an angle of about 45 degrees to the edge of the window frame.

CARCASS CONSTRUCTION

However the front appearance of cabinets in a row differ, the construction behind can be the same for nearly all of them. Where heights and depths are the same along the line, construction details can be the same, whether you make single, double, or long units. Much of the construction is similar to that of the cabinets below the countertop, but because of the shallower section, the work is simpler. Differences in appearance are largely due to the doors (cabinets which are different because of changes in section or shape are discussed later).

There are two main ways of making the carcasses. You can use plywood panels and add a front frame to cover the edges, in the way described for bottom cabinets. You then mount the doors on the front with ordinary hinges. Alternatively you can use particleboard with wood or plastic veneer skins, veneer any exposed edges, and then hinge the doors directly to it, using a hinge that will throw the door clear (FIG. 3-12). In this construction, you do not need a front frame. You could use this method with plywood, too, providing that you lip the exposed edges with solid wood. The throw-clear hinges need a level inner surface and cannot be used with a wider frame.

The size of the carcasses will depend on the overall design you are using and how long the assembly is to be. You could make single units, double ones, or even more, then join them in position. Door widths can be up to 18 inches, so you have to consider the bulk and weight of a carcass. Three compartments at a total of 50 inches long is as much as you are likely to want to handle, both in the shop and while fitting it to the wall in the kitchen. A double unit might be a better choice; you can then make up a total length with another single unit, if necessary. A double or triple unit can have divisions, and a double unit can have a pair of doors over a single interior space, which close against a post.

If you use faced particleboard, the carcass is a simple box on edge (FIG. 14-4A). The particleboard should be ⅝ inch or ½ inch thick. You could use plywood for the back. The sides overlap the bottom and top and the back comes within the other parts (FIG. 14-4B). If you are making a double unit without a division, add a post about 1½ inches wide and 1 inch thick (FIG. 14-4C) for the doors to close against.

Where heads will not show, you can use screws to hold the parts together (FIG. 14-4D), but in other places use glued dowels; ¼-inch-diameter or ⁵⁄₁₆-inch-diameter dowels are suitable (FIG. 14-4E). Screws or dowels at 4-inch intervals should be satisfactory in most joints.

If you want the shelves to be removable and adjustable, drill the sides for peg supports (FIG. 12-2). If you prefer the shelves to be secured in place, dowel them in during construction.

If you are joining several units, make them together so you can compare sizes as you cut all parts. Although the backs will hold the assemblies square, check the fronts by comparing diagonals and testing them against each other.

When you mount the cabinets on the wall, first screw them together. At the same time however, you can put a strip (a 1-inch × 2-inch section should do) at the top and

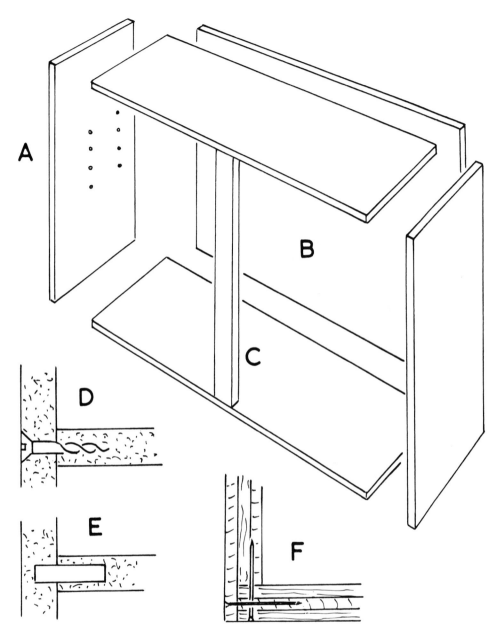

*Fig. 14-4. Typical carcass construction for wall cabinets
made from particleboard or plywood.*

bottom fronts over all cabinets (FIGS. 14-5A, B). You could make the doors to overlap these strips, or at the top you could make the strip wider so it overlaps the doors (FIG. 14-5C) or face it with molding (FIG. 14-5D).

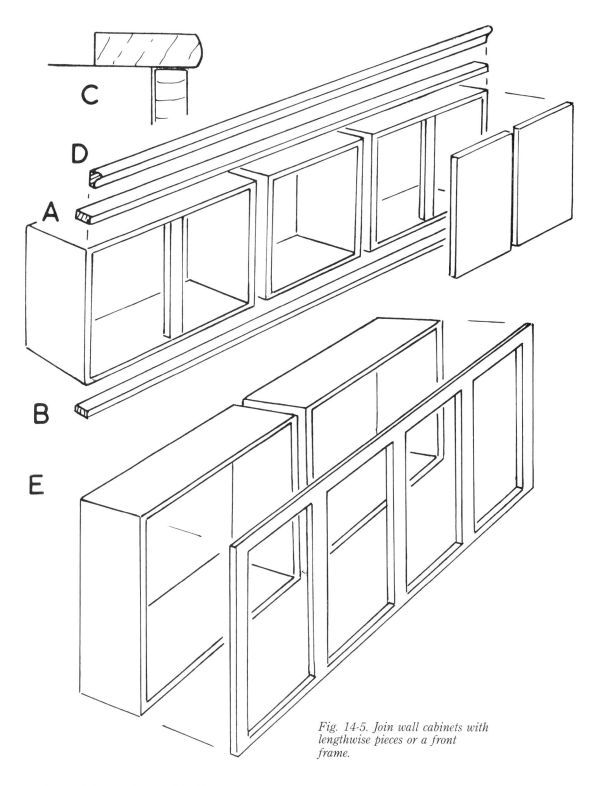

Fig. 14-5. Join wall cabinets with
lengthwise pieces or a front
frame.

Particleboard doors with throw-clear hinges need only a small clearance between edges, if they are over the double thickness material of adjoining cabinets.

Cabinets that are to have front frame and doors on ordinary hinges can be made in a similar way, with an allowance at the front for the thickness of the frame. The frame will hide the front edges, so you can use plywood. The only place where exposed plies might be a problem and difficult to cover with veneer is at bottom corners. You could use a rabbeted joint there to reduce the amount of end grain showing (FIG. 14-4F).

Unless the group of units is very long, you should be able to make a front frame to cover all of them (FIG. 14-5E). The doors fit on the front of the frame in the same way as on the lower cabinets. You could put a top piece with a molding front above the doors, as in the particleboard assembly discussed earlier in this section.

LONG CABINET

For maximum storage on a wall, you could extend the cabinets to the ceiling, either for the whole length or partially. Higher cabinets at the end could have lower ones in-between, with their tops as open storage space. You could also put shelves between high end cabinets, possible with small drawers. The effect would be like a built-in Welsh dresser.

The cabinets could have tall doors, with the inside divided by shelves. Or the cabinets could be on two levels, with the parts you can reach from a normal position behind one door and the parts that require a step-stool behind an upper door. Dividing fronts by using two doors on each cabinet provides a very pleasing appearance.

You will have to relate the cabinets' sizes to the available space. Shelves could be any length. Drawers would have to be low and comparatively small, but these would be useful for the many small items used frequently and needing accessible storage. FIGURE 14-7A suggests sizes for the unit shown in FIG. 14-6, but you might have to alter these considerably for your situation.

You can make the carcasses using either of the methods described earlier in the chapter, but the example assumes you will use front frames. The doors could be any type, but they are shown with shaped frames and panels, which could be molded with a router or spindle molder. Following are the basic steps of construction:

• Make the two carcasses and their front frames, which are identical. The bottom of the frame should match the thickness of the plywood, but the other rails are deeper than the sides of the frame (FIGS. 14-7B and 14-8A). You could make the carcass backs individually or carry one back across the whole assembly. For the narrow shelf arrangement shown, one back would be satisfactory, but if you plan a long center section it would be easier to make that as a unit, with its own back and sides. For the arrangement shown, the back goes across and the shelves are fitted directly to the carcass sides. Make any shelves you require inside the cabinets.

• The parts between the carcasses are 12 inches long. Make the shelves and the case for the two drawers (FIG. 14-8B). At the top, the horizontal piece across has a front apron

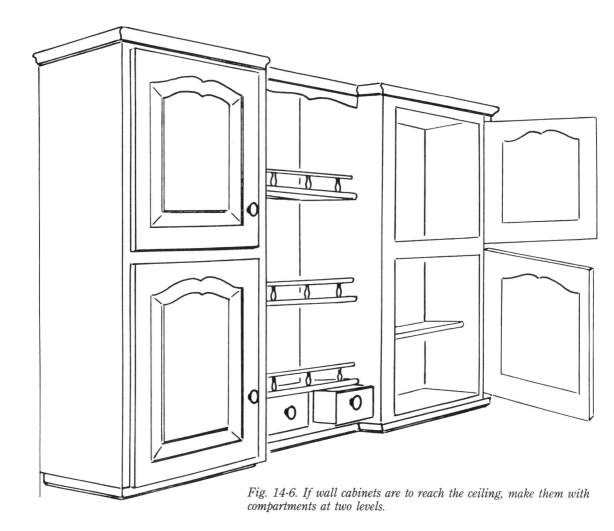

Fig. 14-6. If wall cabinets are to reach the ceiling, make them with compartments at two levels.

whose lower edge you could shape (FIG. 14-8C). The shaping could be any design you wish or it could match the shapes molded on the doors. Prepare the ends of all these parts for dowels to the carcasses.

• You could leave the fronts of the shelves plain and open, or mold the edges and fit rails and spindles similar to those described for other projects in this book (FIG. 14-8D).

• Assemble the two carcasses and fit the parts between them. Use the back to hold the assembly square. Put the assembly on its back and sight across to make sure there is no twist. Attach the front frames. If you do not think the back plywood is strong enough for screwing to the wall, put strips across inside the backs of the carcasses under the tops.

• Put molding around all top edges, unless one end goes into a corner of the room. The molding can go on the surfaces (FIG. 14-9A) and be mitered at the corners.

• At the bottom, you could add a molding or a strip with a molded edge set back a little

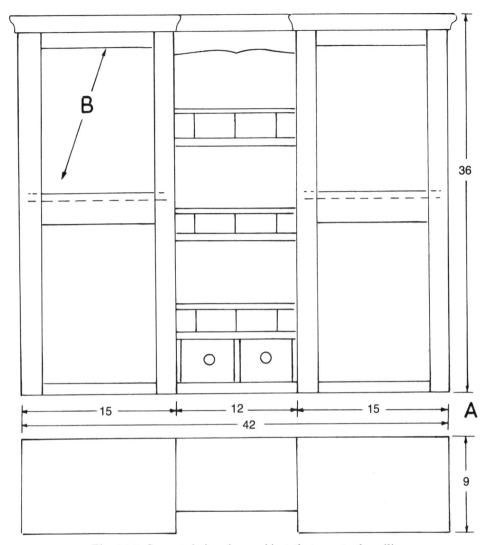

Fig. 14-7. Suggested sizes for a cabinet that goes to the ceiling.

(FIG. 14-9B) and carried all around with mitered corners. If you want to put lighting under the cabinets this front molding can act as a screen and keep light out of your eyes.

• The drawers are simple boxes. You could make them to fit flush at the front or use overlapping false fronts (FIG. 14-9C). Any sort of pull, would suffice, but for these small drawers turned knobs usually look best.

• You can fit any type of door, from plain to ornate, depending on your wishes or the need to match other furniture. The doors illustrated (FIG. 14-9D) have molded internal edges to the frames and matching moldings on recessed panels (FIG. 14-9E). You could let in ordinary hinges here, but this type of door looks best with exposed shaped hinges

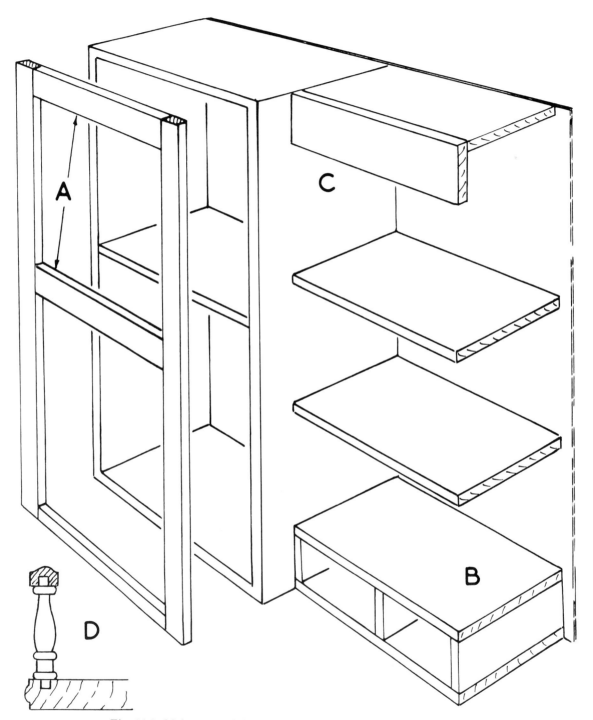

Fig. 14-8. Main parts of the cabinet that goes to the ceiling.

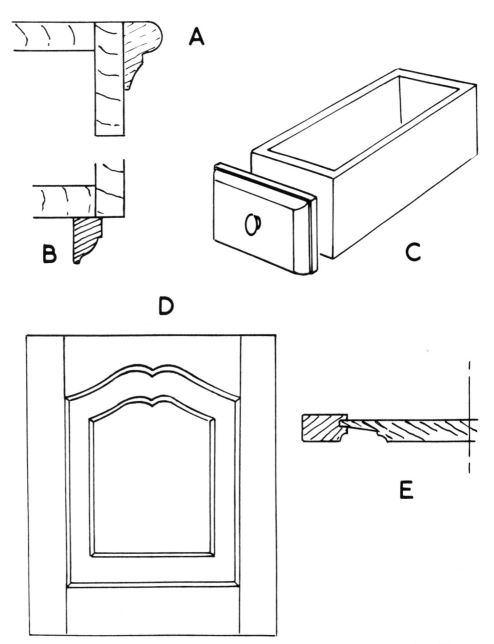

Fig. 14-9. Molding, drawer, and door details for the cabinet that goes to the ceiling.

with an antique finish. And although spring or magnetic catches would be fine, this is an ideal place for knobs of the older type, which go through to turn a latch inside.

• Finish the cabinet to suit the wood used and the surroundings. However, if you have used a good hardwood, a dark stain and a moderate gloss finish will look particularly good.

Materials List for Long Cabinet

4 carcass sides	9 × 38 × ¾ plywood
2 carcass tops	9 × 17 × ¾ plywood
2 carcass bottoms	9 × 17 × 1 plywood
2 carcass divisions	9 × 17 × ¾ plywood
4 front frames	1 × 2 × 38
4 front frames	1 × 4 × 17
2 front frames	1 × 1 × 17
4 shelves	¾ × 7 × 14
1 center top	¾ × 6¼ × 14
1 top apron	¾ × 5 × 14
3 drawer dividers	½ × 5 × 9
2 drawer fronts	½ × 5 × 7
2 drawer fronts	½ × 6 × 7
4 drawer sides	½ × 5 × 9
2 drawer backs	½ × 5 × 7
2 drawer bottoms	7 × 9 × ¼ plywood
1 cabinet back	36 × 44 × ½ plywood
Top molding	72 × 2
Bottom molding	72 × 1½
3 shelf rails	½ × ¾ × 14
9 shelf spindles	¾ × ¾ × 5
Doors to suit	

CORNER UNIT

If you want to carry hanging wall units around a corner, you could deal with the change of direction in a manner similar to that described for under-the-counter cabinets. Wall cabinets however, are shallower and lighter, making a corner unit simpler. The diagonal distance in a corner is obviously longer than the square distance across a counter, so a corner unit can project more without causing an obstruction.

The corner unit shown in FIG. 14-10 is intended to be made of veneered particleboard, using throw-clear spring hinges. Its edge is 11 inches wide and it could butt against straight cabinets projecting 9 inches. Experiment with head clearance in the corner before deciding on the width to use. As drawn, (FIGS. 14-10 and 14-11) the unit has plain veneered particleboard doors. If you want to use other doors or use a front frame, you will have to modify the design slightly. You can change 21-inch height without affecting the method of construction.

The unit has two sides compartments, with doors hinged on the sides away from the corner, and a compartment with a lifting door. Divisions are fitted squarely, so the corner compartment is quite roomy. Spring throw-clear hinges should hold the diagonal door up. If not, you could use a strut, as described in Chapter 13. Following are the basic steps of construction:

• Make the top and bottom the same (FIG. 14-11A).

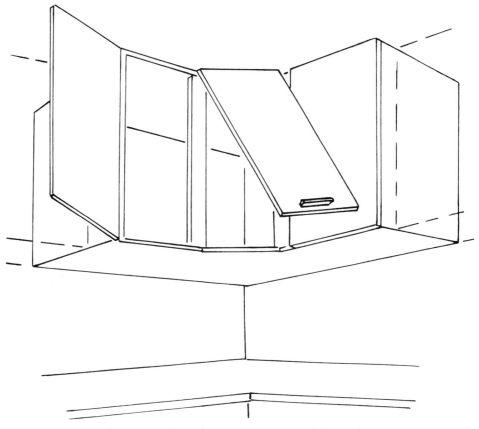

Fig. 14-10. This corner unit has a central lifting door.

• Make the backs (FIGS. 14-11B and 14-12A, B). They overlap each other at the corner and fit between the top and bottom and inside the ends.

• Make the two ends (FIG. 14-12C) to fit over the other parts.

• Mark the positions of the divisions and the doorposts. Each doorpost overlaps the corner miter by 1 inch, and its division goes squarely against it (FIG. 14-12D). Veneer any edges that will be exposed.

• Join all these parts with screws where the heads will not show and with stopped dowels elsewhere.

• Make the side compartment doors to overlap top and bottom and to overlap the doorpost by ½ inch. If there is too much overlap on the post, the door edge might interfere with the action of the diagonal door.

• Make the diagonal door the same height as the other doors and make wide enough to rest against the top and bottom diagonal edges (FIG. 14-11C). Hinge the side compartment doors to the ends and the diagonal door to the top so that it lifts and springs to a nearly square position.

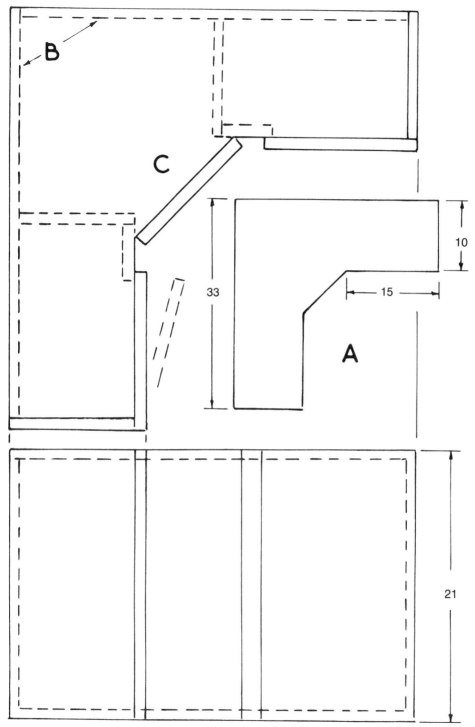

Fig. 14-11. Sizes of the corner unit.

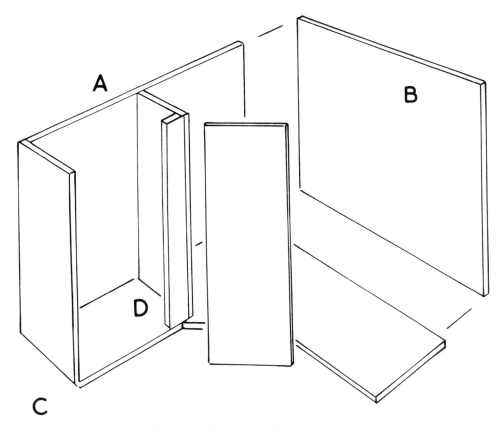

Fig. 14-12. Main parts of the corner unit.

Materials List for Corner Unit

1 top	33	× 33
1 bottom	33	× 33
2 backs	20	× 33
2 ends	10	× 22
2 divisions	9¼	× 22
2 doorposts	4	× 22
2 doors	15	× 22
1 door	12	× 22

15
CHAPTER

Special Bathroom Cabinets

In general, bathrooms have much less space than kitchens, so the possibilities for adding cabinets to a bathroom are fewer. Furthermore, it is difficult to adopt a standard for bathroom cabinet units as you can with kitchen cabinets. If there is any space which can be used for cabinets. To make the most use of available wall and floor space in a particular bathroom, you will have to construct cabinets to specific sizes. In almost any bathroom you can add cabinets of some sort, but you might have to exercise your ingenuity to fit them in without reducing the area required for movement in the room.

The actual construction of bathroom cabinets is usually the same as for kitchen cabinets; this book describes many designs as applicable to either room. What you make for a kitchen can be made in the same way, but narrower if necessary, for a bathroom. You might want to store mostly smaller items, but you can still find uses for many compartments and drawers, which could be smaller and lighter than similar ones in a kitchen. However, because of the additional plumbing that needs occasional attention, you have to carefully fit bathroom cabinets to allow access.

Even if a bathroom is well ventilated, its atmosphere will often be wetter than that of a kitchen. Steam will penetrate most things in the room, and splashed water might not always be wiped away. Therefore, surfaces should be water-resistant. Laminated plastic is usually the best choice for tops. Woodwork should be protected by good paint or varnish, and you should paint inside surfaces that you might leave untreated in a kitchen. Dampness does not usually affect plastic-veneered particleboard, so that may be a better choice than wood for many parts of the structure.

What you add to a bathroom will affect the overall appearance. Sanitary ware and the bath and shower are usually made to be just functional. Their color might be attractive, but these fixtures bear no added decoration. You can brighten the whole effect with color on the wall and a patterned floor covering. A cabinet can be a welcome addition to the visual scheme, besides being practical. It can have fairly plain, easily wiped surfaces, but you can brighten it with contrasting handles or edges. Or you could use paneled doors, perhaps with moldings and raised panels. Molding might edge the tops of high cabinets and there could be an uneven front line, due to shelves being set back and cabinets brought to different levels.

Most designs will fall between the two extremes of visual effect: clinically plain and very ornate. In a compact bathroom, plain is often best. If there is more space, paneled and molded furniture might have a place. Consider cleaning when you plan your bathroom cabinets. Steam tends to deposit dirt in crannies which are difficult to clean out. A smooth surface can be cleaned in seconds.

One advantage of constructing your own bathroom cabinets and other furniture is the ability to make the best use of space. If you build in these items, you will be getting the most out of the space in a way that nothing bought can do. Even if what you make is freestanding, it can be a close fit. To take full advantage of this space, spend some time planning—perhaps even constructing a mock-up of cardboard or hardboard to visualize how the addition will look and fit.

VANITY UNIT

The vanity unit shown in FIG. 15-1 and discussed in this section is ideal for bathrooms in which the washbasin has to be a short distance from a corner. The unit takes advantage of the space between to provide a block of drawers. As shown, the top is made of thick particleboard bought with a laminated plastic top that curves over the front edge. It is cut to width and intended to fit against a tiled wall, but you could add a splash-back as was described for some of the kitchen cabinets discussed in this book. The basin provides space underneath enclosed with a door, and the drawer fronts do not require handles, so anyone with soap in his eyes can reach anywhere along a drawer front to pull it out.

Inset basins vary in size, so get yours before making the top and other parts. The basin in the example is 18 inches × 24 inches overall but the hole needed is smaller. A top height of 32 inches will probably suit your needs. Following are the basic steps of construction:

- Start by setting out the end that will be against the wall (FIG. 15-2A). Allow for the thickness of the top, and cut out for the toe board. The drawers are shown all the same depth, but you can make them different depths to suit your needs.
- So the drawers will have ample clearance near the wall, pack their guides out a little. The amount depends on the width of the upright of the front frame. Check this and prepare strips to go across (FIGS. 15-2B and 15-3A) with their bottom edges level with the bottoms of the drawers. Put another strip to go under the bottom of the cabinet and another on edge at the top to take screws upward into the countertop.
- Make the opposite end in the same way but without the drawer strips (FIG. 15-3B).

Fig. 15-1. This vanity unit has a block of shelves with sloping fronts.

The outer surface of this piece will be exposed, so if you are using plywood it should have a suitable veneer.

• Make the division that fits above the cabinet bottom (FIGS. 15-2C and 15-3C). Put a strip at the top for screwing upward into the countertop. Mark the drawer positions to match the wall end piece, but do not put strips across, as the drawer guides can fit directly to the surface. Notch the division for the rear top strip to go through (FIG. 15-3D).

• The bottom (FIG. 15-3E) fits between the ends. The location of the division depends on the space needed for the bowl, but as shown it is at the center. Join the ends and the division to the bottom with screws where the heads will not show and stopped dowels elsewhere. Fit in the rear top strip (FIG. 15-3F) to hold the parts vertical. Nail or screw on the back (FIG. 15-3G). Its edges will be hidden everywhere except at the end away

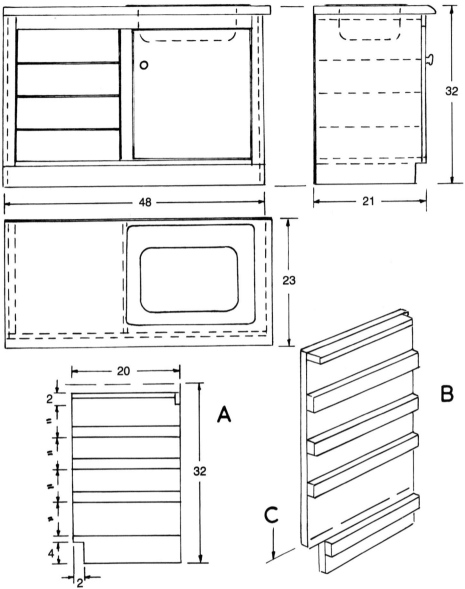

Fig. 15-2. Suggested sizes for the vanity unit.

from the corner wall. You can let in a narrow strip of thin wood there or cover the end with a narrow half-round molding.

• Fit the toe board (FIG. 15-3H). The parts should now be square if the assembly is stood on a flat surface.

• Make a front frame (FIG. 15-3J). The piece that covers the division should be level with

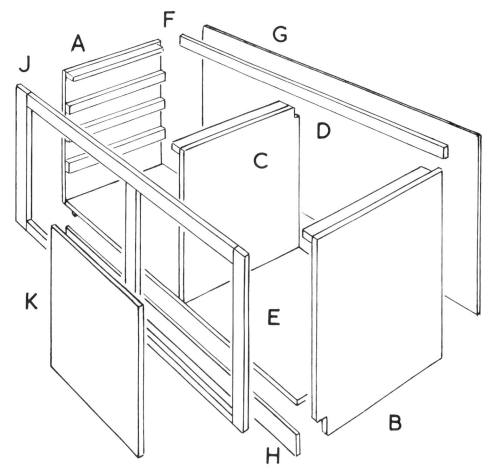

Fig. 15-3. Main parts of the vanity unit.

the surface on the drawer side and its other edge should project into the compartment under the basin. Attach the frame to the other parts.

• The door (FIG. 15-3K) is shown flush, but you could put it on the surface. It should be plain, with a suitable veneer on the front, and you should cover the edges with solid wood or veneer. You could use decorative hinges on the surface or ordinary brass hinges let in. Open from either side to suit the situation. Fit a catch and handle to the opposite side. You could put a shelf in the compartment, but make it removable for easy access for plumbing.

• The drawers could fit flush, with handles or knobs; have fronts overlapping the frame; or, as shown in FIG. 15-4, have false fronts providing a grip and fitting within the frame, so there is no projection. This last arrangement could be ideal for a confined space.

• If you use metal or plastic drawer guides or runners, allow for their thickness (about

½ inch) on each side of the drawer, but make the false fronts to extend over them and make a comfortable fit within the width of the front frame.

• Make each false front tapering in section from 1 inch to ¼ inch (FIG. 15-4A). Round the narrow front and shape the underside of the thick edge to provide a finger grip (FIGS. 15-4B, C).

• You can make the drawers by any of the methods described earlier in this book, with the width reduced to allow for the guides. The drawer front-to-back length should allow for the false front coming just inside the front frame when closed. Fit each drawer front behind its false front (FIG. 15-4D) and attach the guides to the drawer and the cabinet sides.

• Prepare the top by cutting the opening for the basin and covering the outer end with laminated plastic. You should probably screw the carcass to the wall, after cutting out any spaces for pipes, and then screw the top on from below.

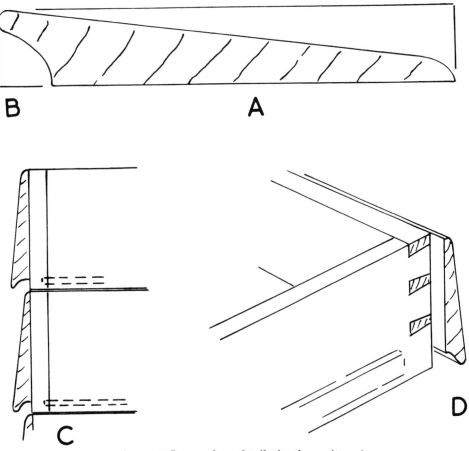

Fig. 15-4. Drawer-front details for the vanity unit.

Materials List for Vanity Unit

2 ends	20 × 33 × ¾ plywood
1 division	20 × 30 × ¾ plywood
1 bottom	20 × 48 × 1 plywood
1 door	22 × 28 × 1 plywood
1 back	32 × 50 × ¼ plywood
8 crosspieces	1 × 2 × 22
1 back strip	1 × 2 × 50
1 toe board	¾ × 4 × 50
1 front frame	1 × 2 × 50
3 front frames	1 × 2 × 30
1 front frame	1 × 1 × 50
8 drawer fronts	1 × 6 × 24
4 drawer backs	⅝ × 5½ × 24
8 drawer sides	⅝ × 6 × 21
4 drawer bottoms	21 × 24 × ¼ plywood

MODULAR UNITS

If the bathroom already has a washbasin and it is a pedestal-type unit or is bracketed to the wall, it probably has curves in all directions. Therefore, you would face careful scribing if you tried to fit a cabinet to it. A better solution is to simply provide cabinets in the vicinity of, but not attached to, the washbasin. You could have cabinets with tops at counter height and others, possibly joined by a shelf, on the wall above—all fairly close to the washbasin, but not joined to it.

The design shown in FIG. 15-5 is for basically similar modular units which can be brought together to form a pleasing and useful pattern around the washbasin. The counter units extend farther from the wall than those higher up, but are made in the same way. The upper ones could be independent, but they could have a common bottom which forms a shelf. You could join the tops in the same way and include a mirror. They are shown only joined at the bottom, with a mirror independently mounted.

You could use plywood or veneered particleboard, although solid wood might be good for many parts. As shown, doors are single pieces with half-round molding applied to give a paneled effect. Backs extend over the other parts. If you want to use thin plywood backs, you will need rabbets in the other parts. As shown, joints are all doweled; ¼-inch or 5⁄16-inch-diameter dowels at 3-inch intervals should be satisfactory, with slightly closer spacing for strength near the front edges (FIG. 15-6A). The instructions below are for making one side unit; but could make another to match. You could make a pair of higher units in the same way, with the projection from the wall reduced and the bottoms continued in a one-piece shelf.

• Make the top and bottom, which are the same (FIG. 15-6B) except that you might wish to give the top a surface of laminated plastic. Mark the positions of the other parts on them. The back comes inside, and it and the ends may be set in ½ inch so the top and bottom overlap (FIG. 15-7A). When marking the positions of the two uprights, allow for

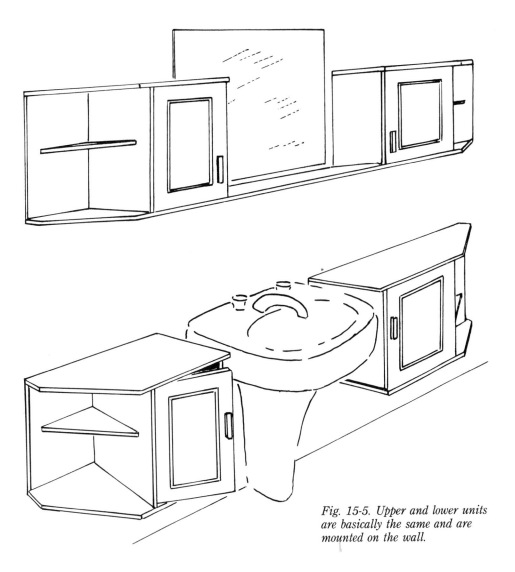

Fig. 15-5. Upper and lower units are basically the same and are mounted on the wall.

the thickness of the door. In the finished unit the door is between the top and bottom and should be set back about ⅛ inch.

• The two upright pieces and the back must all be the same height. As shown inside and outside shelves are at the same level (FIG. 15-6C). Mark the shelf positions on the uprights (FIG. 15-7B).

• Prepare the two shelves. The triangular one (FIG. 15-7C) should be parallel to the edges of the top and bottom.

• Drill all parts for dowels. You could use screws in a few places, provided that their heads would not show. Elsewhere, stop all dowel holes. Where the two shelves meet, you can take dowels through into both edges.

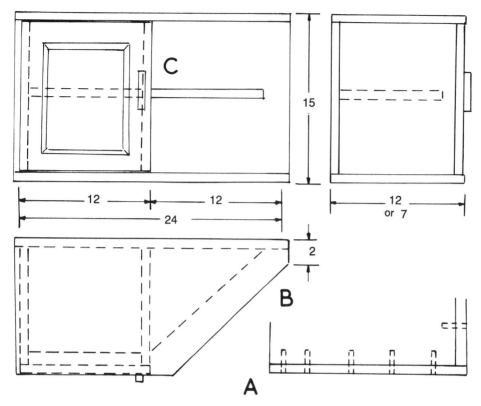

Fig. 15-6. Details of a modular unit.

• Drill the back for screws to the wall. Glue all parts together. Check squareness, particularly at the door opening.

• Make the door to swing easily between the top and bottom. Glue and pin-on-the-half-round molding. Provide a knob or handle. Hinge the door at either side and fit a catch.

• If you want a pair of units, make all parts for both at the same time, to ensure uniformity.

• In general, upper units should not project as much from the wall as lower units. A projection of 7 inches is suggested, but it could be as little as 5 inches. Except for that difference in measurement, construction of the top and bottom units is the same. If you plan to have a shelf connecting the upper cabinets, however, make their bottoms as one with the space between to suit your needs.

Materials List for Modular Unit

(one cabinet only)

1 bottom	¾ ×	12 × 26
1 top	¾ ×	12 × 26
2 uprights	¾ ×	10½ × 15
1 back	¾ ×	13½ × 26
1 shelf	¾ ×	9 × 12
1 door	¾ ×	12 × 15

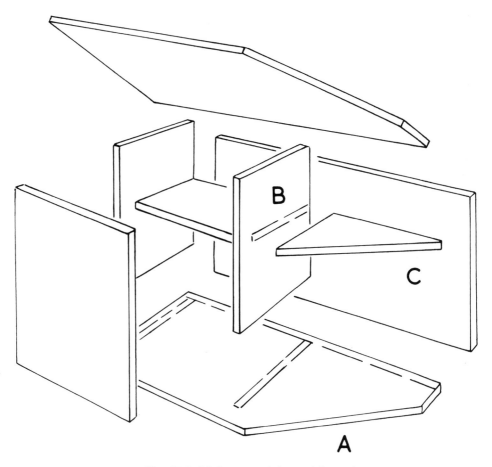

Fig. 15-7. Main parts of the modular unit.

STORAGE CABINET

If there is space along a wall in the bathroom, you can add a narrow cabinet for storing a variety of items, including folded towels. You will have to make the cabinet to suit the available space, but FIG. 15-8 shows a basic arrangement. It has an open compartment, shelves for towels, a broad drawer, and space below to store a stool. Instead of a door, it has a curtain suspended from a rail at the top.

As shown, the unit is made of plastic-veneered particleboard, but you could use solid wood or plywood. You can leave the top plain or cover it with laminated plastic, and you can cover its outer edges with plain or molded wood strips. The back is faced particleboard, which provides rigidity, but it could be thinner plywood. Make sure to veneer all exposed edges. Following are the basic steps of construction:

• The sizes shown may have to be modified, but when you have settled on sizes, mark out the intermediate upright (FIGS. 15-9B and 15-10A) first. Mark the drawer rails on one

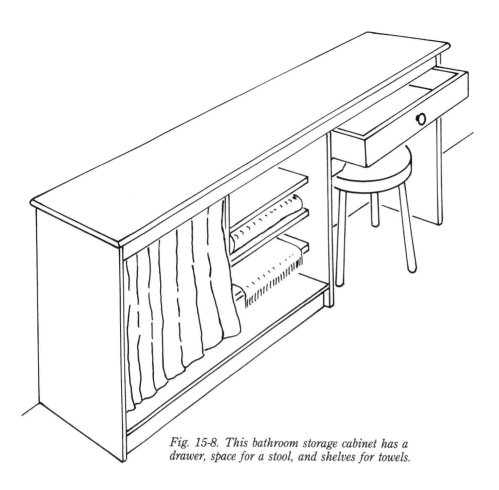

Fig. 15-8. This bathroom storage cabinet has a drawer, space for a stool, and shelves for towels.

side and put all other marks on the other (FIG. 15-9C). Use this as a pattern for marking the other parts.

• The outer pair of uprights are the same size as the first one, but you do not have to cut them out for the top rail. Mark the positions of the drawer rails on the right-hand one (FIG. 15-10B).

• The shelves and the upright to support their ends are kept back 3 inches from the front (FIGS. 15-9D and 15-10C) to leave space for the curtain. Make these parts and mark them for dowel holes.

• Shape the front drawer rail (FIG. 15-9E) to allow ample leg room for anyone sitting at the unit.

• Make the bottom (FIG. 15-10D) and the toe board to go below it. Set this back about 1 inch and join the two together.

• Prepare parts for joining. You will have to make the most of the joints with stopped dowels, but in a few places you can use screws without their heads showing.

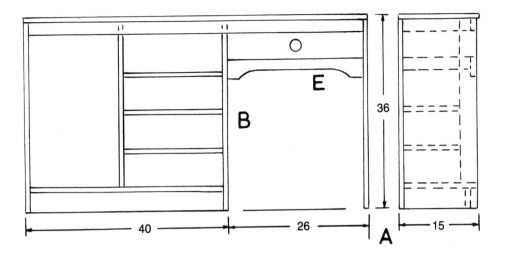

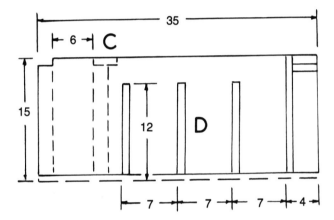

Fig. 15-9. Sizes of the bathroom storage cabinet.

• Join the shelves to their uprights, then add the bottom. Have the back ready; then join it, the front rail, and the ends, while the assembly is on a flat surface. The back should pull the assembly square, but check that the drawer opening is true at the front.

• Put drawer runners behind the front rails (FIG. 15-10E). Make the drawer by any of the methods described elsewhere in this book. As shown, it fits flush, but you could make it with a false front overlapping the frame.

• Before fitting the top, screw a curtain rail behind the front top rail. Check that the curtain will hang and slide properly.

• The top should overhang at the front. If one end goes into a corner the top must be level there, but if either or both ends are exposed, overhang the top a similar amount there.

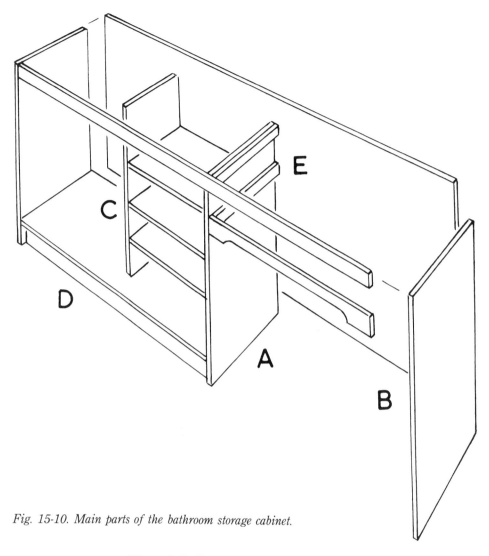

Fig. 15-10. Main parts of the bathroom storage cabinet.

Materials List for Storage Cabinet

3 uprights	¾ × 15 × 36
1 uprights	¾ × 12 × 32
3 shelves	¾ × 12 × 22
1 bottom	¼ × 15 × 40
1 back	¾ × 36 × 68
1 front rail	1 × 2 × 68
1 drawer rail	1 × 4 × 26
4 drawer guides	1 × 2 × 15
1 toe board	¾ × 3½ × 40
1 drawer front	¾ × 6 × 26
1 drawer back	⅝ × 5½ × 26
2 drawer sides	⅝ × 6 × 15
1 drawer bottom	15 × 26 × ¼ plywood

Glossary

There are hundreds of woodworking terms, but those that follow are applicable to the subject of this book and include some alternatives which may be seen elsewhere.

apron—A rail below a drawer, which can be straight or have its lower edge decorated by shaping or molding.

arris—The sharp edge between two flat surfaces.

backboard—The piece of wood closing the back of a cabinet or other piece of furniture.

bail—A swinging loop handle.

barefaced tenon—A tenon shouldered on one face only.

batten—Any narrow strip of wood. When fitted across other boards, also called a *cleat*.

blind—Not all the way through. Examples are a mortise for a short tenon or a stopped hole for a dowel.

blockboard—A form of thick plywood in which the core is made with solid-wood strips. Also called *lumber-core plywood*.

book-matched—Arranged so the grain pattern on one piece of veneer is a mirror image of the adjoining piece.

butt-hinge—The most common type of hinge, usually let into edges.

carcass—The main assembly parts that compose the skeleton of a piece of furniture, such as the framework of a cabinet.

chipboard—See *particleboard*.

clamp—A device for drawing parts together, particularly when closing joints. Also an alternative name for a *cleat*.

cleat—A strip of wood across other parts to join and support them and to prevent them from warping.

contact adhesive—An impact adhesive that adheres as soon as the parts are brought together.

cornice—A molding above eye level that projects around the top of a cabinet.

counter—The working top of a cabinet.

counterbore—To drill a large hole over a small one so a screw head can be driven below the surface and then be covered with a plug.

countersink—To bevel the top of a hole so a flat-head screw can be driven level with the surface.

dado joint—A groove cut across the surface of a piece of wood to take the end of a shelf or other part.

dovetail—The fan-shaped piece that projects between pins in the other part of a dovetail joint; made that way to resist pulling out.

dovetail nailing—A method of driving nails so they slope slightly at opposite angles to give an increased resistance against parts being pulled apart.

dowel—A cylindrical piece of wood used as a peg when making joints. Dowel rods have other uses, such as for spindles.

drawer kicker—A piece of wood across and above a drawer edge to prevent it from tilting when pulled out.

drawer runner—A piece of wood, matching the drawer kicker, on which the drawer runs.

dust panel—A piece of sheet material put between drawers to separate them from each other.

fielded panel—A panel with a raised center part.

figure—A decorative grain pattern, such as the medullary rays prominent in quarter-sawn oak.

fillet—A narrow strip of wood, such as that used for holding glass in a rabbet.

Gothic arch—An arch with a pointed top and rounded sides.

hanging stile—The upright on which door hinges are attached.

hardboard—Thin manufactured board with one smooth side.

hardwood—Wood from a deciduous tree that is usually, but not always, harder than softwoods.

haunch—The short piece of a tenon which is cut back where it joins another piece near its end.

housing joint—See *dado joint*.

impact adhesive—See *contact adhesive*.

jointing—The making of any joint. Also means planing edges straight.

kerf—The slot made by a saw.

knot—A flaw in the wood where a branch projected from the trunk of the tree.

knuckle, hinge—The pivot point of a hinge.

laminate—Building up layers with several pieces of wood glued together; used with thin strips to make up curved parts.

lineal—Length only; sometimes used when pricing wood.

locking stile—The upright against which a door shuts.

louvers (louvres)—Horizontal overlapping strips with ventilating gaps between.

lumber-core plywood—See *blockboard*.

matched boarding—Boards joined edge-to-edge with matching tongues and grooves.

medium-density fiberboard (M.D.F.)—A manufactured material with a wood base and a density between softwood and hardwood.

molding—Decorative-strip edging or border.

mortise-and-tenon joint—One of the most common joints (with many variations); characterized by the projecting tenon on the end of one piece fitting into a mortise cut in the other.

mullion—A vertical division of a window.

nosing—Curved or semicircular molded edge.

particleboard—Board manufactured with wood chips or particles and resin. Also called *chipboard*.

pedestal—In furniture, a supporting post or built-up section.

piano hinge—A long, narrow hinge, which may be cut to length.

planted—Applied, instead of being cut in the solid wood. Molding attached to a surface is *planted*, but if it is cut in the solid wood, it is described as *stuck*.

plastic laminate (laminated plastic)—A hard-surfaced decorative, thin plastic sheeting, used for countertops. Its best-known trade name is ''Formica.''

plinth—The base part of a piece of furniture. Its front edge is often called a *toe board*.

plywood—A sheet material made with layers of crossing veneers.

rail—A horizontal framing member.

rod—A strip of wood marked with lengths of construction parts; used instead of a rule, for comparing sizes.

root diameter—The diameter at the bottom of a screw thread.

scribing—Fitting one edge closely to another uneven or curved part.

seasoning—Drying to a controlled moisture content; applies to wood.

self-tapping screw—A hardened screw designed to cut its own thread in metal or other materials.

sett (set)—To punch below the surface; applies to nail heads.

slat—A narrow, thin wood strip.

softwood—Wood from a coniferous needle-leafed tree.

stile—A vertical member in a door frame.

stretcher—A lengthwise rail between the lower parts of a table or similar assembly.

toe board—A board set back at the base of a cabinet might be part of a *plinth*.

underbracing (underframing)—The arrangement of rails and stretchers to provide stiffness between the legs of a table or similar assembly.

varnish—A nearly transparent paint-like finish.

veneer—A thin piece of wood, usually decorative, to be glued to a backing. Also applies to the plastic surface applied to particleboard.

veneer pin—A very fine nail with a small head.

working drawing—A drawing showing sizes—usually in elevations, plan, and sections—from which measurements can be taken to make the furniture. Not a pictorial view.

worktop—The working surface or *countertop* of a cabinet.

Index

A

access, 4-7
angled end cabinet, 112
appliances
    countertop installation and, 143
    oven cabinet, 125
    standard sizes of, 5

B

basic cabinets, 52-63
    wall hanging (see cupboards)
basic shelf units, 198
bathroom cabinets, 274-286
    modular units, 280
    storage cabinet, 283
    vanity unit, 275
bin, tilt, 80
blockboard, 15
blocks of shelves, 196
bottle rack, 82
breadboard slide, 79
breakfast bar, 184
built-in breadboard, 79
built-in tables, 172-193
    breakfast bar, 184
    cabinet extension, 188
    counter-height, 181
    end, 177
    folding, 174
    sliding shelves for, 172

butcher-block countertops, 131-133
butt hinges, 28

C

cabinet extension table, 188
cabinets
    angled end, 112
    basic, construction of, 52-63
    cloth-hanging compartment in, 78
    enclosed two-drawer, 58
    ends of, 108-129
    fitted two-part, 54
    height of, 5, 6, 7
    modular, 280
    oven, tall, 125
    parts of, 53
    raised end, 117
    reach to, 5-7
    storage, 283
    tall end, 121
    vertical storage compartments in, 75
    wide units, 84
    with drawers, 71
    with shelves, 70
carcass construction, cupboards, 262
chipboard, 15
cloth-hanging compartment, 78
color schemes, 2
construction, 17-35

wall hanging cupboards carcasses, 262
cook's tool cupboards, 240
cookbook rack, 249
corner cupboards, 245, 270
corner shelves, 201
corner unit, 96
corners, 89-107
    corner unit for, 96
    cupboards for, 245, 270
    curved edges in, 106
    diagonal unit for, 99
    external, 101
    folding doors for, 96
    large shelf corner, 102
    overlapped, 92
    shelves for, 201
    small shelf corner, 105
    squared, 101
    top-access, 94
counter-height tables, 181
countersinking, 19
countertop shelves, 206
countertops, 88, 130-143
    appliance installation and, 143
    butcher-block, 131-133
    layout of, 131
    planning for, 131
    plastic laminate for, 133
    plastic laminate, home-made, 136
    post-formed, 135

shelves for, 206
sinks in, 142
stone, 139
tiled, 140
turning corners with, 89
wood, 131
cupboards
  basic, 229-255
  carcass construction for, 262
  cook's tool, 240
  corner, 245
  corner unit, 270
  long, 265
  matching, 236
  mirrored, small, 233
  planning and layout for, 257-261
  single, 230
  with lifting door, 253
  writing-flap, 249
cupping, 12
curves, 106, 109

D

design, 7-10
diagonal corner unit, 99
diagonal lines, 10
display shelves, 203
doors, 2
  corner arrangement for, 90
  decorative moldings applied to, 37
  design of, 36-37
  doorstops for, 85
  folding, 96
  framed, 40-42
  handles and catches for, 32-35
  hinges for, 28
  louvered, 47
  molded, 43
  painting, 39
  paneled, 40-42
  plain, 37-40
  raised panel, 43-45
  shaped-frame, 45-48
  sliding, 48-51
doorstops, 85
dovetail joints, drawer using, 24
dowels, 19-21, 32
drawers, 10, 22-28, 58, 71
  design of, 36-37
  handles and catches for, 32-35
  runners for, 26

E

edging, 21-22, 57
  curved, 109

enclosed two-drawer cabinet, 58
end shelves, 86
end table, 177
extension table, 188
external corners, 101

F

fiberboard, 16
fitted two-part cabinet, 54
floor space, 1, 4
folding doors, 96
folding tables, 174
framed doors, 40-42

G

grain, 12

H

handles and catches, 32-35
hardwoods, 11, 16
heights, 5-7
hinges, 28-32
  folding door, 98
  hidden, 30
hoods, range, 7

I

island bench, 155
island units, 144-171
  island bench, 155
  multiple island units, 153
  side shelf unit for, 158
  square island cabinets, 149
  with trays, 164

J

joints
  dovetail, 24
  plywood, 17
  rabbet, 25

K

kitchen table, 145
kitchens, 1
knots, 12

L

large shelf corner, 102
layout, 2, 3
  worktops, 1, 7
ledged shelves, 108
lifting door cupboards, 253
lighting, 2
long cupboards, 265
louvered doors, 47

M

matching cupboards, 236
materials, 11-16
measurements, 2-5
mirrored cupboards, small, 233
modular units, bathroom cabinets, 280
molded doors, 43
multiple cupboards, 256-273
multiple island units, 153
multiple wall cabinets (see cupboards)

N

nails, 17

O

oven cabinet, 125
overlapped corners, 92

P

paneled doors, 40-42
particleboard, 15
  edging for, 21-22
  screwing into, 19
piano hinges, 29
plain doors, 37-40
plastic laminate, 15-130
  countertops of, 133, 136
plate rack, 225
plywood, 13-15
  edging for, 21-22
  grades of, 13
  hardwood, 13, 14, 15
  joints for, 17
  lumber-core, 15
  screwing into, 19
  softwood, 13, 14, 15
post-formed countertops, 135
pot frames, 2
preparations, 1-10
proportion, 8

R

rabbet joints, drawer using, 25
racks
  bottle, 82
  cook's tools, 240
  cookbook, 249
  plate, 225
  towel, 78
railed shelves, 110
raised end cabinets, 117
raised panel doors, 43-45
range hoods, 7
reach, height of cabinets and, 5-7
runners, drawer, 26

S

scale drawings, 2-4
screws, 17-19
  countersinking, 19
shaped-frame doors, 45-48
shapes, 8
shell construction (units), 67-69
shelves, 70, 194-228
  basic unit, 198
  blocks of, 196
  corner, 201
  corner, larger, 102
  corner, small, 105
  countertop, 206
  curved edges on, 109
  display, 203
  end, 86
  island units, side, 158
  ledged, 108
  plate rack, 225
  railed, 110
  simple, 195
  sliding, 172
  spindle-supported, 222
  tall, 212
  wide, 217
simple shelves, 195
single cupboards, 230
sink, countertop setting of, 142
sliding doors, 48-51
sliding shelves, 172

sliding trays, 71
small mirrored cupboards, 233
small shelf corner, 105
softwoods, 11
spindle-supported shelves, 222
spindles, 110
square corners, 101
square island cabinet, 149
squaring, 4, 5
stone countertops, 139
storage cabinet, 283

T

tables
  built-in, 172-193
  counter-height, 181
  end, built-in, 177
  extension, 188
  folding, 174
  kitchen, 145
tall end cabinet, 121
tall shelves, 212
templates, 2
tiled countertops, 140
tilt bin, 80
toe boards, 88
top-access corners, 94
trays
  island units with, 164
  sliding, 71

U

unit construction, 64-88
  finished assembly for, 88
  shell construction in, 67-69
  style choice in, 65-67
  unit sizes in, 67
  wide unit, 84

V

vanity unit, 275
veneers, 21-22
  plywood, 14
vertical storage compartments, 75

W

wall cabinets
  basic (see cupboards)
  multiple (see cupboards)
warps, 12
wide shelves, 217
wide units, 84
wood, 11-13
  grain pattern in, 12
  lumber sizes, 12
wood worktops, 131
worktop layout, 1, 7
worktops (see countertops)
writing-flap cupboards, 249